Dramatherapy

Dramatherapy

Reflections and Praxis

Edited by Richard Hougham and Bryn Jones

First published 2017 by
PALGRAVE

Palgrave in the UK is an imprint of Macmillan Publishers Limited,
registered in England, company number 785998, of 4 Crinan Street,
London, N1 9XW.

Palgrave® and Macmillan® are registered trademarks in the United States,
the United Kingdom, Europe and other countries.

ISBN 978–1–137–60433–0 hardback
ISBN 978–1–137–60432–3 paperback

This book is printed on paper suitable for recycling and made from fully
managed and sustained forest sources. Logging, pulping and manufacturing
processes are expected to conform to the environmental regulations of the
country of origin.

A catalogue record for this book is available from the British Library.

A catalog record for this book is available from the Library of Congress.

This book is dedicated to the memory of Billy Lindkvist.

Contents

List of Contributors

Antonia Batzoglou, PhD, MA, BA Hons

Antonia (Tania) Batzoglou is an actor, performance artist, dramatherapist and lecturer in higher education. Her praxis looks into the participatory, engaging and intangible ways that the arts nurture relationships and enhance wellbeing and reflection. Her work is applied in various settings from theatre, performing arts and education to hospitals, museums and other cultural venues. Her clinical practice specialises in working with young people with Autistic Spectrum Disorder and multiple learning disabilities, adults using mental health services and elderly people living with dementia.

Naomi Bonger, MA

Naomi is a dramatherapist trained in the Sesame approach. She practises as a therapist, supervisor and trainer, and has recently specialised in therapeutic work with survivors of childhood sexual abuse. In 2012, Naomi set up The Dramatherapy Partnership with a colleague, providing therapeutic services for public sector organisations and charities and in private practice.

Alyson Coleman, PhD, MA, PG Cert.

Alyson has carried out doctoral research exploring the experiences of dramatherapists working with children with life-limiting/threatening conditions. She is a lecturer on the MA Drama and Movement Therapy training course at the Royal Central School of Speech and Drama, University of London.

Laura Francis, MA

Laura is a dramatherapist working with young people with learning difficulties, young people experiencing mental health issues, and refugees and asylum seekers. She has a background in human rights, storytelling and body-based meditation. Laura graduated with an MA in Drama and Movement Therapy (Sesame) from the Royal Central School of Speech and Drama, University of London, in 2016.

Alanah Garrard, MA

Alanah is a psychotherapist and dramatherapist. Her training includes integrative and existential approaches. She is currently working as a therapist in a residential treatment programme in addiction. Other specific areas of work include working with adolescents and young people and bereavement. Areas of research interest include philosophy and phenomenology.

Jo Godsal, MA

Jo is a dramatherapist and clinical services manager at Chroma, where he supports a large team of dramatherapists, music therapists and art therapists. Jo worked at the Mulberry Bush School for six years until 2016. He specialises in working with children and complex trauma and therapist management and supervision.

Richard Hougham, MA

Richard is Principal Lecturer at the Royal Central School of Speech and Drama, University of London, and course leader for the MA in Drama and Movement Therapy. Areas of research interest include a mythopoetic approach to training in the arts therapies and the links between education and Jungian psychology. He is Chair of the European Consortium of Arts Therapies Education (ECArTE) and a conference Director of its biennial conferences.

Bryn Jones, MA

Bryn is a dramatherapist, supervisor and mindfulness-based therapist. His current clinical practice includes work with adolescents in Tier 4 Child and Adolescent Mental Health Services (CAMHS) and work with adults as part of an addiction therapy programme. Bryn lectures the drama strand on the Drama and Movement Therapy MA at the Royal Central School of Speech and Drama, University of London. Alongside his clinical and teaching practice, Bryn continues his practice as a theatre director. Most recently he has directed work for Arcola Theatre and Punchdrunk and an annual environmental art project in Japan.

Alison Kelly, BEd. MA

Alison is a dramatherapist. She co-runs a children's bereavement service within the NHS and teaches on the MA in Drama and Movement Therapy at the Royal Central School of Speech and Drama, University of London. Alison is Joint Coordinator of the Creative Arts Supervision Training (CAST) and has a private dramatherapy and supervision practice.

Sophie Lasek, MA

Sophie is a newly qualified dramatherapist coming from a background in education and community work. Her practice is in primary schools and both acute inpatient and community NHS mental health settings. Her research interest lies in building the evidence base for dramatherapy and she sits on the British Association of Dramatherapists Executive Committee to support and forward research initiatives.

Aleka Loutsis, MA, PG Dip

Aleka practises as both a dramatherapist and a dance movement therapist working in education, social services and NHS Forensic Services. She is currently employed by the NHS in Acute and Community Mental Health Services and also with the National Specialist Unit for Personality Disorders. Aleka teaches the Laban Movement strand on the MA in Drama and Movement Therapy training course at the Royal Central School of Speech and Drama, University of London. Aleka is actively promoting an embodied approach to therapy drawing on her clinical and research experience and specialist training in the treatment of trauma.

Enda Moclair, MA

Enda is a dramatherapist with 20 years' experience as a creative facilitator working cross-culturally with vulnerable groups in countries experiencing conflict. His background is in learning and capacities development, and community and organisational development. His work is grounded in developmental psychology and systemic thinking.

Eran Natan, MA

Eran is a dramatherapist, voice practitioner and creative supervisor. He is a graduate of the MA Drama and Movement Therapy (Sesame) course at the Royal Central School of Speech and Drama, University of London, where he is currently a visiting lecturer for voice. Eran uses voice in his dramatherapy practice with various client groups, including refugees, patients with psychosis and people with learning disabilities. Eran also facilitates voice sessions and workshops in Israel and Europe. His main focus of interest is the role of pre-lingual vocal expression.

Rachel Porter, MA

Rachel Porter is a dramatherapist and a theatre maker. After a career as an actor and puppeteer, she gained an MA in Drama and Movement Therapy (Sesame) at the Royal Central School of Speech and Drama, University of London, in 2001. She has worked as a dramatherapist in London with a special focus upon pre-linguistic communication. She teaches Movement with Touch and Sound on the MA Drama and Movement Therapy training at the Royal Central School of Speech and Drama. Other teaching includes Agape dance and movement therapy training and Arteveldehogeschool's dramatherapy programme in Belgium. She is also a co-director of Feral Theatre in the UK.

Mark Saban, MA (Oxon)

Mark Saban worked as an actor and performer for twenty years before training as a Jungian analyst with the Independent Group of Analytical Psychologists. He is now a senior analyst with a practice in Oxford and London. He has taught Jungian psychology on the MA Drama and Movement Therapy training at Royal Central School of Speech and Drama for more than ten years and also lectures on analytical psychology at the Centre for Psychoanalytic Studies at Essex University. Recent publications include 'Jung Winnicott and the Divided Psyche', Journal of Analytical

Psychology, 2016, 61, 3, 329–349. He also co-edited (with Andrew Samuels and Emilija Kiehl) Analysis and Activism: Social and Political Contributions of Jungian Psychology, Routledge, 2016.

Marianna Vogt, MA

Marianna comes to dramatherapy from a background of theatre directing and devising, cabaret performance and actor coaching. She works in schools with children and their families as well as in private practice, and lectures on the Movement: Directing and Teaching MA at the Royal Central School of Speech and Drama, University of London.

Foreword

Professor Phil Jones

This book moves between worlds of deep, centuries old archetypal myth and moments such as a therapist's response, one day, on arriving at a residential centre to find that the client they were to work with, along with others, had been left 'in a row for a number of hours, so they could only see the back of the chair in front' (p. 96). Can such seemingly different perspectives have anything to say to each other? Within the chapters of *Dramatherapy: Reflections and Praxis*, clients in therapy and dramatherapists together offer us many varied, stimulating ideas and experiences born out of such juxtapositions and interconnections. In creating contact between elements that are unlikely to be brought into relationship, potential is unleashed and this offers us, as readers, challenge. This book is full of such dynamism.

One of the opportunities for any discipline is how enquiry or research challenges its ideas, practices and boundaries. The energy created between what is already known and what has yet to be discovered is crucial to any form of therapy. This is as true for the intimate weekly contact between clients and therapists as it is for larger-scale work of policy makers, care providers and those involved in training or the setting of professional guidelines. Much of this book's energy is created by the interaction between contemporary experiences and time spent with clients and an older fund of knowledge that connects wellbeing and the arts, such as drama and movement, to ancient Greece or to the work of frontierswomen such as Lindkvist over a half-century ago. The case studies, accounts and analyses create fresh knowledge and insight, offering the field of therapy views and challenges from this lively combination of experience and experiment.

The art forms within this book are explored by clients and therapists in spaces and relationships that are also illustrative of this 'combining', challenging energy. The spaces of the therapy take place, on one level, in everyday rooms in schools, social care settings and centres but, at the same time and on a different level, they are created by carefully crafted ideas and passions about clients bringing into these ordinary rooms the symbolic, the numinous and the imaginative. The therapist as an individual becomes, as Hougham says in Chapter 3, a guide, witness and 'actor' within this process offering, as Coleman and Kelly assert in Chapter 8, support for the client to explore their self-expression and agency as these new connections emerge and the numinous becomes the everyday within the dramatherapy space.

The book has much to offer about the value of such work as a direct challenge to those contemporary political landscapes which foreground hatred of difference and the different. We are introduced to new insights into the potency of drama and movement in therapy as a way of connecting to the other and to others, and to community as a living hope of increased collaboration, inclusion and growth. One way of interpreting Jung's writing about the 'Conscious, unconscious, and individuation' is to see a part of it in the light of such connection and difference:

> Conscious and unconscious do not make a whole when one of them is suppressed and injured by the other. Both are aspects of life. Consciousness should defend its reason and protect itself, and the chaotic life of the unconscious should be given the chance of having its way too – as much of it as we can stand. (Jung, 1981, para 522)

Here, in ways that are similar to the discussion in this foreword, potential is enabled through the creation of interconnection and interaction between areas deemed as different. This book represents many lucid and moving examples of the ways in which therapeutic opportunities are made by the bringing together of the separate or separated.

Smith (2011) has argued that 'praxis' is not simply 'action based on reflection', but is action that embodies certain qualities. These, he argues, include a commitment to human wellbeing and respect for others: 'praxis is creative: it is other-seeking and dialogic'. Looked at in this way, *Dramatherapy: Reflections and Praxis* is a perfect example of this interpretation of praxis in its dialogues with difference, in its accounts of therapeutic action and reflection deeply connected to concerns for wellbeing and respect for the other.

Professor Phil Jones, University College London, Institute of Education, November 2016.

References

Jung. C. G. (1981). Conscious, unconscious, and individuation. The archetypes and the collective unconscious. *CW*, 9i. London: Routledge and Kegan Paul.

Smith, M. K. (2011). What is praxis? In *The Encyclopaedia of Informal Education*. http://infed.org/mobi/what-is-praxis/.

Foreword

Dr Olu Taiwo

My time spent as external examiner for the MA in Drama and Movement Therapy (Sesame) greatly increased and deepened my understanding of the creative processes with particular regard to psychodynamic praxis. I came to appreciate the significance of the use of symbolic languages in the creation of meaning and their effective application in the process of therapy. The individual chapters in this collection articulate a breadth and depth of knowledge available to both students and practitioners. Within this, a praxis emerges informed by a diversity of influences including Jungian psychology, and contemporary research in neuroscience and phenomenology. The guiding philosophy of this book brings attention to the use of myths, symbols, movement and play as ways to obliquely engage with dramatherapeutic processes.

The primary focus addresses the philosophy and practice of dramatherapy, where the dramatherapist is free to philosophise and contemplate the nature of the profession and its contemporary relevance. There is a crucial distinction to be observed here, as we are not talking about a juxtaposition of practice and theory. Rather we see praxis steering us towards a 'triumvirate' comprising clinical practice, reflexivity and scholarship. In the context of training, this becomes a pedagogical approach where percipients integrate critical thinking, embodied practice and interpersonal skills. These chapters present fresh ideas derived from practice, contemporary research and education. Let me offer a few examples.

Jo Godsal's chapter brings together new insights from neuroscience with its application to current practice within therapeutic community settings. His praxis focuses on early childhood trauma, comparing Bruce Perry's Neurosequential Model with the progressive phases of the Sesame approach. Aleka Loutsis focuses on a taxonomy of five developmental gestures: yielding, pushing, reaching, grasping and pulling. She, too, explicates new ideas from recent developments in neuroscience and emphasises the importance of the physical journal as the principal channel for information in the therapeutic encounter.

Richard Hougham concentrates on the symbolising process within the Sesame approach. The use of Jungian analysis, deep experimentation and a mythopoetic approach to reflexivity can be seen as tools for the 'secular clinical shaman' as both therapist and patient engage in a dialectical relationship with each other's psyches. Jung's influence on dramatherapy is further explored by Mark Saban who gives us some inventive perceptions concerning how Jung's archetypal ideas, particularly the myths surrounding Dionysus, can function as metaphors that are utilised in both theatre and contemporary dramatherapy.

With regards to the scholarly aspect of the triumvirate, Antonia Batzoglou discusses an historical perspective by taking us back to an original examination of psyche in Ancient Greece. This chapter draws on philosophical as well as pragmatic elements of the Socratic concept of psychagogia. By deconstructing this concept, we are taken to the ancient foundation of contemporary theatre practice and dramatherapy. This exercise in cultural excavation leads us into the landscape of ancient Greek thought as a cultural ancestor of dramatherapy. Batzoglou's chapter explores untold stories, cultural assumptions and misperceptions of meaning. Naomi Bonger has another angle on misperception as she addresses and critiques burgeoning narratives, with reference to the commodification and normalising function of wellbeing and cognitive therapies. This raises crucial questions of constructed assumptions based on cultural relevance. She offers a different perspective which emphasises diversity, contexts and duration, arguing for dramatherapy as a counter-cultural force.

In this book we hear from practitioners who seem to avoid privileging the mind over the body. The volume steers away from linear or dualistic thinking, exploring instead different approaches which shed new light on meaning-making which is supported by the artistic process. For this reason, it speaks not only to practitioners of dramatherapy, but also to those interested in the conversations between art and psychotherapy. This dialogue raises fundamental questions concerning the role of drama, music, dance and art in society as a whole.

Timeline of the Sesame Approach to Drama and Movement Therapy

NB: Marian Lindkvist – the founder of the Sesame approach preferred to be called Billy. The following timeline uses this chosen name.

Marian (Billy) Lindkvist listens to an interview on the radio with Dame Sybil Thorndike addressing the question "what is drama?" Thorndike discusses how drama is psychology, planting the seed in Billy's mind.

1963

Billy Lindkvist has a dream of how the arts can support people with mental health problems.

1964

Billy runs first workshop at the York Clinic in Guys Hospital at the invitation of Dr. D. Stafford Clark

The first booking of KATS (Billy's touring group of actors which travelled the UK to hospitals and day centres) in the Midlands for an audience of people with learning disabilities

1965

Billy meets Peter Slade, Audrey Wethered and Chloe Gardener and Sue Jennings

1966

Billy gathers together tutors, colleagues and fellow artists to set up the Sesame Institute

Sesame begins a six month pilot project in a London psychiatric hospital

1967

Billy attends a lecture by Jungian Analyst, Irene Champernowne and then begins analysis with her

1970

Billy begins exploring the work of Marie Louise Von-Franz, James Hillman, Joseph Campbell and C.G. Jung in relation to the emergent Sesame methodology

KATS group invited to work with non-verbal children with autism, with Billy developing her ideas of movement with touch and sound

1973

1974

The first day release course starts, with fieldwork and placements

Billy, along with a child psychiatrist, a representative of the Department of Health her Majesty's inspector of drama for schools (Peter Slade) and a clinical psychologist, develop a manifesto on showing the need for a full-time Sesame training course for movement and drama therapists

1974–76

1975

A day release course at Cassio College, Watford begins, led by Graham Suter

Billy is introduced to Frederick Flower, the Principal of Kingsway Princeton College in London

1976

Full time course begins at Kingsway Princeton

1977–1993

Billy works as a fieldwork placement tutor and is teaching on the course

The formulation and adoption of the Sesame Institute Constitution stating; "For the purpose of this Constitution, the terms 'Arts in Therapy' and 'Arts Therapy' shall be deemed to be the use of any of the major art disciplines as a creative means of self-expression for the purpose of maintaining mental and physical health."

1978

1979

Billy contributes to a conference run by National Association of Dramatherapy (NADT) in the United States

Times Educational Supplement article outlining Sesame approach

Pat Watts introduces the Myth module into the training

1980

Billy visits South Africa and begins her work there with patients in a psychiatric hospital

1985

Billy presents paper of her research in South Africa at international Congress of the World Federation of Mental Health, Brighton, UK

Sesame training moves to Central School of Speech and Drama in London, the same year Central begins to offer degrees

1986

1994

The course changes from Advanced Certificate in Higher Education to Postgraduate Diploma

Publication of *Discovering the Self through Drama and Movement Therapy: The Sesame Approach*, edited by Jenny Pearson (Jessica Kingsley, UK)

1996

1997

Dramatherapy becomes a state registered profession in the UK

Billy publishes *Bring White Beads When You Call upon the Healer* (Rivendell House publishers)

1998

The course moves from Postgraduate Diploma to Masters

2002

Creative Arts Supervision Training (CAST) begins, recognised by the British Association of Dramatherapists (BADth). It is designed and delivered by Sesame trained dramatherapists

Central gains degree awarding powers and is awarded HEFCE centre of Excellence award for theatre related disciplines

2004

2005

Central becomes a constituent college of the University of London

Sesame Institute, supported by the Terpsichore trust initiates a practice-based research CPD course

2007

2008

Fleshing the Psyche conference at Central, a collaboration between the Sesame Institute and Central School of Speech and Drama and David Holt on-line

Central hosts the ECArTE 10th European Arts Therapies Conference: *The Space in Between; The Potential for Change*

2009

Central and the Sesame Institute are successful in their bid for a fully funded Collaborative Doctoral award from the Arts and Humanities Research Council

2010

Award of first PhD exploring aspects of the Sesame approach to Dramatherapy

Research project culminating in the film 'Dramatherapeutic Presence' selected as part of Central's research excellence framework submission

Publication of *Dramatherapy with Myth and Fairytale: The Golden Stories of Sesame*, Mary Smail, Pat Watts and Jenny Pearson, JKP: London

2013

Central awarded Royal status as recognition for 'world class institution for exceptional training in theatre and performance studies'

2015

Sesame Institute closes. Royal Central continues to deliver Masters programme which teaches the Sesame approach to drama and movement therapy

Following a review the course is formally extended to become a 2 year full time programme

2017

Launch of the Central Dramatherapy Graduate Network

1

Introduction

Richard Hougham and Bryn Jones

This book traces and is inspired by an accumulation of ideas, discussions and provocations that formed substantial parts of the termly MA Drama and Movement Therapy team meetings at the Royal Central School of Speech and Drama, University of London, from 2013 to the present day. The dramatherapy course has been delivered at Central for 31 years at the time of this publication and while it has been through many periodic reviews and progressions, there remain core principles and pedagogic approaches. This book captures some of these and articulates them at a moment when the programme moves into a new phase. Now the formal partnership with the Sesame Institute is no longer in place, Central has the opportunity to recalibrate its articulation of the Sesame method and generate new work. From evidence-based research to 'foundation courses which aim to cultivate a diversity of applicants to the full-time pre-registration training, this is a moment of transition. While the core principles of the symbolic approach remain, along with key influences from Jung, Laban, Slade and Lindkvist, now is a time for refreshment and renewal. As many recent graduates press forward with contemporary practice and research, new intersections of knowledge and collaborations are beginning to emerge. The idea of praxis, with its capacity to bring together the old and the new, seemed a good guiding principle.

The heart of this book explores some of these articulations of contemporary dramatherapy praxis by bringing together a selection of chapters which illustrate elements of current thinking and practice. Many of the authors are members of the teaching team on the Masters programme. Praxis is the engaged activity linking theory with practice. More specifically, it is the processes by which initial understanding is enacted or embodied towards actualisation. A diverse range of thinkers, artists and writers have drawn on notions of praxis to examine and progress their work. Writing on the importance of sensuous activity in actualising the potential power of social humanity, Karl Marx writes: 'All mysteries which lead theory to mysticism, find their rational solution in human practice and in the comprehension of this practice ... The philosophers have only interpreted the world, in various ways; the point is to change it.' (Marx, 1969, pp. 13–15) In more prosaic terms Tony Wilson of Factory Records talks of praxis when he describes the innovative creative process of his artists as 'doing something, and then only afterwards, finding out why you did it' (Channel 4, 1984). In discussing how the band worked on their seminal album *London Calling*, Joe Strummer and Mick Jones of punk group The Clash describe their process:

> All I remember is playing football until we dropped and then playing music ... writing and rehearsing and then recording it ... a real intensity of effort ... but we always left a little bit undone ... we didn't do these things by thought. We did these things by accident (Letts, 2004).

In this, Strummer and Jones allude to the praxis imperative that there can be no pre-formed idea or anticipated knowledge of where precisely the deliberate action will lead. Rather we are following an informed and considered choice to step on, in search of that which is presently beyond our reach but worthy of our stretch. Praxis requires an evolving willingness to be meaningfully diverted, surprised, shaped and shifted. To have our plan altered by the experience of that which we encounter is to change what we might have previously been aiming for. It is central not only to art, but also to epistemology. This is the dynamic quality of praxis; an evolving and continuing dialogue, a constant interplay between ends and means. Praxis, then, is a considered and committed form of action, of doing, which develops from a basic level of understanding towards the deeper waters of discovery, revelation and direct knowing. Praxis appears to be an expression of freedom, while at the same time requiring discernment. It moves towards risk in venture but is deliberate in action. Praxis takes us off plan and brings into view knowledge and experience previously unseen.

As an approach to training, praxis is well known in Eastern spiritual traditions. Here, the teacher provides the student with a rudimentary outline of a specific meditative practice. The student will then be encouraged to value and investigate his or her personal 'taste' of this practice. The lineage of such traditions can still be found today in contemporary mindfulness practice. Encouragements towards 'participating fully', 'engaged acceptance' and observing experience via the 'sensing mode' can all be considered aspects of praxis. The key in understanding this rests with the view that our 'being' is not a permanent, fixed and static state but one of continual revision and flux. It is *being* viscerally engaged with the process of our becoming in the very moment-to-moment messiness of our daily lives. In contrast to the increasingly convenient and packaged 'mindfulness-lite' approaches to mindfulness practice, Hannah Arendt argues against the Western philosophical tendencies towards the contemplative life (vita contemplativa) and provokes us towards an active life (vita activa) (Arendt, 1998). Speaking to the human capacity for action she cites praxis as an actualising force for freedom, expression and human togetherness (Arendt, 1998).

In this book each chapter is written by an author/practitioner trained at Central and many of the contributors are teaching or supervising students. The writing seeks to expose and reveal examples of praxis within current dramatherapy discourse and an emergent articulation of the Sesame approach. The work illustrates, through a collection of direct, first-hand and first-person narratives how the leading edge of active experience grapples, tests and twists its way towards fuller comprehension and insight. The enquiry is intentionally broad in scope, with a diversity enriched by a geographical and epistemological mix. It is hoped that this further serves to evoke and capture the vital processes of reflection and action which fuel the transformative capacity inherent within praxis and its relationship to the arts. Individual chapters offer comment on several key and related themes including: the nature of the dramatherapeutic relationship; intersections between dramatherapy and other therapeutic modalities; and new emergent languages of dramatherapy. The work tests assumptions, interrupts slumber and surprises the reader through trespassing, and following a non-linear yet incisive purpose. Its collective composition provides a compelling and cohesive montage of contemporary dramatherapy practice as it is being practised, developed and advanced today.

The writing plays out across three areas: philosophical, developmental and practice-based, highlighting particular and specific applications of dramatherapy from various perspectives. The heartland examines how drama, with its taproot in play, voice, movement and touch, offers the chance to facilitate connection and meaningful communication between people. There is acknowledgement of the psychodynamics of this relationship and how the art forms of drama and movement offer clear containment and opportunities for the expression of unconscious material. The writing reflects on the complexity inherent within these dynamics and steers more towards their mystery than a prescription of exact methods or techniques. In the spirit of this, chapters offer reflection on philosophical concerns such as the nature of silence, the ancient Greek idea of psychagogia and the phenomenology of the gaze.

The text also carries a recurring examination of how contemporary dramatherapy practice positions itself within current theoretical and practice landscapes. There is enquiry into the nature of the relationship between dramatherapy and the two key spheres of influence from which it emerged: drama and therapy. The book elaborates on themes which offer contemporary markers for dramatherapy both as an allied health profession registered with the Health and Care Professions Council (HCPC) and a form of psychotherapy. It exposes contextual and academic similarities and differences between dramatherapy and other disciplines including contemporary theatre practice, neuroscience and psychology. In honouring the spirit of the book's origin and in examining the role of praxis, authors have been encouraged to trust their own distinctive voice and to write following their curiosity and passion. It was an invitation to mark, in these pages, what matters to them, their clients, their practice and their profession. As such, the writing arises from areas of personal testimony, clinical work, training and artistry. The weave of the text is held by the overarching themes of reflection and praxis as contributors mine a wide range of subjects and disciplines. Ideas from theology, anthropology and philosophy help to unearth broader questions of the relevance of the arts therapies today and the efficacy of the languages they use.

From the outset the book engages with the subtleties of praxis as the meeting of ideas and practice, of action and thought. Chapter 2 by Antonia Batzoglou offers an historical lesson in examining the philosophical and pragmatic meaning of psyche in Ancient Greece. She outlines the Socratic concept of psychagogia as a foundation for problematising contemporary theatre practice and dramatherapy, and in so doing takes us into the terrain of ancient Greek thought and an idea at the roots of dramatherapy. In Chapter 3 Richard Hougham writes specifically about training in drama-therapy and the cultivation of a symbolic attitude as a cornerstone to the Sesame approach. He introduces the combined pedagogy of the Central programme which aims to cultivate this, including Jungian analysis, intensive experiential work and a study into the mythopoetic approach to psyche. Drawing on Jung's ideas of the value of the healing symbol he navigates a path which refers to Keats's negative capability, the Greek idea of poiesis and examples from working with myth and fairytale in both teaching and practice. Eran Natan then sounds the call in Chapter 4 for dramatherapists to support the humming, growling and roaring of voices with an integrated use of the voice in dramatherapy practice. He draws from sources both ancient and current, to articulate a powerful argu-ment for the enduring meaning and relevance of primal and pre-lingual vocal expression. His writing provides a distillation of how practitioners might grow their personal experience of this approach towards integrat-ing it into their clinical practice. In contrast, Bryn Jones in Chapter 5 blends research and practitioner testimony with personal experience and observation to examine the role and function of silence within the dramatherapeutic relationship. He examines how to make space for silence within the therapeutic endeavour and how that space might be used to promote and progress the therapist and client relationship. He examines how silence can be used skilfully to counter and balance the world of words, where doing and conceptual thinking can dominate and drown out and obstruct the quieter, intuitive language of the Self. Alanah Garrard continues to draw out philosophical themes in Chapter 6 and discusses Merleau-Ponty's theories of perception and the body to grow self-awareness and assist the therapeutic endeavour. Garrard brings into play phenomenology and shines a light on nuances and subtleties within the human interaction, examining how this might inform the practice of dramatherapy. Jo Godsal goes on in Chapter 7 to reflect on his recent work in therapeutic community settings. He outlines a unique development in which the community's interest in neuroscientific theory inspires and supports the introduction and development of dramatherapy as a key clinical intervention. Godsal's work focuses on children who have experienced early trauma. His approach addresses not only the impact of a single trauma but also environmental failure, which is often termed developmental or complex trauma. He examines how Bruce Perry's Neurosequential Model informs his practice and how in his view it corresponds with the graduated stages of the Sesame approach. Alyson Coleman and Alison Kelly then reflect in Chapter 8 on their shared professional experience as co-facilitators working for a bereavement service. They bring candid insight in to the development of their own working relationship and reflect on the benefits and challenges of co-facilitation. The emergent narrative of their chapter outlines a model and an argument for the efficacy of this approach; the particular discipline of two therapists working together in clinical settings.

In Chapter 9, Aleka Loutsis discusses recent developments in neuroscience which are confirming the centrality and importance of the body and the primary relationship in the therapeutic encounter. She introduces compelling ideas in terms of the psychological importance of five developmental gestures; yielding, reaching, pushing, grasping and pulling. These are framed and explored within a writing convention which identifies the definition, deficit, observation and potential intervention of each gesture. Rachel Porter continues a focus on the body in Chapter 10 and explores how her interest and research into multimodality has coincided with post-Eriksonian perspectives on developmental psychology. She introduces the reader to a persuasive argument for the work of Colwyn Trevarthen and Daniel Stern as key theorists underpinning her progressive approach to Movement with Touch and Sound as a vital component of the Sesame method. Porter explores these influences in her roles as trainer, clinician and performer. Sophie Lasek and Laura Francis in Chapter 11 move the focus to questions of training, writing fresh and open reflections on their experience as recent students on the Central programme. They offer eloquent and engaging testimony to the value of developing a relationship with the unknown in both training and clinical contexts. In Chapter 12 Marianna Vogt takes an autoethnographic approach to exploring the psychological significance of relationship to place and the role place plays in the therapeutic encounter. The style here offers a freshness and vulnerability, witnessing the author's relationship with feelings of belonging and identity through place. Continuing the theme of place, in Chapter 13 Enda Moclair introduces his work in Syria and the application of dramatherapy in conflict zones and within the experience of refugee communities. His writing critiques existing tropes of therapeutic work with refugees, bringing into play the importance of creating environments for people to connect within. He reflects on his experience working with a group of Syrian volunteers with whom he adapted dramatherapy exercises to support shared experience and redeveloping a sense of home. The focus then returns to Jung in Chapter 14 with Mark Saban offering new and innovative perspectives on how some of Jung's ideas translate across to dramatherapy and the Sesame approach. Specifically, Saban draws out substantial resonances between the Greek god Dionysus and the early functions of theatre and the contemporary practice of dramatherapy. And the book ends with a most engaging chapter by Naomi Bonger who addresses the groundswell of narratives of wellbeing and cognitive interventions through a critique of their commodification and normalising function. Her writing poses questions of relevance and offers counterpoints via a diversity of approaches, settings and durational scopes. She critiques the prevailing culture and commodification of wellbeing and draws attention to, and forms an argument for, the notion of dramatherapy as a countercultural force. This final chapter destabilises assumptions about wellbeing and argues for the importance of the complexity of the dramatherapeutic relationship as a fundamental aspect of psychological insight.

In editing all of these individual chapters we have been struck and encouraged by the naturally occurring dialogues and convergent themes linking them. This rich and lively interplay seems to reflect the varied and diverse ways Sesame-trained dramatherapists are developing their practice, as well as the joined-up and shared language that exists between them. All authors have been encouraged to tap into and write from their own sources of inspiration, experience and curiosity. We imagine that in similar ways, as a reader of this book, you will turn the pages alive with your own motivations and existent areas of interest. It is our hope that you can easily find your way to those sections which strike an immediate chord and that in reading one chapter you will discover links to another. In any case, we very much hope you will stumble across or navigate a pathway of meaning, where connecting threads emerge from the work presented here. Readers who prefer starting at the beginning and progressing through the text sequentially will hopefully appreciate the narrative mapping from philosophical to developmental to practice. We have attempted to ensure consistency of style in ways which don't dim or inhibit the unique and individual voices of each contributor. We have also worked with chapter authors to preserve confidentiality and ensure all appropriate consents have been gained.

References

Arendt, H. (1998). *The Human Condition*. London: The University of Chicago Press.

Channel 4. (1984). *New Order: Play at Home*. Available at: http://www.mojo4music.com/4831/new-orders-naked-80s-art-experiment/. Accessed 26 May 2016.

Letts, D. (2004). *The Last Testament*. London: Sony Music Entertainment (UK) Ltd.

Marx, K. (1969). *Theses on Feuerbach: II, VII, XI/Engels Selected Works, Volume One*. Moscow: Progress Publishers.

2

Psychagogia

Antonia Batzoglou

Introduction

This chapter reflects on the praxis of drama within dramatherapy and examines its connection to theatre as *psychagogia*. The relationship of drama and theatre with therapy can be traced back to their archaic roots in ancient Greece and especially in the healing practices of Asclepius. For this historical and philosophical journey, I am drawing on Socrates' pedagogical concept of *psychagogia* and its relationship to theatre as outlined in Aristotle's *Poetics*. Scouting the origins and sources of this relationship, *psychagogia* is examined through selected philosophical, religious, psychological and psychoanalytical discourses spanning from ancient Greek times to the present. Psyche is thus discussed and examined in order to clarify its conceptual and pragmatic meaning. Following the ancient Greek perspective, the entirety of human soul, mind and body, the Apollonian and Dionysian qualities, the personal and the archetypal are seen as intertwined in the notion of psyche. For the examination of the concepts of psyche, therapy and theatre and their relationship, the chapter resurrects and re-contextualises the Socratic concept of *psychagogia* as a starting point of reference for this critical endeavour. This archaic excavation is sketched out by drawing from philosophical discourses of that period as well as facts and discoveries about theatre and therapy's respective practices. The findings of this relationship are then examined in parallel with the contemporary praxis of dramatherapy and specifically the Sesame approach. The focus remains on the use of myth and drama in the Sesame approach, re-contextualised through the lens of *psychagogia*.

> *Life is too rational,*
> *there is no symbolic experience*
> *in which I am something else,*
> *in which I am fulfilling my role*
> *as one of the actors in the divine drama of life.*
>
> (Jung, 1977, p. 273)

My personal experience of drama reflects the perception that theatre possesses an attitude of curiosity and exploration about the human psyche; it also remains one of the few collective activities where a communication of the psyche, on both conscious and unconscious levels, takes place between its participants. Theatre is perceived as an act of engagement, a medium to communicate, express and create movement in the psyche. Based on this perception, we find, in practice and theory, theatre's connection with psychology and therapy. My approach and praxis within this chapter reflects Barba's suggestion that 'we should not ask what the theatre means in general but rather what the theatre means for oneself' (Barba, 1995, p. 8). More specifically, in an era of postmodern and post-dramatic aesthetics, the chapter asks what qualities of drama and theatre remain relevant within contemporary dramatherapy praxis. In a series of deconstructed events, I am imagining performing a 'post-mortem' examination to rediscover the rooted connection between theatre and therapy by re-invoking the concept of *psychagogia* and prompting this connection to elicit contemporary transformations.

From mime to physical interpretations of stories, re-invented performance rituals, improvisations and plays, drama in dramatherapy practice has taken many forms. Outside the therapy room, drama, theatre and performance's aesthetics and boundaries have also been questioned and deconstructed. In this process of a 'post-mortem' examination, the chapter aims to excavate or to 'cut through' history and to concentrate on finding the philosophical roots of this connection regardless of the performance's aesthetic form. The archaic connection of drama, theatre and therapy had its beginnings in ancient Greece, where the Asclepeion sanctuaries of health and treatment were adjacent to theatre venues and it is there we look for answers.

Psyche, Theatre and *Psychagogia* in Ancient Greece

In ancient Greece, we identify a significant evolution in the understanding and study of psyche, since philosophy and psychology were not distinct disciplines, in contrast to their positions in modernity. The subject of the human psyche preoccupied many great thinkers of antiquity, and I will explore some key writings in order to critically integrate the ancient understanding of the individual psyche in relation to the socio-political functions of theatre. To start with, we need to remember what the purpose of theatre in ancient Greece was and to re-contextualise its purpose in relation to psyche and the Socratic pedagogical concept of psychagogia.

Aristotle's (384–322BC) *Poetics* is the only complete work of his time that discusses theatre, its dramaturgy and performance. Aristotle acknowledges a psychological function of theatre when he describes it as an act of mimesis of great and complete actions, manifested using poetic language and passions that lead to catharsis through empathy (Αριστοτέλης, 1992, p. 193 [Aristotle, *Poetics* 1449b25–29]). The purpose of theatre, as Aristotle defines it in the *Poetics*, is to create an action (the Greek term *praxis*) which does not mean physical activities, events or deeds but rather a motivation from which actions spring in order to shift the mind and the psyche of the spectators (Αριστοτέλης, 1992, p. 120). Fundamental to Aristotle's philosophy is the theory that sees external movements or actions resembling the movements of the psyche so that action/*praxis* is the outward expression of an inner state. Butcher (1951) in his critical analysis of Aristotle's theories points out that:

> An act viewed merely as an external process or result, one of a series of outward phenomena, is not the true object of aesthetic imitation [referring

to mimesis]. The πρᾶξις [*praxis*] that art seeks to reproduce is mainly an inward process, a psychical energy working outwards; deeds, incidents, events, situations being included under it so far as these spring from an inward act of will, or elicit some activity of thought and feeling. (Aristotle and Butcher, 1951, p. 123)

Theatre as an art of mimesis does not imitate real life but rather represents it from a reflective and interpretative view. Aristotle makes it clear that poetry – referring to all forms of drama and literature – is an imitation not of men but of an action and of life that implies personal agents of intellect and character. Aristotle refers to this integration of intellect and character that informs the performance of the action as ethos. The Aristotelian ethos can be associated with the German word *Haltung* translated into attitude, stance, manner and posture; the way our actions are guided by our beliefs.

In Aristotle's psychology, character is less fundamental than action. He defines character as 'habitual action' that is formed and influenced by the parents and the environment, and argues that as the person grows they begin to understand these actions rationally and become ethically responsible for their character (Αριστοτέλης, 1992, p. 193 [Aristotle, *Poetics* 1450a1–5]). Here Aristotle refers to the character as the psychological, intellectual and behavioural qualities of an individual. The actor is called to perceive the *action* of this character they portray, and then recreate it in their own thoughts and feelings as truthfully as possible in order to make the character's actions believable for the spectator. Actors utilise their intellect and personal ethos to understand and portray the actions of the character on stage. In that sense the actor is creating the ethos of the dramatic characters from the basis of their own ethos. Interesting to note is that the word 'actor' in Greek [*ethopoios*] means the maker of ethos.

Aristotle states that this kind of mimesis induces motion in the psyche and inspires reflection. Following this conception, theatre was aiming to educate, to raise questions and thoughts about ethos and morality, to express ideas and to amuse. For that reason the performance of a dramatic play, especially of tragedy, was called *didaskalia* – meaning instruction – and so the spectators, on leaving the theatre, had gained awareness from witnessing a theatrical piece. In that context theatre was *psychagogia*, a Greek word freely translated as 'education for the psyche', meaning the education or cultivation of psyche by guiding the spectator towards reflection and critical thinking. Aristotle declares tragedy as the greatest form of *psychagogia* (τά μέγιστα, οίς ψυχαγωγεί ή τραγωδία) and highlights myth as the most important agent through which tragedy serves as *psychagogia* (Αριστοτέλης, 1992, p. 197 [Aristotle, *Poetics* 1450a33]).

In order to define *psychagogia* and the connection between theatre and therapy, I will start by sharing a fictional story that takes us back to the late fourth century BC in ancient Greece. Miltiades was unwell, both mentally and physically, and so he sought treatment at the Asclepeion at Pergamos. The Asclepeion was a sanctuary of health dedicated to Asclepius, the god of healing, where body, mind and spirit were treated as inseparable. There Miltiades' therapy consisted of participation in rituals, meditative practices and physical activities under the supervision of the healers. In the majority of these ancient sanctuaries, theatres stand in or adjacent to them. At Pergamos, an underground passage connected the theatre venue with the patients' sleeping hall in the sanctuary, called the *abaton*. When the initial cleansing rituals had taken place, Miltiades, with other ambulatory patients, followed the underground passage and attended theatre performances of tragedy or comedy to assist in their recovery. Attendance at the theatre could initiate or advance the therapeutic process by enabling the individual to undergo inner rearrangements and to expand the possibilities of seeing oneself in relationships with the self and the other. After watching the performance, Miltiades and the other patients returned to the *abaton* where they slept, awaiting the nocturnal visit of the healing god Asclepius in human or animalistic form in their dreams.

Asclepius was a semi-god, or rather a demon whose identity is both mythical and real. He was both mantic and chthonic in character and associated with animals and specifically with the dog and the serpent which symbolise healing. According to the myth by Hesiod, he was the son of Apollo with a mortal woman and was born in Epidaurus. Asclepius learned the art of healing from Chiron the centaur and is considered the god of medicine, religion and mythology. His cult grew enormously in reputation in Ancient Greece, and sanctuaries devoted to his name were built in several cities. The recognition of the healing effects of his practices was widely spread and focus has been given to the connection between theatre and therapy.

Asclepius recognised the value of theatre's therapeutic qualities and the role of the theatre within the community as an art form that corresponds to the psyche and soma as an inseparable union of spirit and matter. His cult was attested in Epidaurus, as his birthplace, from the sixth century BC. As the sanctuary in Epidaurus grew in prosperity by gaining fame and popularity, more and more people needed to be accommodated and so a theatre was built next to it. The ancient theatre of Epidaurus, with a seating capacity of 14,700 people, became a significant cultural and healing centre in ancient times and still hosts performances during the summer months.

In the ancient world, Asclepius's therapy or healing cared for soma and psyche undivided, and so physical sickness and psychic imbalance were treated as inseparable. The medical symptom in antiquity is seen as the point of correspondence between the psychic inner reality and the outer somatic manifestation (Meier, 1989). The information we have about the practices that were taking place in Asclepius's sanctuaries is collected mainly by testimonies, written documentation or through artistic representations like statues and vases as well as from archaeological excavations (Edelstein, E.J. and Edelstein, 1998). These discoveries offer knowledge and facts about the cult of Asclepius but we can only arrive at a hypothetical understanding as to how exactly healing was applied and perceived.

Nevertheless, what we do know is that the treatment took the form of an incubation ritual that preserved both physical and psychical aspects of the human condition. This consisted of an initial cleansing bath for the soma and psyche, followed by preliminary sacrifices, attendance at the theatre and, finally, the sick person slept in the *abaton*, the innermost sanctuary, in order to dream the healing dream. Thus the healing process or incubation had the characteristic of a mystery or initiation during which the healer god or healing symbols were summoned to visit the patient's dreams. In ancient Greece the attitude towards dreams was purely religious in the beginning and so dreams were seen as prayers or divine messages. Meier (1989) notes that Plato has no specific theory about dreams but that in his view the content of a dream is determined by the part of the psyche that is active. In *Prometheus Bound,* Aeschylus mentions dream interpretation as one of the cleverest inventions of Prometheus. What is constant in the development of the Greeks' theological, philosophical and theoretical approach to dreams is the dreamer's attitude towards the irrational. Meier points out that:

> Anagogical readings (especially in Greek rhetoric) are spiritual or allegorical interpretations. Therefore medical practice would have an essential connection with the irrational. We may then say that what works in medicine is irrational. (Meier, 1989, p. 25)

The proposed treatment in Asclepius's sanctuaries is seeking to contemplate the irrational and its symbols and thus find meaning and awareness as a way to find cure for the body and mind. Modern psychiatrists and psychotherapists agree that 'good therapy and good theatre have in common a set of inner processes' (Simon in Hartigan, 2009, p. 13) and that 'the psychology of drama and the phenomenology of human experience march together. It is deeply grounded in the fact of self-consciousness, the awareness of our existence which involves the ability to stand back and look at life' (Grainger, 2004, p. 6).

This ability to stand back and attend or reflect on life's experience is the exact meaning of the Greek word 'therapy', deriving from the Greek verb *therapeuo* meaning 'I wait upon'. Thus, 'therapy' not only signifies healing or the treatment of a trauma or problem but the amplification of self-awareness. Theatre then becomes a place of encounter, for waiting upon or reflecting on psychological human situations of archetypal significance. It becomes the place for a dynamic exchange between actors and spectators, a place where the irrational is acted out and therefore a meeting place for the unconscious and conscious aspects of the human psyche. Theatre is acknowledged as a praxis where archetypal questions about human existence are being acted out, asking the audience to interpret its symbolic meaning. In the sanctuaries of Asclepius, theatre and dreams have similar qualities that promote the amplification of self-awareness and thus healing. It is in that sense that drama and theatre are the greatest form of *psychagogia*, for both educational and therapeutic purposes.

The Notion of Psyche in Ancient Greece

A discussion about *psychagogia,* as the art of guiding the psyche, becomes highly problematic if psyche is translated as soul, influenced by the religious connotations that the word predisposes. The following section will look at the etymological and philosophical meanings of the words *psychagogia* and psyche and its relation to the ancient Greek polytheistic religion.

Psychagogia derives from the ancient Greek ψυχαγωγός found in the *Oxford English Dictionary* as 'psychagogue': '1. conjuring up the dead, (noun) a necromancer, leader of departed souls – said of Hermes' and also describing '2. a person who directs the mind; a teacher, an instructor and 3. a medicine that restores consciousness or revives the body'. Etymologically, the word *psychagogia* is a compound of the words 'psyche' and 'agogy', meaning leading or guiding (*OED*). In modern Greek the term *psychagogia* is translated in English by the words 'recreation, entertainment and amusement' (Collins Greek-English Dictionary, 2003). Although entertainment defines an activity designed to give people pleasure or relaxation, as theatre does, it lacks a main aspect of the word that is lost in translation. Entertainment and amusement, meaning an 'action of upholding or maintaining, of occupying a person's attention agreeably; interesting employment; of amusing, or a thing done to amuse' (*OED*) do not reflect any aspect of the words 'psyche', 'guidance' or 'education'.

The word 'psyche' is derived from ancient Greek and its paradoxical meaning refers both to breath, spirit or mind and to the butterfly, the colourful and beautiful ephemeral insect that has been dramatically transformed from a caterpillar. For the ancient Greeks, psyche was a way of referring to life, the vital principle that animates all living things.

Before Plato the early Greek philosophers of Orphism recognised immortal substance and divine qualities in the principle of psyche, considering that the secret thoughts, the deep feelings and the imagination constitute aspects of an 'inner being' (Αρβανιτάκης, n.d., p. 146). Plato saw psyche as an idea that produced an eternal entity, describing it as complex referring to a tripartite psyche divided into the aspects of the psyche that form the intellect/thinking (*logos*), the passions/emotions (*thymos*), and, thirdly, the desires/physical appetites (*epithumia*). Aristotle's naturalistic conception of the psyche returns to its literal meaning as the form of a living body, i.e. a living organism, and that the psyche is an organism's active functioning, all that it characteristically does, its deeds and ethos which are inseparable from the shape of its body.

Even for the contemporary philosophers of antiquity it is difficult to establish a common definition since each one recognises indisputable uncertainties about the nature of psyche and its relation with the body, death and reality. Nevertheless, where all agree is in the idea that psyche is creating motion/movement, that it exists prior to motion, that it exists before the soma/body and so their relationship is of principal and auxiliary, that it is responsible for everything, good or bad, and is present in everything that moves (Αρβανιτάκης, n.d., p. 139). This clarification is of great importance to the contemporary conceptual understanding of *psychagogia.* Therefore, when Aristotle refers to tragedy as the greatest art of *psychagogia,* he is referring to theatre's ability to create motion within psyche and therefore to guide the psyche towards distinctive capacities of comprehension, empathy and contemplation. Furthermore, the theatrical praxis was further related to the ritualistic and religious aspects of the ancient Greek society.

According to Otto (1955), a society expresses in religion 'what is most venerable to man', and all essential questions about existence, love and death are being confronted within the religion's content (Otto, 1955, p. 5). The polytheistic religion in ancient Greece recognises the imperfection of human nature and does not assert absolute distinctions between man and gods, good and evil, rational and irrational, chaos and harmony. Otto in his study of the Homeric gods declares that 'the ancient Greek religion comprehended the things of this world with the most powerful sense of reality possible, and nevertheless recognised in them the marvellous delineations of the divine' (Otto, 1955, p. 10). Therefore, the Greek's magical or metaphysical thinking, in contrast to the rational, comes from the depths of natural experience, and therefore it stands for itself in 'the glory of the sublime and divine' (Otto, 1955, p. 7). These naturalistic and humanistic aspects of the Greek religion are encountered in their philosophy, poetry, theatre and plastic art. For theatre, this amalgamation of the natural, the spiritual and the divine manifests itself through the significance and appreciation of the gods Apollo and Dionysus. The opposite aspects of their divinity are being reflected not only in the art forms of dramatic poetry and theatre performances but also in everyday life, philosophy, mythology and medicine. Olympic religion 'never speaks through conceptual formulization in the way of dogma but is expressed as a vital force in everything that happens or is said or thought' (Otto, 1955, p. 15). Otto suggests that:

> it is difficult if not impossible for a modern [man] to acclimatise himself to this peculiar mode of thought, and it would be better to let the myths stand upon their own terms than to falsify them through the persistent intrusion of one's own categories of thought. (Otto, 1955, p. 29)

Theatre thus becomes the arena for the myths to stand upon and reflect the metaphysical and philosophical thoughts intrinsic in them. Martin Esslin (1999) recognises theatre's purpose for the contemplation of the ordinary and extraordinary when he states that:

> The theatre is defined as an assembly of human beings striving to establish contact with the profound mainsprings of their own being, the dark forces of physical emotion which lie beyond the trivialities of their everyday existence. (Esslin, 1999, p. 83)

Psyche is poetically personified in the myth *Psyche and Eros*, and the irrationality and archetypal dimensions of this myth elicit to its audience a symbolic understanding of psyche that is multifaceted and open to individual interpretations. In my reading, I see Psyche's laborious journey as an allegory for everyone's efforts to love her- or himself and I relate it with the impossibility of fully unveiling and understanding the whole of human psyche. From another perspective, Derrida (1987 in Derrida and Kamuf, 1991) in his reading of *Fable* by Francis Ponge remarks that 'the She in this fable I shall call Psyche from the fable of *Eros (Cupid) and Psyche*', and he points out that in French the word 'psyche' also refers to an old-fashioned kind of round mirror set on a pivot (p. 204). By this reading, Derrida wishes to underline the play in language between irony and allegory, the psyche as soul and round mirror represent the distance between the two 'selves', the subject's two selves, the impossibility of seeing oneself and touching oneself at the same time and the 'permanent *parabasis*' and the 'allegory or irony' (p. 213).

The mythological personification of Psyche and her recognition as a deity underline the humanistic aspect of the polytheistic religion as well as the way that Greeks contemplated and studied complex concepts through imagination, symbols and stories. Those two readings and interpretations of psyche, philosophically and metaphorically, reflect the methodology of the Sesame approach that conceptualises psyche following the analytical psychology of C. G. Jung. Jung (1960 [1946]) describes the Self as an archetype that is the coherent whole that unifies both consciousness and unconsciousness; the core of the human being that is impossible fully to see and grasp despite the human's constant endeavours. The creation or understanding of the Self is a continuous process of individuation, where all aspects are brought together as one. Imagination, creativity, symbolism and play are all aspects that aid this continuous process. Based on the above, I further connect *psychagogia* with Jung's analytical studies of psyche and their application within the methodology of the Sesame drama and movement therapy approach.

Socrates' Educational Concept of *Psychagogia*

When Aristotle mentions theatre as the highest form of *psychagogia,* he is borrowing the term from Socrates who uses it in reference to philosophical and ethical teachings about education. In this section, this pedagogical concept is re-contextualised within contemporary psychotherapeutic practices. *Psychagogia* is the central theme in Plato's *Phaedrus* where rhetoric is called *psychagogia,* referring to the Socratic conception of education as 'soul-leading'. According to Muir (2000) it means the educational art of leading the soul towards the 'good', providing an account of the way in which the individual's psyche is drawn towards dialectical examination of the 'good' (Muir, 2000). Muir argues that the dialogue in *Phaedrus:*

> provides a unified argument concerning rhetoric and philosophy, which are false and true *psychagogia* respectively (*Phaedrus* 271d), and their relation to education. Central to this argument is Plato's examination of the relative merits of speech writing and dialectic as means to achieve true *psychagogia,* and the roles of Love (or Eros), knowledge, and the criterion of truth in such 'soul-leading.' (Muir, 2000, p. 234)

Socrates' intention is to use the conception of truth as a starting point, concerning both the educator and the student, for the integration of three components of *psychagogia:* love, the psyche and the psyche's desire for 'good'. We should consider here that the Greek language distinguishes at least four different ways as to how the word 'love' is used: *agape, eros, philia,* and *storge.* For example, the word *philia* is the first component in *philo*sophy meaning love for wisdom and knowledge.

Psyche's love and desire for 'good' suggests being a pursuit of knowledge, knowledge that comes from within the individual rather than given from an external authority. Based on this relationship with the truth, Muir interprets *psychagogia* as 'a dialectical enquiry concerning the good' (Muir, 2000, p. 235). But love and 'good' are relative and absolute, in as far as our opinion of the good influences our knowledge of the 'good' and our choices in life. This means that one understands and questions what is 'good' based on the individual's perspective of life and humanity. Thus, 'truth' and 'good' are judged on the individual's ethos. Furthermore, according to Socrates, our opinions and choices are both relative to our level of knowing ourselves, according to his maxim 'know thyself'.

For Socrates the dialectical relationship based on love between the educator and the student is of supreme importance for *psychagogia.* The most vivid experience of the ultimate goal of being in itself comes from the recognition of qualities in other human beings. The variety of perception and depth depends on the individual. Muir (2000) takes this further by acknowledging what Plato recognises as the most important thing in educational terms:

> the movement of two souls toward each other, and then together toward knowledge of the good, constitutes not only a binding friendship but also the process of mutual education of the two friends. This mutual education culminates, ultimately, in these friends' participation in the philosophical (and according to Socrates, the best) life. (Muir, 2000, p. 240)

These ideas reflected on the art of theatre, recognising theatre as an absolute art of speech and movement that in a compelling and convincing way tries to persuade its audience for the good and truth of what it represents. Furthermore, we could draw parallels between the relationship of theatre with therapy. As we have already discussed, Aristotle examines the relationship between actor and spectator as one that motivates the psyche or creates a movement towards each other subsequently corresponding to *psychagogia*. This correspondence is achieved if both parties of this relationship are pursuing the 'good' or 'truth' for their self-development. When the actor is replaced with the dramatherapist and the audience with the client, and by following Socrates' paradigm, I interpret *psychagogia* in dramatherapy praxis as a methodology that employs theatre and drama for facilitating engagement and movement in the psyche. The 'movement of the two souls towards each other and then together toward knowledge of the good' (as quoted above) constitutes the basic principle of a psychotherapeutic relationship.

Theatre as Therapy

As discussed, the therapeutic dimension of ancient theatre can be detected by the attendance of patients being treated in the sanctuary of Asclepius at theatre performances. The witnessing of tragedies, comedies and satiric plays aimed to activate a psychic motion, and therefore promote healing by the contemplation of archetypal manifestations of mythology, reality, dreams and the divine. This, in turn, helped create internal contact and dialogue, resulting in the patient achieving inner understanding and potential transformation. Theatre, particularly tragedy, provides masterpieces of the kinds of actions and archetypal situations which induce empathy and contemplate sufferings. Thus, theatre corresponds to *psychagogia*. According to the Oxford Greek-English Lexicon (Oxford University Press, 1977), *psychagogia* contains the meaning of therapy when describing an action during which the psyche, 'beguiled from what she witnesses, experiences empathy at the contemplation of another's suffering' (1977, p. 2026).

This kind of healing by contemplating the irrational, dreams, psyche and archetypal mythological or divine qualities resonates with the theories of depth psychology on dreams and the unconscious. Freud and Jung placed high significance upon dreams and the symbols arising from them. According to Jung (1960), dreams are glimpses into the unconscious realm of the mind, a way for the unconscious to confront its irrational messages.

Jung (1954) points out the significance and effectiveness of education through example as the kind of education that can proceed wholly unconsciously and he recognises this learning through examples from the environment as a primitive feature of the psyche. In his analysis, 'education through example rests on this fundamental fact of psychic identity, and in all cases the deciding factor is this seemingly automatic contagion through example'. Jung (1954) continues to describe this type of education, borrowing the term *participation mystique* from the French anthropologist Lévy-Bruhl (Jung, 1954, p. 149). Based on these ideas, Jung believed that a therapist could guide their patient's inner exploration for as far or deep as they had been themselves. This pedagogical approach corresponds with the Socratic concept of *psychagogia* during which the educator guides the student towards a dialectical examination of human nature. In the case of dramatherapy praxis and by embracing the concept of *psychagogia,* the therapist acts as 'psychagogue', who, indirectly and with non-analytical means, suggests an attitude of self-reflexivity and exploration of the lived experience without offering direct answers, interpretations and solutions. The dramatherapist's ethos and cognisance of psyche is manifested obliquely in their praxis.

The Sesame Approach to Drama and Movement Therapy employs drama, myths, stories and movement, aiming to facilitate relationships and spontaneous embodied associations from the inner life. The principles of the Sesame approach rely on the importance of encountering the unconscious to inspire imagination and a symbolic attitude. The approach emphasises symbolic images, metaphors and allegories guided by the Jungian theory 'that the unconscious psyche has the chance to find expression through the emergent symbols within the art forms of drama and movement, with the therapist acting as guide, witness and "actor" at different times' (Hougham, 2009, p. 31). For Jung, symbols are the product of the 'transcendent function' in the psyche, 'which serve to unite psychic opposites and … are recognised for their duplicity and numinosity' (Hougham, 2009, p. 31). This transcendent function is activated through theatre and the communication between actors and spectators or therapists and participants. The roots of the Sesame approach belong to theatre and especially mime and movement. It is through Lindkvist's encounters with the in-patients and the numinous experiences that they had through the touring company which visited various psychiatric institutions in the 1970s – the 'Kats' – that Sesame as a therapeutic approach emerged. Furthermore, Lindkvist's encounters with traditional African healers embraced the symbolic and healing dimensions of movement, enactment and ritual (Lindkvist, 1998; Sesame DVD, 2009).

The Use of Drama and Myths

Paralleling the methodology of the Sesame approach with the concept of *psychagogia,* the focus rests on the use of drama and myths. Both in theatre in Ancient Greece and in the Sesame approach, myths are seen as mediums to motivate the psyche; as vehicles for an inner journey, a journey to the 'abyss or the unknown' exploring the archetypal dimension of human psyche. The irrationality and mystery within the myths offer the ground for inner expression of unconscious feelings and images. Jung notes that 'the more critical reason dominates, the more impoverished life becomes; but the more myth we are capable of making conscious, the more life we integrate' (Jung, 1954, p. 98).

Myths and traditional stories are widely recognised and studied as holders of truth and knowledge about human nature. With the advent of psychoanalysis, Freud and Jung opened the way to a new recognition of myth and dream as homologous agents to comprehend neurosis and the unknown psyche. Their psychological readings of mythological phenomena demonstrate the identity and relationship of the mythological realm with the unconscious, dreams and imagery. Mythology is recognised as 'the womb of mankind's initiation to life and death' or as 'the picture language of metaphysics', through which the second birth is achieved for the individual's life facilitated through the mythological rites (Campbell, 1990, p. 51). Through dreams and myths we come into contact with the mysteries of human life and with a wiser inward Self.

When using myths, participants are asked to reflect on the images or characters or events from the story that resonate with them. The inner ripples of this resonance are the movement that Aristotle identifies in a theatre that aspires to *psychagogia*. In dramatherapy praxis, the story is not merely witnessed or heard but enacted and improvised by the participants and expressed through image and symbol rather than a literal dramatic representation. This inner reflective dialogue is expressed through the metaphorical language of drama and movement.

This engagement of the participants within a ritualistic structure resonates with the practices in Asclepius's sanctuaries. Myths and archetypal manifestations are encountered in order to activate an inner movement. In the ancient sanctuaries, the participants are 'acting out' this inner resonance in their dreams. In dramatherapy praxis and specifically in within the Sesame approach, this movement takes form in an enactment. Thus, the way the myth is portrayed resembles the perplexing language of dreams. It may not have a direct, rational meaning but the myth's meaning permeates the consciousness for the participant who experiences it through their sensations. The embodied meaning is more powerful for the individual than an intellectual encounter with the story when reading it or hearing it. Pat Watts stresses this significance:

> In using the myth within the context of drama we are working with powerful energies and this must be respected and taken seriously. It is one

thing to hear or read a myth, but enacting is quite another. Enacting means engaging with the myth with the whole of our being – feeling, thinking and using our bodies; we are also relating to other people who are participating in role. No repetition of myth enactment will be identical; how a group works with the material depends on the chemistry of the individuals within the group and upon the particular mood at the time. (Watts in Pearson, 1996, pp. 28–29)

The application of the myths encourages a reconnection with archetypal principles that illuminates 'mythopoetic' aspects of our psyche. Mythopoetic describes the human ability of relating and imagining life experiences through myths. Hougham (2009) states that the focus of Sesame's approach is a pedagogical cultivation of a 'mythological intelligence' that amplifies the images, symbols and metaphors within the myths. To reflect on the images arising from the psyche within a mythological context minimises analytic reductionism and a pathologising of the psyche (Hougham, 2009).

In the context of dramatherapy, the embodiment of the myth in combination with the avoidance of any interpretation of the symbol allows the participant to give artistic expression of the image without losing any of its psychic force. This means that a key aspect of dramatherapy's methodology is located in praxis enabling a communication based on *psychagogia* to be achieved. The relationship of the actor with myths is not a quest for scientific or analytic interpretation of the given images or symbols, but rather a feeling of immediacy with true mythology. Mythology is not only 'possessed of meaning' but rather 'explanatory, that is assigner of meaning' (Jung and Kerenyi, 2001, p. 5).

McGlashan (1994) notes that to see the objects around us in stories or in reality as symbols:

is to intensify almost painfully the vividness and concreteness of the actual ... Archaic man spontaneously saw life in this way, but today perhaps only the artist understands that an object has not merely a concrete actuality, but also a transcendent reality, and perceives that this reality is something which the phenomenal world reveals rather than contains or engenders. (McGlashan, 1994, p. 71)

The capacity to understand an object or nothingness beyond a concrete reality is consistently found in the act of playing. The child plays with the objects around them to transcend their apparent actuality. The child's imagination expands with ease as an inherited aspect of their being. Artists are called not to abandon their capacity for play but to amplify it through their artistic mediums. As Pablo Picasso said, 'Every child is an artist. The problem is how to remain an artist once he grows up.'

Theatre is an act of playing; the actor is 'playing a role'; actors and spectators are playing a game based on pretence and belief; the actor 'plays' with their body and self, seeking the most truthful transformation. The actor is required to behold their creative playfulness with the same intensive curiosity and liveliness as a child. The Sesame approach emphasises the importance of spontaneous play and encourages the awakening of intuition. Myths are approached with spontaneity and a playful attitude led by the body. Participants are not seeking an interpretation of the myth's characters and situations but rather an intuitive response to the myth. The meaning of the myth is not sought outside but rather within each individual and the gained knowledge is an embodied knowledge. This knowledge has arrived through reflexivity and self-awareness, not given from outside as a recognised 'truth'. This praxis for me is *psychagogia*.

It feels like we have completed a full circle questioning the philosophical and pragmatic relationship of drama and theatre within dramatherapy methodologies. As Aristotle suggested, only by looking back can you move forwards. The operation of this chapter searched back to the archaic roots of the relationship between drama and therapy to rediscover and re-contextualise it for the contemporary dramatherapy practice. It concludes by signalling the subtle motion that drama and theatre can create in the human psyche regardless of its aesthetic forms.

References

Aristotle & Butcher, S. H. (1951). *Aristotle's Poetics*. New York, NY: Hill & Wang.

Barba, E. (1995). *The Paper Canoe: Guide to Theatre Anthropology*. London: Routledge.

Campbell, J. (1990). *The Hero's Journey.* New York, NY: Harper & Row.

Campbell, J. & Moyers, B. (1988). *The Power of Myth.* Reissue. New York, NY: Bantam Doubleday Dell Publishing Group.

Derrida, J. & Kamuf, P. (1991). Psyche: Invention of the other. In J. Derrida (Ed.), *A Derrida Reader: Between the Blinds* (pp. 200–220). New York, NY: Columbia University Press.

Edelstein, E. J. & Edelstein, L. (1998). *Asclepius, Collection and Interpretation of the Testimonies.* London: The Johns Hopkins University Press.

Esslin, M. (1999). *Antonin Artaud, The Man and His Work* (New edition). London: Calder Publications Ltd.

Grainger, R. (2004). Theatre and encounter. *Dramatherapy, 26*(1), 4–9.

Hartigan, K. V. (2009). *Performance and Cure: Drama and Healing in Ancient Greece and Contemporary America.* London: Gerald Duckworth & Co Ltd.

Hougham, R. (2009). Stone Soup: Towards a mythological intelligence. In S. Scoble, M. Ross & C. Lapoujage (Eds.), *Arts in Arts Therapies: A European Perspective.* Plymouth, MN: University of Plymouth Press.

Jung, C. G (1954). *The Development of Personality: Collected Works* (Vol. 17). London, Routledge and Kegan Paul.

Jung, C. G. (1960 [1946]). *Structure and Dynamics of the Psyche* (New edition, Vol. 8). London: Routledge and Kegan Paul.

Jung, C. G. (1977). The *Symbolic Life: Miscellaneous Writings Collective Works* (New edition, Vol. 18). Princeton, NJ: Princeton University Press.

Jung, C. G. & Kerenyi, C. (2001). *The Science of Mythology* (2nd ed.). New York, NY: Routledge.

Lindkvist, M. (1998). *Bring White Beads When Calling on the Healer.* New Orleans, LA: Rivendell House Ltd.

McGlashan, A. (1994). *Gravity and Levity.* Einsiedeln: Daimon.

Meier, C. A. (1989). *Healing Dream and Ritual.* Klosterplatz: Daimon.

Muir, D. P. E. (2000). Friendship in education and the desire for the good: An interpretation of Plato's Phaedrus. *Educational Philosophy and Theory, 32*(2), 233–247.

Otto, W. F. (1955). *The Homeric Gods: The Spiritual Significance of Greek Religion.* London: Thames and Hudson.

Oxford University Press (1977) *A Greek-English Lexicon.*

Pearson, J. (1996). *Discovering the Self Through Drama and Movement: Sesame Approach* (illustrated edition). London: Jessica Kingsley.

Hellenic References

Αρβανιτάκης (n.d.) Τάσος (απροσδιόριστη) *Πλάτων περί της κινήσεως*. Αθήνα, Ζήτρος.

Αριστοτέλης (1992) *Περί Ποιητικής*. Αθήνα, Κάκτος.

3

Symbolic Attitude

Richard Hougham

*I am looking down into a pool of water. It is quite a large pool and looks deep.
I am standing above it, on a sort of walkway, or bridge, with iron railings.
There are small rounded outlets on the ground, positioned at regular spaces
along the path. Perhaps these are for ventilation. I look down at the water,
which is about 30 feet below and see the reflections of the buildings around.
These buildings are tall and for workshops or factories. Diagonally to my right,
I see an area next to the water, which is an open-plan work yard. It is square
in shape and feels prepared for work. It is close to the water and used to make
and construct. I have a sense of this as a place of engineering, of manufacture,
of building. It reminds me of the landscape of canals of Birmingham.*

The Sesame Approach to Drama and Movement Therapy, evolved
over the past 31 years within the Royal Central School of Speech and
Drama, University of London, has variously been described as 'oblique',
'symbolic' and mythopoetic (Pearson, 1996, p. 39). Early innovative
practice over half a century ago by Marian ('Billy') Lindkvist has evolved
in many ways but an essence remains: the symbolic image is core to the
therapeutic process and training. One could say this belongs to a very old
tradition of psychic healing which considers therapeutic whole-making
experiences to occur when the personal or conscious psyche is brought
back into a vital relationship with the archetypal, deeper instinctual fun-
dament of the human being. The vehicle for this uniting experience is the
symbolic image, particularly that which Jung called the uniting symbol

(Jung, 1981, p. 189). The pedagogy of the Master of Arts Drama and Movement Therapy programme at Royal Central aims to cultivate a symbolic attitude in both the students and the learning and teaching milieu. By symbolic attitude, I am suggesting a relational and aesthetic sensibility to images which appear in dreams, the arts and myths and fairy tales, linking the personal psyche to archetypal experience. This pedagogic approach places value on the student's active attitude to the developmental possibilities inherent in various kinds of symbols or symbolic experience and attributes meaning to the images produced by the unconscious. Jung refers to the image being symbolic when 'it has a wider unconscious aspect that is never precisely defined or fully explained' (Jung, 1990, p. 21). In other words, the symbol has a uniting and mediating function, between the intellect and the individual experience of 'being-in-the-world'. Jung discusses this in terms of the contrasting virtues of an attitude guided by the world of ideas (*esse in intellectu*) and the vitality of an individual experience of the senses (*esse in re*) (Jung, 1981, p. 51). These are brought together by *esse in anima*, a reality of the psyche which Jung refers to as a 'constantly creative act', in which fantasy reveals the products from the unconscious (ibid.). *Esse in anima* paves the way for a pedagogy that seeks to relate to, but not jump to interpret, fantasy images and to live with the unknown yet dynamic aspect of the living symbol. It is this tension that the following chapter sets out to examine.

In the first section, I outline elements of the programme and the teaching of the Sesame approach, offering reflections on the requirement for students to undertake Jungian analysis throughout the training. I also refer to the different subject areas in the course as they present challenges to the students to cultivate a relationship with image and symbolic attitude. In the second, I discuss the Ancient Greek idea of *poiesis* in relation to the learning process in dramatherapy, as a force of creation which leads to formation and transformation, a bringing forth of something new into existence. This is Heidegger's 'blooming of the blossom', and the 'plummeting of a waterfall when the snow begins to melt' (Zimmerman, 1990, p. 233). Poiesis is the root of the modern word 'poetry' and prompts questions about the creative moment and the nature of symbolism. As an aspect of poiesis I refer to Keats's idea of negative capability as a capacity to be with the unknown without striving after fact or reason. The final part offers a closer look at myth and how different teaching practices give students an opportunity to wrestle with the fabric of myth and its enactment through improvisation. These reflections on Jungian analysis, poiesis and myth aim to offer some definition and form to the pedagogy of the Sesame approach and more broadly the articulation of a distinctive perspective on educational practice in the arts therapies.

The two year full-time course at Royal Central is a combined pedagogy which includes individual Jungian analysis, experimental studio practice, group process, academic seminars and placement practice. The seminars introduce students to Jung's own work as well as other key voices in analytical psychology such as Marie-Louise von Franz, Rafael López-Pedraza and H. G. Baynes. Students are in weekly Jungian analysis throughout the training and often beyond. Alongside this a weekly analytically oriented process group offers the opportunity for students to verbally reflect on the dynamics at play in the group, with a developing sense of the influence of the unconscious and the nature of projection. Beginning analysis, the group process and a simultaneous curriculum of daily physical experiential work activates the unconscious life of the student and a simultaneous discipline of reflection. Attending to images from dreams in analysis alongside expressive work in drama and movement workshops are initial ingredients for the cultivation of a symbolic attitude. At the outset, students are guided towards developing a sensibility to the images which is not simply representational. They are steered away from any 'dictionary of symbols' and instead encouraged to read fairy tales and myth alongside the theories of analytical psychology. A central part of individual Jungian analysis is to work with dreams, and students will often say their dream lives are enlivened at the beginning of the training. Experiencing the symbolic image through reflecting on dreams is a touchstone in the student's overall learning and can offer new and experienced insights into the depths and dimensions of psyche. The compensatory nature of the dream balances the ego's stance and attitudes, and vivid dream characters can play out an inner drama. This wildness in the psyche has immense energy and these images serve the function of rebalancing the psyche and revivifying the body. This is often both a period of excitement for the students, but also disorientation, as images from the shadow inevitably perturb the status quo and disturb existing perceptions of Self. The guidance offered by the analyst gives them a means to start to develop an understanding of the parts of the Self which may have been cast out by the ego. Meanings emerging from reflecting on dreams may be the first foundations of an understanding of the symbolic nature of the psyche and a sensibility to the unconscious as neither chronological nor rational. There is a developing sensibility to Kairos. Methods of amplification, which will often be guided by the analyst, start to train the students in looking both inward and outward at the reverberations of the symbols as they play out in their internal and external worlds.

The pedagogic function of Jungian analysis alongside the course challenges some students' existing ideas about psychotherapy, which they expect to be more geared towards autobiographical narratives and developmental ideas. But the beginning of the analytic journey is often a milestone for the student, as they begin to realise the imaginal nuances of the therapeutic relationship in psychotherapy and the mystery of the unconscious exhibited through the dream images it creates. It is also an opportunity to experience and reflect on the messages from the unconscious, as the analyst begins to offer interpretations and ideas about what the dream points to in the personality structure. This often marks a realisation that dramatherapy is not simply an application of technique, but an intricate and mysterious encounter, within which the unconscious relationship plays a significant role. It brings into play Jung's admonition that 'Life is too rational, there is no symbolic existence in which I am something else, in which I am fulfilling my role, my role as one of the actors in the divine drama of life' (1977, p. 274). Jungian analysis remains a foundational aspect to the training and one which psychologically anchors all the dramatherapy methods and techniques. Perhaps most importantly, it enhances the students' realisation that therapy rests largely on the discipline of self-knowledge and the importance of their own experience of a symbolic life and what this means to each of them as individuals.

How then, do the philosophy and practice of the subjects and units of the course combine with this introspection and learning in Jungian analysis? All parts of the curriculum aim to cultivate a symbolic attitude through immersive experience in group sessions, collaborations, individual facilitations, planning and reflection on fieldwork. In the first phase of the training, this happens specifically through work in the subjects of drama, movement with touch and sound, Laban movement and myth. These sessions are immersive, and while also framed academically, the teaching encourages praxis – that is, an experiential route into understanding. In other words, the learning experience is not only propositional, but brings the experiential and the dialogic into the frame before the theoretical construct. For example, students keep an 'arts journal' as a means to document and develop their artistic and symbolic attitude, and mark and reflect on their experience of the practical sessions. In this first phase of the training, but often throughout, they use montage, audio and poetry to portray and capture moments of meaning. They are invited to write in their first language. They mark vulnerabilities, hunches and sparks of ideas through lead, texture, shape and colour. The arts journal is a place to create a mandala rather than a sequence of learning. It is a means of documentation and amplification where inner images may link to associative images in myth, literature and contemporary arts practices. This is freedom from specific tasks and encourages praxis where the experiential is in the foreground and existing scholarship and knowledge come into play only after the experience itself. In other words it is encouraging the artistic qualities of the student and the cultivation of an individual aesthetic as formative aspects of a symbolic attitude.

In Laban movement sessions, for example, the symbolic field of gestures bridges inner and outer worlds and offers experience both individually and in relationship without working towards a particular 'understanding'. The poise of a still sculpt, the connection of the gaze with another, the evocation of a dream image through a shared and spontaneous dance is all material which is experience in the broader sense. It is experimenting with connection in the relational field which is not using the spoken word. But what does this word 'experience' mean? In this context, it is aligned with Wilhelm Dilthey's *erlebnis*, which speaks not only of experience as cognition, data, or the 'diluted juice of reason', but of expectations, feelings and impressions (Dilthey, 1976, p. 161). In other words it is bringing the question of affect squarely into the dynamic of the relationship and as a form of knowledge. In drama, the capacity to enter into spontaneous play and improvisation draws on conventions which emphasise the capacity to be in the present moment and move away from representational or autobiographical drama. This too, is a move towards the abstract, the augmented and the mutative image. The subject of Movement with Touch and Sound introduces teaching which focuses on presence, distilling the question of gesture and movement down to a rarefied sense of what it means to be attuned and spatially connected with another. This unique element of the Sesame methodology works in this symbolic realm, noting the bold and raw as well as the small and intricate movements between people as the language of contact and communication. This intersubjective landscape, explored through symbolic expressions, gestures and sounds gradually supports students to work intuitively and non-verbally with clients in dramatherapy. In addition to these core subject areas, students participate in a weekly core process group throughout the first three academic terms. This verbal group presents another set of challenges, as early patterns of behaviour and attachments are unearthed and become apparent. Group process sessions allow for specific attention to the dynamics of the cohort and an opportunity to explore the unconscious processes which are influencing relationships. The *raison d'être* of group process in the curriculum is for students to experience the powerful dynamics that groups can generate, such as the potential for 'pairing', the impact of regression and the dynamic of projection. The symbolic image in this context can be a core feature, as the 'group image', facilitates a movement in the group which can take a group deeper into its nature (Foulkes and Anthony, 2003). All these subjects carry an implicit educational practice which places the process of creation above the working towards any 'product' or performance. Learning is not conceived only as the building of a set of skills, but the development of an ear to the unconscious, a capacity to listen to its murmurings. In other words, it is learning as *poiesis*.

Poiesis is a philosophical idea which predates the languages of psychoanalysis and analytical psychology, beginning with Aristotle's poetics (Janko, 1987). *Poiesis* translates from the ancient Greek 'to make' and describes an emergent experience which has its source in the root of our being and adds to the discussion on the nature of symbolism and the symbolic attitude. This 'making' springs from a deeper, more instinctual part of the psyche and manifests in what Levine calls 'an inherent truth' through the process of creation (Levine, 1997). *Poiesis* is a root idea examined in the earliest formulation of phenomenology and speaks to the importance of how we perceive and relate to image (Miettinen, 2015). It points to the innate expression within an image, happening or moment, which is 'waiting in the wings'. In this process of unveiling, the image has a natural autonomy, reminding us of Corbin's mundus imaginalis and the inherent animation within nature which he observed (Corbin, 1971). This touches on the whole idea of teaching in that the emergence of knowledge is not an act of will, nor is it prefigured. Instead, it is a ground and a posture which requires in both the student and the teacher a capacity to be moved, affected and also surprised by autonomous images which arise from the unconscious. As Levine suggests, *poiesis* casts forward new possibilities of 'being-in-the-world', which are then framed in a work of art, whether it be a moment during a physical sculpt, a piece of music, a dance or a sound as the source of song (Levine, 1997, p. 37). Just as praxis speaks of the convergence of experiential practice and existing knowledges, so *poiesis* speaks of the creative process of an idea coming into being. *Poiesis* requires listening (in contrast to hearing) and the cultivation of a particular sensibility. Kereyni (Jung and Kereyni, 2002) refers to how we are open to be moved by images: 'a "special "ear" is needed for it, just as for music or poetry. Here, as well, "ear" means resonance, a sympathetic pouring out of oneself' (p. 5). The image cannot be grasped, it needs to be nurtured into being. For example, the discipline of remembering dream images upon waking requires reverie and a sense of mystery in relating to the poetic image. As Jung points out, 'it can never be precisely defined or fully explained' (Jung, 1990, p. 21).

This emergent quality of *poiesis*, which actively nurtures images into being, was at the heart of Jung's work, where the psyche brings forward symbolic communications which are compensatory, unifying and ultimately healing. In this constant interplay between the inner and the outer, Jung points to the autonomous nature of the symbolic image coming to light, suggesting that 'in no case was it conjured into existence through purpose and conscious willing, but rather seemed to be borne on the stream of time' (1981, p. 92). This offers a dynamism and sense of mystery, the unconscious as a source from which these images come. Poiesis has this sense of autonomy and reflects a teleological force in nature which brings images into being. As Bachelard suggests, it is the 'onset of the image' where 'the image touches the depths before it stirs the surface', (1994, p. xxiii) taking us further into the territory of paradox and reflections which are neither linear nor rational. Indeed, the symbolic image initiates depth, a vertical and dynamic axis between the surface and depth of the psyche. And so we see the image is autonomous, and the experience of the image requires a vulnerability, a sense of destabilising, and an openness. Within a learning environment, such qualities need to be articulated clearly to the students as aspects of their learning. In a climate of the acquisition of knowledge and a context where standards of proficiency are the benchmark assessments, the capacity to remain with the unknown requires clear articulation as a learning outcome. One way to outline it is to open up discussion of how it has been articulated in different discourses, such as the idea of negative capability first penned by the English poet John Keats.

In a letter to his brother in 1817, Keats described negative capability as: 'When man is capable of being in uncertainties, mysteries, doubts, without any irritable reaching after fact and reason.' (Keats in Forman, 1948, p. 72) It contributes to a culture in which experiential practice deepens, becomes less derivative from existing tropes and challenges students to reflect on images as a source of insight. It is a state of readiness to live with the unknown. This may seem counterintuitive in the process of learning, but this apparent inversion is at the core of a pedagogy which encourages students to relate to the symbolic image. In particular, it embraces different kinds of knowledge, carving out space for intuitive, embodied and symbolic ways of knowing. In other words, it is a disposition inclined towards paradox and ambiguity and one which intentionally turns away from positivism. Negative capability allows for and actively encourages disorientation and a step into the unknown, enduring risk and an openness to affect. Jung's work consistently emphasised the importance of lowering the critical faculty of the intellect and turning attention to the images from the unconscious, whether through dreams, play or myth. In his commentary on *The Secret of the Golden Flower*, in which he addresses the ancient Taoist text from c.1668, he suggests that the history of Western consciousness, in striving towards more power and independence, has forced the unconscious into the background (Wilhelm and Jung, 1975). In this movement, the unconscious has been neglected or at the very least relegated in relation to the hubris of intellectual thought. In teaching practice, this '*abaissement de niveau mentale*' is an aspect of negative capability which allows the fantasy to move forward and the symbol to breathe. It is *esse in re*. Learning in this sense is not only an acquisition of knowledge and skills, but also seeks to establish an attitude and environment in which 'obscure possibilities' may reveal themselves (Jung, 1975, p. 92). The idea of negative capability may support students in thinking about how a symbol 'speaks' to them through their intuitive and feeling functions, rather than jumping into an interpretation too soon. This stance invites the wild and the tame, the known and the unknown, the paradox of the crossroads and twilight.

In drawing out ideas such as negative capability, poiesis and esse in re, there is a move towards remaining with the unknown and allowing the nature of the image or the experience to emerge. In this sense, my argument aligns itself more towards phenomenology. But the idea of symbolism can be seen to disrupt phenomenology and it is this tension that I am interested in, whereby the attitude towards the experience, the image, the look, might allow for a phenomenological stance which then also brings in questions which ask 'to what might it point?' a further aspect of the programme at Central which enables these forces to be elicited within the teaching milieu is the introduction of myth and fairytale. As Emma Jung says:

> When a myth is enacted in a ritual performance or, in more general, simpler and profaner fashion, when a fairy-tale is told, the healing factor within it acts on whoever has taken an interest in it and allowed himself to be moved by it in such a way that through his participation he will be brought into connection with an archetypal form of the situation and by this means enabled to put himself 'into order'. Archetypal dreams can have the same effect. Equally, this putting oneself 'into order' or 'becoming one with the higher will' is the content of religious experience.
>
> Emma Jung (Jung and von Franz, 1980, p. 37)

The course introduces myth and fairy tale from the outset, through reading, through shaping, through the discipline of telling. When learning, telling or listening to a story, a symbolic attitude requires a linguistic wildness. Myth resists being pinned down with critical interpretations, moral judgements or historical determinants which make it dry up into

a factual archive. For the story to come to life, there must be a release of pre-ordained understanding, or reasoning. The teller must sit in their mythic ground and tempt the images into the space. They are there, in the air, and ready to be woven together in the telling. The smell of the forest floor as the animal musicians travel to Bremen in the Grimm's story. The frozen wing of Leithen as she flies from the cliffs of the Shannon to visit the black-footed stag Dubhchosach on the slopes of Ben Bulben. As the Nigerian proverb says, 'hold on tightly, let go lightly'. And so the musicality of dreams couples with the tremor of the myth and the personal life takes ground in the collective. The storyteller Martin Shaw speaks of the storehouse of the old myths, which are living and released through telling; we 'dwell within the story, not the other way round' (2014, p. xvi). He talks of 'feeding the image', offering the images which have become alive in the telling to become animated further and nourished through speaking them aloud (Shaw, 2014). The archetypal images within fairy tale and myth prompt a response beyond intellect, opening up a mythic landscape, mythic time. The story animates the space. In a dramatic improvisation, there is a dance between the shaping or 'sculpting' of an image from the story with the negative capability of jumping into the scene and allowing the myth to move the body into a shape. Sometimes it is the image which affects us, moves us. In the Grimm's story of 'The Three Feathers', a student is drawn to the image of the trapdoor, where Dummling's feather falls, and which leads to the steps underground where he finds the magical creatures, the toad and the toadlings in a circle. By virtue of negative capability and poiesis the student doesn't try to understand why they are drawn to this image. Indeed, the *what* is more important than the *why*. Questions to flesh out this moment might be: what is the impression of the trapdoor? What is its atmosphere, its texture, its shape? Such questions move away from representational drama and towards the cultivation of atmosphere, of material substance and sensation. It allows for abstraction and moulding by and from the image (Deardorff, 2004, p. 170). This is a subtle but important distinction. The student amplifies the image aesthetically. It is a release, not an interpretation. And more detail might emerge; the trapdoor might be partly hidden by a fern, the wood has been weathered into a particular shape. Or there is an inscription where the hinge has been lifted. The discipline required in this moment is an openness to affect, and a willingness to allow the fantasy to move further, for *esse in re* to come into being, for the symbol to appear and show itself further. In this way, the myth is inherently poietic, creating manifestations in the moment of enactment. As Emma Jung suggests in the extract above, 'through his participation he will be brought into connection with an archetypal form of the situation'. This connection with the universal can bring the personal psyche into relationship with the healing symbol during the ritual of myth enactment.

The emergence of this unifying symbol is unpredictable but focused. Bachelard (1994) speaks of both a resonance and a repercussion of the image: 'The resonances are dispersed on the different planes of our life in the world, while the repercussions invite us to give greater depth to our own existence' (p. xxii). His philosophical perspective suggests resonance as intersubjective and repercussions as intrapsychic. These musical terms offer a rhythm to the moment of affect from the symbolic image, and a chance for reflection. The thrust of this chapter has been to advocate for the autonomy of the image, to speak against the indiscretion of jumping to interpretation and cognition. But, just as with Jungian analysis, where the images are amplified and also interpreted, an understanding and reflection on the resonances and repercussions of the images is also a part of the training. While I have left this section until last, it is clearly important to ground these ideas in terms of the students' training to become dramatherapists. The combined pedagogy I have outlined is designed to give students the opportunity to cultivate a symbolic attitude, both as a route to understanding their own psychology, and then for this to have a direct impact on their dramatherapeutic practice with clients. Just as Jung emphasised the fundamental importance of the development of the personality of the psychiatrist, so the central effort in teaching the Sesame approach is in the levels of insight students develop into their own nature. Jung refers to an ancient adept: 'If the wrong man uses the right means, the right means work in the wrong way.' (Jung in Wilhelm and Jung, 1975, p. 83)

It is said that in Ancient Greece, when a room which was full of conversation suddenly fell into silence, Hermes had arrived, touching the event with his wand. The Ancient Greeks experienced Hermes as the god who brought this lull in the noise of discourse, and offered a chance for the imagination to come into play. This chapter has tackled the idea of a symbolic attitude in training dramatherapists and how a 'lull in the noise of discourse' might help us create a space for and hear the resonance of the healing symbol, especially in the dramatherapy training context. I hope this chapter contributes towards the groundswell of pedagogical discourses which are mythopoetic, which offer a counterpoint to the influences of positivism and social construction in education (Leonard and Willis, 2010). The arts therapies are perfectly placed to draw on themes which reach beyond the personal narrative and employ myth and image as primary sources of understanding. In this way, there is the opportunity to explore the cultural dimensions to psyche and to not rest solely on personal narrative. It encourages a pedagogy of the imagination and a link between the personal and the collective psyche which can be examined through a combination of depth analysis, experiential movement practice, storytelling and myth enactment. And I should finish by referring to the dream I shared at the beginning of this chapter. As I write, as I challenge myself not to dilute the image with the rational, I reflect on my own roots, my own resonant images. The pool of water is between me and the place of work, the canals are of Birmingham. And unusually a recent dream prompts a correspondence with my analyst which seems strangely fitting for this final part of the chapter. For it is my challenge to cultivate my own symbolic attitude, and it is the teaching, my own weekly analysis and the thirst for wild story which, in some way, keeps me alert to the healing symbol. I would like to share some of my dialogue with my analyst – his comments to me about my dream at the beginning of the chapter, which has been present for me throughout the time of writing. And he says:

> The pond, deep and at same time reflective, suggests contemplation of the unconscious, or more precisely the background of consciousness, where one's depths are, and the unconscious reflects images from the outer world but in its own way, changing them a bit or a lot, arranging them according to its own structures, the archetypes. You are on a bridge, the bridge unites the two, represents the connection, and also a state of transition. I guess Birmingham is the place of business, commerce, exchange, the least poetic of the English towns, as I hear. I don't know because I haven't been there.

And so it is, this dream takes me to the place of my own becoming. A place of both contemplation and manufacture. Birmingham is my roots, poetic or otherwise.

References

Bachelard, G. (1994). *The Poetics of Space*. Boston, MA: Beacon Press.

Corbin, H. (1971). *En Islam Iranien: Aspects Spirituels et Philosophiques, Tome IV, Livre 7*. Paris: Gallimard.

Deardorff, D. (2004). *The Other Within*. Ashland, OR: White Cloud Press.

Dilthey, W. (1976). Dilthey's approach to psychology. In H. P. Rickman (Ed.), *Dilthey, Selected Writings*. Cambridge: Cambridge University Press.

Forman, M. (1948). *The Letters of John Keats*. London: Oxford University Press.

Foulkes, S. H. & Anthony, E. J. (2003). *Group Psychotherapy: The Psychoanalytic Approach*. London: Karnac Books.

Janko, R. (1987) *Aristotle, Poetics 1*. Indianapolis: Hackett Publishing Company.

Jung, E. & von Franz, M. L. (1980). *The Grail Legend*. Boston, MA: Sigo Press.

Jung, C. G. & Kereyni C. (2002). *The Science of Mythology*. London: Routledge.

Jung, C. G. (1981). *Psychological Types*. Oxon: Routledge.

Jung, C. G. (1977). *The Symbolic Life*. London: Routledge and Kegan Paul.

Jung, C. G. (1990). *Man and His Symbols*. London: Arkana.

Levine, S. (1997). *Poiesis, The Language of Psychology and the Speech of the Soul*. London: Jessica Kingsley Publisher.

Leonard, T. & Willis, P. (2010). *Pedagogies of the Imagination, Mythopoetic Curriculum in Educational Practice*. Dordrecht: Springer BV.

Miettinen, T. (2015). Husserl's phenomenology of poiesis: Philosophy as production. *The Journal of Speculative Philosophy*, 29(3), 356–365.

Pearson, J. (1996). *Discovering the Self through Drama and Movement, The Sesame Approach*. London: Jessica Kingsley Publisher.

Shaw, M. (2014). *Snowy Tower, Parzival and Wet, Black Branch of Language*. Ashland, OR: White Cloud Press.

Wilhelm, R. & Jung, C. G. (1975). *The Secret of the Golden Flower*. London: Routledge.

Zimmerman, M. (1990). *Heidegger's Confrontation with Modernity: Technology, Politics, and Art*. Bloomington, IN: Indiana University Press.

4

Primal and Pre-Lingual Voices

Eran Natan

Introduction

Our world is made of words. All around the world, people use a variety of languages to express their feelings and communicate with one another. Words help us to frame our thoughts and give meaning to different stimuli we encounter along our life path. But to what extent can language truly accommodate the human need of expressing deep, primal feelings, such as anger, joy, surprise or fear? In the words of Berry (2000, p. 41), 'today we tend to use language to cover up what we feel, rather than to reveal what we feel'.

Preceding the development of words, pre-lingual voices were used by the human race from ancient times. Ancient people were closely connected to their surrounding nature, and in particular to animals. They obtained food by hunting, used fur to keep themselves warm, took animals out to pasture and used their voice to communicate with them (Armstrong, 1996, p. 75). Animals were an inseparable part of the human environment, and the animals' instinctive behaviour was naturally an inherent part of their life, enabling humans to express themselves similarly in 'the language of the animals ... the primary level of vocal expression' (Pikes, 1994, p. 5). These ancient people were strongly connected to their voice, 'that longs to roar, snarl, holler ... howl, cry and bay at the moon; in short to be the animals we are' (Newham, 1999, p. 114).

In an experiment conducted in 1904, while examining the relationship between 'sound reaction' and human behaviour, Carl Jung hypothesised that in ancient times humankind used 'non-verbal sound and sound associations' as a means of communication, and that language developed as a secondary, conscious process (quoted in Overland, 2005, p. 28). Referring to the use of language in those days, Overland quotes Jung, who asserted: 'Language was originally a system of emotive and imitative sounds, expressing terror, fear, anger, love … sounds which imitate the noises of the elements: the rushing and gurgling of water, the rolling of thunder, the roaring of the wind, the cries of the animal world' (Jung, 2014, p. 12).

As part of my vocal approach to dramatherapy, following the Sesame method, I often work with the notion of animals as a way of exploring a range of pre-lingual voices. My hypothesis is that working with animals offers clients a legitimate way to reconnect to fundamental and unconscious parts of their primal instincts. Various anthropological studies have explored the inseparable link between humans and animals (see, for example: Seeger, 2004; Levin & Süzükei, 2006). This new field of research is termed Anthrozoology – the study of the interactions between human and non-human animals. I shall now give a few examples of such human–animal relationship.

In his study, Eske Willerslev (2007) followed the Siberian hunting community of the Yukaghir people. He describes how Old Spiridon, a Yukaghir hunter, prepares himself for an elk hunt: Spiridon dresses up like an elk, and is moving around the snow and making sounds imitating a female elk, in order to seduce a male elk to get closer to him. As part of the hunting process, Spiridon gradually becomes the elk – however, he does not lose all his human qualities; although he wears elk skin and fur, walks like an elk and imitates its voice, he still carries a weapon and continues watching his prey as a human. Willerslev describes well this dual, seemingly paradoxical phenomenon: 'It was not that Spiridon had stopped being human. Rather, he had a liminal quality: he was not an elk, and also he was not not an elk. He was occupying a strange place in between human and nonhuman identities' (2007, p. 1).

Anna Stevens created an compelling documentary film about the Shipibo tribe in the Peruvian Amazon (2007). The Shipibo people's traditional songs, Icaros, which are passed down through many generations, imitate the power of the elements and the animals in their surroundings. The Shipibo people believe that each animal has a special healing energy and the power to protect people against illness or disaster. The Shipibo shaman women compose elaborate geometric wool designs, capturing this animal power and expressing it. The women 'weave the songs' as they sing them, simultaneously working the cloth with their fingers. Thus, each Icaros encompasses sung metaphors, capturing not only the animal power, but also the rich environment and emotions the animals evoke in the singer. Here is an example of a bird Icaros, sung by the shaman:

> *Birds, listen to this song and transmit it to others.*
> *I am singing with Joy*
> *I am singing with a smile*
> *I am singing this song into your bodies*
> *I am planting the seeds of this powerful song into your hearts.*
> (*Woven Songs of the Amazon*, DVD (Stevens, 2007))

Pre-Lingual Voices in Sesame Dramatherapy Practice

The Sesame Approach to Drama and Movement Therapy uses metaphors as an important ingredient in its practice, offering clients an alternative, non-verbal way of expression. During Sesame sessions, both client and therapist explore the richness of metaphors through movement, drama, touch and storytelling. The metaphor becomes a living entity, echoing different themes the client brings to the session. It also offers the client a new and fresh perspective, allowing them to reflect safely on their life experiences.

The importance of metaphors in myth, dramatic role plays, enactments and movement has always been stressed in the Sesame approach; however, what is yet to be explored is how pre-lingual voices can become a more central element within Sesame, mainly in relation to metaphors. In Sesame sessions, dramatherapists often tend to use language as their main means of communication when enacting characters and expressing various images. Thus language creates a frame, assigning clearer meaning to an otherwise metaphoric non-realistic world, while the therapist is simultaneously aiming to distance this imaginary world from all that is 'real'. By doing so, language paradoxically challenges the safe, dream-like world weaved by the metaphors for the benefit of the clients.

Pre-lingual vocal expression, on the other hand, brings clients back to what Peter Slade called 'the land' (Slade, 1954), a safe play zone where metaphors stay detached from any conscious interpretations. In my work as a dramatherapist I work with various clients, such as people who have experienced trauma and people with learning disabilities, who often cannot fully express verbally how they feel. The possibility for both therapist and client to form a third, shared language during the Sesame session establishes a common ground for the formation of trust.

In my practice, I like to explore the breathing styles, vocal textures, postures and movements typical of various animals. For example, as part of the body warm-up at the beginning of a therapeutic session, I often use an exercise which I call Bear & Tree: I ask clients to pair up, then one partner stands solid as a tree, and the other is a bear that just woke up, hoping to scratch its back against the tree trunk. At the first stage the tree is receptive, responding to the bear's need to scratch. However at the second stage the tree becomes more active, pushing the bear off or trying to tickle it. This exercise is not only used as a body warm-up for both tree and bear, but is also a way to form a non-verbal dialogue of give and receive between the two partners, using body and voice.

Another breathing exercise I use in dramatherapeutic sessions is called the Cow & the Mosquito. One client plays the role of a cow grazing in the field, standing on all fours. The other partner places their fingers against different parts of the cow's back, imitating mosquito bites. As the cow feels each 'bite', it inhales deeply from the area that was touched and exhales gently to the same spot on the back, trying to drive the mosquito away; the mosquito then finds another 'feeding spot' on the cow's back. At the next stage the inhalation of the cow becomes much stronger, sending the mosquito far away. This exercise aims to work on different breathing tempos and various breathing spaces in the back, using play and metaphor.

An important purpose of the two exercises described above is to prepare clients for more in-depth pre-lingual voice work later on in the session. By exploring the slow breath and bass voice of a sleepy bear, or the quick breath and high-pitched voice of a hungry mosquito, we encourage clients to rediscover the rich qualities of their voice. The vocal discoveries that spontaneously occur in the dramatherapeutic setting are often silenced outside, as our modern society tends to categorise them as unacceptable, 'non-human' voices. This is a defence mechanism used in order to protect us from the truth these voices hold about who we really are – humans with animal instincts. Our goal as dramatherapists is to create a safe container for clients to celebrate these instincts and play with pre-lingual animalistic voices, allowing them to find the bear and mosquito elements within themselves, the animalistic within the human.

In the following sections we shall explore how pre-lingual voices can be used and integrated into the Sesame Approach to Drama and Movement Therapy. The first section examines the role of breathing: breath is the most basic function we are all born with and has a calming effect on the body, and it can be used in dramatherapy as both an assessment and a creative tool. The second section demonstrates how the use of archetypes can enable dramatherapy clients to discover a new range of pre-lingual voices and express their deepest feelings. The third section looks at how the pre-lingual voices a storyteller uses in their narration can stimulate further vocal expression, as part of the 'main event' enactment of a Sesame dramatherapy session. The chapter concludes with a short summary.

Breathing Voices

About Breathing

The Greek word *psyche* means both 'soul' and 'to breathe'. Breathing is the link between body and mind; it is our most basic pre-lingual vocal expression.

The autonomic nervous system (ANS) is responsible for maintaining the balance of our main bodily functions, including our heart rate and breathing. It consists of the sympathetic (SNS) and parasympathetic (PNS) systems. The PNS conserves energy in the body, and is responsible for ongoing and mellow activity; it helps in regulating our breath while keeping the body relaxed in a 'rest and digest' mode. The SNS, on the other hand, reacts to immediate changes in our environment, and is responsible for the 'fight or flight' mechanism that turns our breath fast and unsteady (Hanson, 2007).

The two sets of breathing mechanisms distinguished above are embedded in the Sesame dramatherapy session structure. During the initial 'check in' stage, clients are usually guided to look inwards, relax and ground their breath and body as they move into a more balanced state of being. Later on, as the session develops towards the 'warm-up' and 'main event' stages, the body, imagination and breath are reactivated, aiming to energetically explore a chosen theme. During these stages, the characters we enact and the movement styles we perform constantly manipulate our breath dynamics, keeping us alert. The 'grounding' stage at the end of each session supports clients in reconnecting with their body and breath, before gradually letting go of the session theme and getting ready to leave the therapeutic space.

I wish to point out two common types of breathing techniques I apply in my voice work as a dramatherapist: costal breathing and diaphragmatic breathing (Calais-Germain, 2006, p. 24). In costal breathing, we expand the ribs when inhaling and close them when exhaling. In diaphragmatic breathing, the abdominal area expands during inhalation and contracts during exhalation. I find the diaphragmatic breath useful especially when working with clients who come to the session feeling unbalanced and in need of support in grounding their body and mind. In such situations I often use guided imagination, with the image of an anchor grounding a boat in a stormy ocean. The costal breath, on the other hand, provokes the expansion of the chest muscles, creating a lighter and more open sensation in the body as it moves around the space. In such cases, the image of a feather or a boat sailing freely is often used.

Case Study: Anchored Boat Sailing Free

Ben (pseudonym), aged 50, has been in individual dramatherapy intervention for the past three years. He describes himself as having a successful career with a well-paid job, but nevertheless he feels unhappy; his real dream is to become a professional painter. Breath work has become central to our weekly sessions, in order to help Ben relax after a long, stressful day at work. In one of our sessions we explored the theme of freedom/restriction with the breath. Ben mentioned the image of a sailing boat as a symbol of both freedom and restriction, perceiving the boat's anchor as a restricting, heavy object tying him to the bottom of the ocean and preventing him from fulfilling his dreams; he said that the boat wishes to sail freely, but is obliged to stay where it is.

We went on exploring the anchor metaphor using diaphragmatic breathing, focusing our attention on the body as it pulls heavily towards the deep, dark water. We then continued the imagery work, exploring costal breathing when lifting the anchor and allowing the boat to float gently on the waves. It was only during the verbal reflection at the end of the exercise that Ben realised the anchor quality, which he perceived as an obstacle at first, actually became a source of stability and order in his mind. The untamed sailing boat, which until then was a dream-like image, was now experienced as chaotic, symbolising the lack of control Ben felt over his life.

The dynamics and tempo of our breath is constantly affected by emerging thoughts and feelings we experience in our daily routine. When we are calm, our breathing is slow, rhythmic and deep; when we are excited or in danger, the breath tends to become quick and shallow; when we are startled, we usually gasp in surprise. The breath also helps the body to self-regulate, and supports clients in becoming more present and connected during the sessions. Furthermore, when clients breathe naturally, they produce a wide spectrum of sounds. For many clients who feel embarrassed to project their own voice, listening to the natural sound of their breath becomes an important step, leading to stronger confidence and the belief they have the right to voice themselves in additional ways.

Breath and Metaphors

Breath can be successfully integrated within metaphoric work. When using metaphors, it is not 'I' that breathes, but rather it is the 'thing' I become; the metaphor or character becomes a 'breathing body', enabling the client to feel freer to discover new textures of breath qualities – round and deep, quick and direct, or short and shallow. As argued by Linklater

(2006, p. 43), for an actor to truly embody a character, he should first let go of his natural breathing pattern and then establish a new breathing, which reflects the events in the life of the dramatic character.

Exploring animal breathing can be an inspiring stimulus for many clients to explore different breathing patterns. The variety of bodily postures animals offer, the unique body formation each species represents, and their interaction with their natural habitat – all affect the way animals breathe. For example, an alert tiger that runs after a hunt will have a different breath energy than we might imagine a floating jellyfish cradled by the waves in the middle of the ocean to have. For a client wishing to explore more grounded, assertive and instinctive parts of themself, the short and sharp breathing pattern of the tiger can become a way for self-discovery. However, for another client, seeking for more flow, space and freedom in their life, the moving image of the jellyfish, with its soft and prolonged breathing pattern, can be a useful metaphor at times of tension.

Other metaphors which are interesting to work with in relation to breath are natural images such as trees, mountains or rocks. These images support clients in finding a better sense of solidity and gravitation, and help slow and ease the breath. For example, a huge rock that is stuck deep in the ground for millions of years is a useful image to explore in order to maintain a slow, deep and long breathing pattern. However, the same image can develop into something different and thus change the breath and movement dynamics completely: what would happen to the client's breathing energy if the solid rock were to be suddenly detached from the ground and to begin rolling frantically down a steep hill? The breath and the body will probably roll with it, quickly, uncontrollably and powerfully. Similarly, an old tree with a wide trunk and long roots can be associated with a solid, gravitated pattern of breath; but simultaneously, the treetop can express lighter qualities of breath, represented by the gentle swaying of its branches and leaves.

With some clients, where gravity and centre are needed, we can work with more anchored, gravitated breath qualities represented by the solid rock and the old tree metaphors; the breath will then be slow, deep, travelling from the bottom of the earth through the feet and all the way up to the thighs, abdomen and belly. With other clients, on the other hand, who are more passive and require an energetic breath quality, the metaphors of the rolling rock or the swaying treetop can be helpful.

In Sesame dramatherapy sessions, we use the 'warm-up' and 'bridge in' stages as a means to physically and metaphorically prepare the clients for the 'main event' stage, where a story is being told and enacted by the group. During the bridge in, we often explore specific images from a given story. One exercise includes asking clients to create a moving sculpture of these images, thus helping them make a gentle transition from the 'here and now' world into the dream-like unconscious world the story entails. When sculpting the images, clients should focus on their breathing and examine how breath can support the creation of the image they become. For example, in the well-known story *Ali Baba and the Forty Thieves* clients are sometimes asked to embody the shape of the cave where Ali Baba discovered the treasure. Though it is always interesting to watch the variety of physical shapes clients use to form the cave, it is unfortunate to notice that the breath, which is the life force generating every living image, is often absent.

What if dramatherapists encourage their clients to use their breath to imitate the sound of air travelling through the cave passages, leading us deep into the underworld? What if clients use the breath to embody a deeper physical image of the cave, rather than an external visual one, one that encourages grounding of the cave in their nose, neck, chest, torso, etc.? From my experience, body, breath and image then become integrated, supporting clients to explore the theme of the story at a deeper, more unconscious level.

Breath in Assessment, Grounding and Touch

By listening to the client's breathing, the dramatherapist can find clues indicating their emotional state – nervousness, distraction, lack of energy or over-excitement can all be heard in the tempo of breath. The dramatherapist can also observe how air travels along the client's body and examine areas of blockage. Breathing can help in expanding different spaces in the body (such as the chest, lungs and abdomen), soothing tensions in various body parts and marking the body boundaries, thus grounding it.

Austin (2008, p. 26) also emphasises the importance of deep breathing in slowing down the heart rate and calming the nervous system.

Different breathing exercises can be used effectively in different parts of the session, especially at the beginning and the end. Breathing as part of the warm-up of every session helps clients to focus, to connect to their bodies and gradually to make a transition from the outside world into the dramatherapy space. We should always ask ourselves, what is the story the breath is telling us about the client today?

Case Study: Group Breathing

I once worked with a group of school children aged 8–10 for a period of one year. The children used to enter the dramatherapy space, which was located inside the school, just after the lunch break – straight from the playground. They were usually excited, breathless, and were jumping all over the dramatherapy room, unfocused and shouting. Instinctively I asked all of them to kneel to the floor and lie down in any position they wished, and so they did – some lay on their bellies, others on their backs. It was interesting to see the powerful effect the floor had on their breath energy: its solidity grounded the ecstatic movement of their bodies, soothing their breath and softening their muscular tension.

Dramatherapists may also find touch useful when wishing to help clients connect more easily to their breath. The touch of palms or transitional objects, such as pillows, fabrics and bean bags, on specific body parts, can help clients focus their attention and their breath on those specific body parts and release physical tension that has accumulated in them. Touch also offers both clients and dramatherapists a simple way to connect and become one breathing unit; it can help to build intimacy and mutual understanding in the therapeutic relationship.

In addition, the therapy space itself, with its walls, floor, chairs and curtains, can help clients mark the body's boundaries and support it while breathing: clients can lean against walls, be supported by the floor or cover themselves up with curtains. Leaning, pushing or rubbing our backs against our partner or a wall, gliding our belly along the floor or leaning on a chair in different postures can provoke new, interesting qualities of breath.

The Snoezelen room is another setting in which a more focused dramatherapeutic work with touch can be explored. The Snoezelen is a multi-sensory room developed mainly to answer the needs of severely disabled people: cushions, fabrics, a water mattress and other sensual stimulations, such as light and sound effects, create a safe therapeutic environment to work with (Fowler, 2008, p. 76).

Case Study: Snoezelen Room

These days I am working with Pete (pseudonym), an adult client with learning disabilities, in a Snoezelen room. Pete is overweight, and has body image issues. His physical state is unstable, as he moves from extreme undereating to episodes of extreme overeating followed by constant vomiting. He always covers himself up with long sleeves, making sure no one ever sees his hands or legs.

Our dramatherapy sessions are usually non-verbal. Pete often asks to be covered from toes to chest with big soft cushions. As I touch the cushions surrounding his stiff body, I ask him to breathe in and out; I then add a gentle hum while pressing down the pillows. The cushions create a safe and protecting 'bubble' feel for Pete, which he greatly enjoys as he closes his eyes; the soft cushions are an external support helping him mark his body boundaries while softening his muscular tension. Pete is encouraged to use breath and voice during the session, thus building another layer of presence in the space. The exercise helps him form a healthy dialogue with his injured body self-perception.

In this section we examined the role of breath in supporting clients, allowing them to connect to their body and stimulating a more creative type of therapeutic work. Breath is a basic need all humans and animals have shared for millions of years, and it is a necessary foundation for any voice work we practise later on in the session. Exploring breath on its physical, emotional and metaphorical levels prepares the clients for an in-depth dramatherapy experience; it also helps connect us to unconscious parts of our psyche, inherited from our primal ancestors. These ancestral shadows are shaped in the form of archetypes, described in the next section. We shall now examine the possibilities of working with pre-lingual voices using archetypes, in order to support clients when exploring emergent themes in dramatherapy sessions.

Archetypes and Voice Work

About Archetypes

Carl Jung talked about two levels of unconscious: the first is the 'personal unconscious' and the second is the 'collective unconscious'. The first holds a range of complexities and images that connect to our life experience (Newham, 2000, p. 27), and consists of 'all contents that are still too weak to become conscious' (Jung, 2014, p. 133); while the collective unconscious contains all the patterns we have inherited as humankind.

Jung believed that one person's psyche holds various voices, instincts, passions and feelings within it which are unique living entities that need to be expressed. These archetypal entities have existed from the dawn of human history – the Trickster, the Mother, the Devil, the Child, etc. As suggested by Von Franz (1995, p. 2), 'whenever known reality stops, where we touch the unknown, there we project an Archetypal image'. Jung also mentioned the power of music when aiming to reach 'the deep archetypal material that we can only sometimes reach in analytic work with patients' (McGuire & Hull, 1977, p. 275).

Voicing the Archetypes

The medium of dramatherapy offers clients various ways to explore archetypal qualities through their voice. Assuming we have all inherited the primal voices of the archetypes, we should all have the capacity to express them. Clients are thus encouraged to work vocally with archetypes, as they express aspects of their psyche – the dark side and the light one, the beautiful and the ugly, the loving and the hating, etc. The primal instincts, drives, needs and actions of the archetypes project the client's real 'self', allowing them to dive into new play zones where these 'bigger than life' vocal qualities could be experimented with.

Each archetype has a unique vocal identity that distinguishes it from other archetypes. Every one has a set of 'archetypal behaviours' that can be projected through the voice: for example, the Child archetype's quality is a soft, dreamy and playful vocal energy, which is opposite to the direct, fixed and solid vocal energy that the King might express. The Witch has a sharp nasal quality of sounds that differentiate her from the low, deep moans and growls the Ogre produces.

We can also identify specific body parts or vocal spaces that serve as the archetype's 'vocal container', that is, a centre in the body which is the core of the archetype's vocal energy. For the Witch, for example, it is the nose; for the King, it is the chest; and for the Ogre – the abdomen. In addition, each archetype has a set of movements that affects the colour of its unique voice.

When working with the King, for example, clients may explore two contrasting qualities: on the one hand, the soft and loving King, and on the other hand, the harsh and controlling King. When exploring the first quality, I usually ask clients to stretch their arms horizontally; then the King's bodily posture seems open, communicative and ready to interact. But it is the horizontal stretch of the arms which also expands the chest muscles, pulling the rib cage with them and widening the breathing space, thus allowing more air into the lungs. The breath then becomes deeper, steadier and calmer, supporting the production of soft airy voices: *ahhhhh* ... On the other hand, when exploring the second King's quality, which is more controlling and demanding, I usually ask clients to quickly point one of their hands forward in command. In this position the chest is contracted into the centre of the body, making the breathing space tighter and the voice sharp and direct: *ha!*

Working with specific archetypes involves the preparation of both body and mind. The session begins by warming up the body with focus on specific organs, which, later on, will be the centre from where the archetypes breathe. Deep, shallow, relaxed or quick breathing styles help the client transform their body from normal to irregular breathing patterns. The heartbeat then becomes faster or slower, chest or abdominal muscles expand and contract as they support the breath, and the body posture changes as air comes in and out. I often ask clients to gently voice the breath, sometimes using the image of letting the voice 'surf' on the 'breath wave', colouring it with different pitches and vocal energies. By placing the palms on different parts of our body, we can also feel the vibration of the voice as it travels around.

The physical sensations described above help clients feel present and confident enough gradually to leave behind the 'here and now' world and to delve into the unconscious. The different breath and voice styles experienced in the warm-up encourage clients to dare to metaphorically explore their primal needs. Metaphors create an atmosphere that allows archetypes to surface; the unique vocal quality of each metaphor, be it a tree, lake, animal or a weed, transform into the 'playground' of the archetype, offering new, rich vocal dimensions to relate to. For example, how will the Ogre's voice be affected by the image of swimming in a sensual mud pond? We can assume a possible sense of pleasure, with gurgling voices centred in the abdomen; yet what would have happened if then suddenly another 'monster' had invaded its territory, trying to take over? We could expect a possible expression of anger, through chesty shrieks.

The example above clearly demonstrates how inseparable archetypes are from the metaphors surrounding them. The archetype cannot exist in a vacuum, since it draws from its communication with the world; it affects the world with its voice and gestures, while being affected and changed by the stimuli around it. This is also why archetypes can be so useful when working with clients on various themes. On the one hand, the archetype helps in building a stronger sense of presence and confidence for a client who might lack it in real life. On the other hand, the metaphors nourishing the archetype symbolise the relationship the client has with their own surroundings. For immigrants or refugees, for example, this type of work can be quite helpful as a transition from one society to another. For other clients who struggle with basic communicational skills, such as those on the autistic spectrum, working with archetypes can contribute to their establishing constant communication and the exchange of ideas with the world surrounding them, with obvious therapeutic value.

Archetypes are present at every dramatherapy session, offering clients permission to play and voice unconscious aspects of their psyche. For example, a client who has issues of low self-esteem may find the assertive King's voice helpful to gain more confidence, whereas another client, who might feel too serious in life, can use the Trickster's voice to connect to their more playful aspects. Although dramatherapists occasionally work with archetypal qualities during sessions, they often focus on exploring them in more verbal, dramatic or movement-related techniques. By doing so, I believe they lose the rich vocal potential of archetypal work.

To illustrate this point, I wish to give a common example from an exercise often used in dramatherapy sessions: Sesame dramatherapists sometimes use the children's game Simon Says in the warm-up stage, as a way to bring the group together and warm up the body: one participant becomes the group's King, demanding everyone to follow their instructions by saying 'Simon says to … jump on one leg\scratch the nose', etc. But as the game develops the King also tries to fool the group as a trickster, by skipping the statement 'Simon says' (which should result in the instructions not being obeyed). Consider what might happen if we play Simon Says more freestyle, allowing the King to command the group in gibberish, using pre-lingual voices – just to fool them and enrich the game.

Another dramatic exercise dramatherapists often use in warm-ups is Leading Body Part. In this exercise, the facilitator chooses a specific body part for the participants to follow as they move around the space. The same exercise can also be used for exploring the movements and voices of different archetypes. For example, the nose can lead participants to discover the range of pre-lingual nasal voices of the Witch, and the belly more animal-monster like archetypes. These vocal discoveries can be used later in the session in enactments during the main event stage, where different 'evil' roles appearing in the story can be explored.

Imaginary objects or real ones can also be used during the dramatherapy session in order to support clients and ease their way into the archetypal land. For example, with clients who wish to explore the notion of lightness, we can use light handkerchiefs at the warm-up stage, throwing them up in the air and gently catching them. When the upper body parts – chest, shoulders, hands, neck and head – are engaged in the soft play, we can shift our centre of gravity from the legs and the abdomen (Hunter, Ogre, King) to the upper body parts, mainly the neck and head (Child, Witch, Princess). In this way, the upper dimensions of movements we explore can invite and support surprising light and high-pitched qualities of voice. In the following case study, an example of archetypal work with objects can be seen.

Case Study: Warrior, Child, Mother and Objects

Johanna (pseudonym), aged 24, underwent an individual dramatherapy intervention for a period of one year. Johanna wanted to attend voice-based dramatherapy sessions since she felt shy to use her voice freely in her daily inter-actions; she also hoped to find ways to address her suppressed feelings. Johanna was sexually abused in her childhood, and the mental scars the trauma has left in her were one of the complexities we explored in the course of the sessions.

Johanna had great difficulty in breathing naturally. At first we started every session with a set of breathing exercises; when she tried to breathe, I noticed how stiff her body would become, with her breathing becoming constricted. Her throat and chest were tense, preventing air from travelling down towards the belly and abdomen. Referring to the physiological effects of trauma, Jung called the throat 'a ring of fear', describing the locking of the throat muscles in its wake. Pearce (2005, p. 28) supports this view, mentioning that in a state of stress or trauma the muscles in the body tighten, impairing breathing, and the sounds we are able to utter become fainter. It is also believed that from a psychological perspective, the belly and the abdomen hold the human emo-tional and sexual sides (see, for example, Austin, 2008, p. 25). By blocking her breath from reaching further down towards these organs, Johanna uncon-sciously tried to protect painful emotions and memories linked to her trauma. I felt Johanna strived to find a key to these hidden emotions, but could not discover the way. It then occurred to me that dramatic work with archetypes could be helpful in this case; it was then that the Warrior archetype appeared in our sessions.

In one of the sessions, I brought two pieces of cardboard roll one metre long, as they seemed interesting vocal objects to experiment with. At first we held between us both sides of one of the rolls, and started exchanging gentle breaths through it while the other was listening. Later we exchanged gentle voices. Then gradually the two rolls turned into tribal objects: we stood facing one another and bounced the rolls in turns on the floor. We moved to a 'call and respond' exercise, where movements and voices are exchanged. The rhythmic movement of our bodies while holding the rolls-turned-sticks, and the sound and vibration they made when beating them against the wooden floor, gradually transformed the dramatherapy room into a tribal ceremony space. Slowly the rolls became fighting, ritualistic objects of the Warrior: we raised them in the air as spears and hit them on the ground as drums. Johanna's movements, cries and growls became more primal, when suddenly, instinctively, she took the roll she had in her hand and smashed it against the wall while shouting. Next she grabbed the other roll from my hands and smashed it as well. She then collapsed to the ground, and sat exhausted on the floor.

After a few seconds of rest she took one of the smashed rolls, and started rolling it on the floor while humming gently. I joined her with the other ruined roll. The vocal and physical intensity changed dramatically: from the fierce Warrior she had been a moment before, she now turned into a soft, dreamy Child playing in order to soothe herself. Johanna then put aside the roll, lay down on the floor and burst into tears. It was a deep and painful sob that came from the bottom of her body, expressing pain that was held deep inside her for a very long time. I continued to hold the soft hum in the space, but changed my role from an echo of the Child she was to a protecting Mother, vocally supporting her fragile child.

In this section we examined the power of archetypes, showing how they can support vocalisation of hidden parts of clients' emotional world within the dramatherapy scope. Archetypes reside in each and every character and story we enact. The variety of archetypes and their deep connection to our primal needs offer clients the permission to project feelings that are not easily accepted in the outside world, often perceived as embarrassing. For some clients, who feel they have no control over their life because of personal trauma or sexual abuse, exploring the role of an archetype dealing bravely with the problems it faces can be greatly significant. In addition, archetypes allow clients to touch the most lively and healthy parts within themselves, helping them to develop their creativity and the belief that in the imaginary world almost everything is possible.

In the next section, readers are invited to follow the vocal trace of the archetypes into the world of storytelling. The extreme and rich voices, which have been explored in this section, will now be used by the storyteller – inviting clients to further explore primal voices as part of the story's enactment.

Storytelling, Enactment and Voice

Voice of the Storyteller

Storytelling is an art of sound and voice, and each storyteller has their unique vocal style. Nevertheless, the art of storytelling becomes much richer if pre-lingual voices and sounds are integrated into the spoken story. When listening to a story, the clients do not only visualise the images being told but also absorb the vocal scenery the story offers. The storyteller's own voice echoes the sounds of the landscape where the characters and images live, conveying their richness to the listeners: the opening of a squeaking door, a soup stirred by a hungry witch, a hyena feeding in a savanna, a wolf howling at the moon, or a lullaby sung by a child in a forest.

The sound effects a storyteller adds to the narrative fascinate the listeners, since they meet their most primitive and pre-lingual mode of thinking. Krause, a leading expert in natural sound, remembers how as a child he was fascinated by the sound effects his father used when reading him stories:

> I especially liked the tales that evoked acoustic events – pirates' yarns; legends of giants, their huge feet thundering across the landscape; ancient battles; children lost in the woods, obsessed by mysterious noises. In the end, however, it was the faithful combination of the whip-poor-will and crickets outside my window that finally lulled me to sleep. (2013, p. 107)

From the opposite perspective, Mellon, a storyteller, describes the impact the soundtrack has on the storyteller himself, as he expresses the landscape, scenery and characters with his own unique voice:

> As you let yourself open up to each resounding moment of your story, stones, trees, and insects can speak of themselves. Stones can chant their rhythmic purpose on earth. Plants can sing and call with clear voices into your story world. Animals can speak their needs … winds can intone from the depths of the seasons. (1992, p. 14)

Often when telling stories, I like adding to characters' names the sound they make: for example, *Mr. Rabbit clippity-clop*, or *Ms. Frog ribbit-ribbit*.

In this way I create a clear association between the character's name and the sound it makes. It is mainly valuable for those clients who are too shy to dive into the non-verbal world of the character during an enactment. For them, starting to imitate the *clippity-clop* sound of the rabbit in the enactment becomes a safe starting point, from which they can continue to express new authentic pre-lingual voices.

Enacting a Story Through Voice

The narration of myths and stories is one of the core elements in a Sesame dramatherapy session: usually a story is being told, and then the clients choose their favourite roles and the group enacts the story. The variety of characters and images within each story offers clients fascinating ways to express themselves vocally.

Each story enfolds a main theme which the dramatherapist wishes to explore with the group or the individual. For example, if we wish the group to deal with the notion of confrontation, we may choose to work with a myth which has at its centre a battle between two rivals; the enactment could then offer a way for clients to explore assertive parts of their voice. However, if we choose to work with a story which deals with the notion of sharing, we could invite clients to search for gentler, caring types of voices to communicate with one another.

Stories are also the land of the archetypes. According to Smail 'these archetypes are encountered in Sesame through working with the embodied image' (2013, pp. 60–61), and through symbolic play that takes place in the main event. For example, choosing a story with a Trickster as its main character (such as the legends of *Anansi*) enables clients to find lighter and more playful types of voices. On the other hand, choosing a story with a Warrior as its main character invites more earthy voices to be explored.

The beauty of the story world lies in the fact that in a single enactment the ruling King, the bad Witch, the pure Child and the ugly Ogre can all play together, interact and affect one another. For example, in the story *The Emperor's New Clothes*, the two Trickster thieves who pretend to be tailors are gradually turning a mighty King into a Fool. A small and unknown Child becomes the people's Hero when shouting out loud that the King is naked. The transformation from a shy child with a small voice into the people's public speaker is a massive vocal transition for a client enacting that role, who is struggling to find their independent voice in life. For another client who seems to be taking themself too seriously, enacting the foolish king would help them discover funnier, lighter aspects of their voice.

Each landscape has its own unique 'soundscapes' and images. For example, the dark caves of the underworld can be a symbolic womb detached from the upper world. It is a place of solitude and self-reflection, where many clients like to explore their voice and its most deep, authentic and sometimes painful aspects. The underworld is also the land of all sorts of creatures – slugs, cockroaches, ogres and witches – all the 'ugly' and 'weird' natural phenomena live there. In terms of the vocal experience, it is a treasure land with new and unfamiliar sounds and voices to experiment with.

In many stories, different natural elements such as fire, wind, earth and water become living vocal images for clients. In the next case study I describe a dramatherapy session I had with a young girl, where the notion of 'cold' and 'warmth' were explored vocally (see Natan, 2009).

Case Study: The Fire Keeper

Emma (pseudonym), aged 11, was a junior school pupil attending dramatherapy sessions for almost two years. She suffered from social and behavioural problems in and outside class, including getting into physical clashes with other children at school, leading to social ostracism.

In many of our sessions the theme of warmth and cold preoccupied Emma's imagination and inspired our work. In one of our sessions I suggested to Emma that we work on the story The Coyote Steals Fire (Gersie & King, 1990, p. 163), which is centred on the theme of cold and warmth. In this tale, the coyote rescues people who are freezing by stealing fire for them from the fire keepers, figures living at the other end of the world, who do not want to share it.

While telling her the story, I invented a song the fire keepers sing while guarding the fire: 'We are the fire keepers, we keep the fire alive!' Emma loved the song and asked to act the figure of the fire keepers. She wanted to go back to the scene in which the coyote tries to steal the fire. She created an imaginary bonfire, placed stones into it, calling them 'fire stones', which I, the coyote, was to steal. Emma began to walk round the fire in circles, singing the fire keepers' song. At first the song sounded pleasant and soothing, as she walked rather calmly round the fire. From the corner of her eye she observed the coyote, approaching the fire, stooping.

Encircling the fire monotonously and watching the wild animal facing her, snorting, helped Emma dive into 'the land' (Slade, 1954), straight into the world of metaphor, and imbue the fire keeper's figure with life. She behaved more and more wildly and started to circle the fire very rapidly, bent and aware of her body, as though sensing the natural environment within which she was moving. Gradually the song changed its tone, it became rasping, aggressive, belligerent, interspersed with menacing cries and growls. The figure of the coyote I portrayed moved on towards the fire until it exposed itself. Emma screamed at the coyote as it tried to steal the fire from her and drove it away.

Summary

In this chapter I have explored the way pre-lingual voices can be used as a therapeutic tool in the Sesame Approach to Drama and Movement Therapy. The introduction was an overview of the connection ancient people had with the sounds and voices in their natural surroundings; the people used to produce a wide range of voices in imitation of the sounds around them – the animals they were sharing the habitat with and the sounds of the elements they were surrounded by. However, following the development of language, many of the pre-lingual voices that were used as a way of expression and communication have gradually disappeared. In this paper I attempted to prove the great relevance pre-lingual voices have to the Sesame approach, by offering clients non-direct ways to express suppressed emotions using authentic voices.

In the breath section I looked at the place breath has as an assessment, self-regulating and creative tool in dramatherapy. The next section focused on voicing the archetypes; working with those 'bigger than life' figures offers client creative ways to experiment and discover new colours in their voice. The unique voices of the King, Trickster, Hunter or Child turn the drama-therapy space into a vibrant vocal laboratory. In the following section I have explored how pre-lingual voices can be used in storytelling and enact-ments; dramatherapists who integrate vocal elements early in the session encourage clients to use voice also in the main event of the enactment.

In the last few years voice has become more present in the Sesame approach for drama and movement therapy, both in the academic level and in practice with clients. However, many dramatherapists still talk about their lack of confidence in using their voice freely during ther-apeutic sessions. Some feel safer to use songs in the sessions, but are embarrassed to express their voice in its most deep, pre-lingual form; this explains why many clients, who could have benefited from the richness voice has to offer, have no real access to it. This is also why I believe voice has to step forward and become even more prominent and integrated in the Sesame approach, alongside drama, Laban movement, myth and movement with touch and sound.

Much research has already been done regarding the importance of voice for the singer, actor and performer; however, little has been written about the place voice has in dramatherapy. Many research areas can be explored: for example, what is the role of pre-lingual voices when working with people who have 'lost their voice' due to trauma or organic disorder that affected their ability to talk? Links between cultural identity and voice are also an interesting area for further research; can we say that there are 'archetypal voices' that identify a culture? And what vocal interactions may develop between clients from different cultures working together? Research regarding the way voice in Sesame affects image and archetype work, as well as movement styles, is another theme that awaits further examination.

To conclude, in this chapter I have attempted to demonstrate the insep-arable role voice plays within the Sesame approach. Pre-lingual voices are a powerful tool in every aspect of the dramatherapeutic intervention, whether in the warm-up, narration of myth or the enactment stages of a session. It is my hope that voice will continue to grow within Sesame, and be acknowledged also by the larger creative arts therapies community.

References

Armstrong, F. (1996). The unique voice that lives inside us all. In J. Pearson (Ed.), *Discovering the Self Through Drama and Movement* (pp. 72–78). London: Jessica Kingsley Publisher.

Austin, D. (2008). *The Theory and Practice of Vocal Psychotherapy: Songs of the Self.* London: Jessica Kingsley Publisher.

Berry, C. (2000). *Your Voice and How to Use It.* London: Virgin.

Calais-Germain, B. (2006). *Anatomy of Breathing.* Seattle, WA: Eastland Press.

Fowler, S. (2008). *Multisensory Rooms and Environments: Controlled Sensory Experiences for People with Profound and Multiple Disabilities.* London: Jessica Kingsley Publisher.

Gersie, A. & King, N. (1990). *Storymaking in Education and Therapy.* London: Jessica Kingsley Publisher.

Hanson, R. (2007). Relaxed and contented (part one): Activating the parasympathetic wing of your nervous system. *Wise Brain Bulletin, 1*(5), 1–8.

Jung, C. G. (2014). *Collected Works of C.G. Jung: The Complete Digital Edition.* Princeton, NJ: Princeton University Press.

Krause, B. L. (2013). *The Great Animal Orchestra: Finding the Origins of Music in the World's Wild Places.* New York, NY: Little, Brown.

Levin, T. C., & Süzükei, V. (2006). *Where Rivers and Mountains Sing: Sound, Music, and Nomadism in Tuva and Beyond.* Bloomington, IN: Indiana University Press.

Linklater, K. (2006). *Freeing the Natural Voice: Imagery and Art in the Practice of Voice and Language.* Hollywood, CA: Drama Publishing.

McGuire, W. & Hull, R. F. C. (1977). *C.G. Jung Speaking: Interviews and Encounters.* Princeton, NJ: Princeton University Press.

Mellon, N. (1992). *Storytelling and the Art of Imagination.* Rockport, MA: Element.

Natan, E. (2009). The voice and the 'Shadow': How does the use of voice in dramatherapy enable greater expression of 'Shadow' aspects of the psyche? *Sesame Journal, 9* (spring), 13–20.

Newham, P. (1999). *The Healing Voice: How to Use the Power of Your Voice to Bring Harmony into Your Life.* Shaftesbury: Element.

Newham, P. (2000). *Using Voice and Theatre in Therapy: The Practical Application of Voice Movement Therapy.* London: Jessica Kingsley Publisher.

Overland, G. (2005). Voice and DNA trauma. *ReVision: A Journal of Consciousness and Transformation, 27*(3), 26–33.

Pearce, S. (2005). *The Alchemy of Voice: Transform and Enrich Your Life Using the Power of Your Voice*. London: Hodder Mobius.

Pikes, N. (1994). Giving voice to hell. *Journal of Archetype and Culture,55* (spring), 1–14.

Seeger, A. (2004). *Why Suyá Sing: A Musical Anthropology of an Amazonian People*. Urbana, IL: University of Illinois Press.

Slade, P. (1954). *Child Drama*. London: University of London Press.

Smail, M. (2013). Entering and leaving the place of myth. In J. Pearson, M. Smail & P. Watts (Eds.), *Dramatherapy with Myth and Fairytale: The Golden Stories of Sesame* (pp. 55–72). London: Jessica Kingsley Publisher.

Stevens, A. (2007). *Woven Songs of the Amazon*. Santa Fe, NM: Green Spider Films (DVD).

Von Franz, M. L. (1995). *Creation Myths*. Boston, MA: Shambhala.

Willerslev, R. (2007). *Soul Hunters: Hunting, Animism, and Personhood Among the Siberian Yukaghirs*. Berkeley, CA: University of California Press.

5

Silence

Bryn Jones

Introduction

I began writing about silence during the Spring of 2007. Since that time, I seem to have developed a growing awareness of the diminishing opportunities for common silence. By *common silence* I mean those unconditioned, serendipitous moments which punctuate our sensory lives. Moments, when warning, we find ourselves held in a reverie of stillness and quietude. A kind of dropping down beneath the flotsam and jetsam of our daily busyness and into a more clear and becalmed sphere of being. Such occasions seem increasingly rare. I wonder if it's just me? I wonder if it's about getting old? I wonder if, by thinking about silence, I have made myself more sensitive to and more noticing of its lack. Like when John Ruskin talked about 'sketching in order to notice' (Ruskin, 2010), by my noticing silence have I perhaps also become more aware of its infrequency?

In any case, the incessant crackle and chatter in contemporary living seems undeniable. And this relentless increase seems to be insinuating itself into ever more intimate corners of our lives. Those in-between moments provided by our common silences are becoming fewer, faint and fleeting. It's like we are being continually distracted. Kept forever plugged in, connected and in the loop. Assailed and beguiled by a constant stream of audible and visual noise. The relentless outpourings of Instagram, Facebook, Spotify sounds and Twitter tweets holding us on the crest of some perpetual wave.

To me this is the troubling thing. I think about those simple human needs which appear to shore up our wellbeing; recuperation; a rest, a break from it all. I think about the ways we define our sense of place and how some sense of connection with our shared and natural world is key in that. Is it too much to say that the relentless pull of the remote device deprives us of such simple centring and so causes a profound and personal disconnect with our natural world?

Perhaps I'm being overly dramatic. Of course quiet moments remain ever available to us. Even as I write I can gaze from my window and see the solitary figure enjoying early morning sunlight while sitting quietly beneath a tree. In Peckham. Five migratory geese standing in a line in the middle of an empty playing field. The steam shadow from my coffee playing on the opposite wall. Yet I wonder if we have the time to notice. I wonder if we have the space to hear. And as a dramatherapist, I wonder: what might all of this mean to the noisy, messy, disruptive practice with which I am engaged?

In 1999 I was diagnosed with tinnitus. The condition began with an infection in my right ear; within a couple of months I was experiencing bilateral tinnitus. I embarked on a round of 'cure seeking'. This took me to the consulting room of an ear, nose and throat specialist. The subsequent conversation surprised and fascinated me. The consultant asked me what it was about tinnitus that troubled me. At the time I was living as a Buddhist monk, silence was in many ways my field; that which provided the necessary foundation and support for my life and work. In silent surroundings tinnitus appears at its loudest, interrupting peace and distracting the mind. I remember asking: 'Will I ever hear a silence again?' The consultant's answer was appropriately Buddha-like: 'You just have to think about the silence in a different way. Anyway,' he concluded, 'silence doesn't bring peace. Silence is the most stimulating sound there is.' So began a new chapter in my relationship with silence.

Breaking the silence
Of an ancient pond,
A frog jumped into water –
A deep resonance

Basho, 1996

I received treatment for tinnitus in Sheffield, home to the British Tinnitus Association and the UK centre for tinnitus research. It is there because of the miners. South Yorkshire was also the heartland of mining in England and miners were found to be suffering from an inordinately high incidence of hearing loss brought on by the pressures of working beneath the surface. At the time I wondered about the metaphorical similarities between monks and miners; the monk descending within to investigate the inner seams of the mind.

Similarly in the processes of dramatherapy, we mine. The mythical call of 'Open Sesame!' moves a mysterious rock to reveal a passage leading to the inner world of the imagination. There we may find ourselves digging darkly down to explore internal terrains and investigate the unseen, unconscious workings of underworld material. In such transit and toil what blasts and pressures might we encounter and what fissures may become exposed?

A Call to Silence

Silence is something many of us crave. Although frequently submerged beneath the constant ebb and flow of modern living, the distant call of silence reminds us of our quiet hope for a haven. Such romantic distancing perhaps indicates that our craving is fed not by a clear idea of what we want as much as a reaction, an escape from that which we don't; namely the intrusive and incessant clamour and chatter of contemporary life. These days, we may feel, the world seems so loud, with so much noise and yet so little communication.

Conversely there are many who dread and abhor the idea of being with a silence. Their silences are far removed from any soothing and pleasurable sense of tranquillity; these represent the frightening and the unbearable, the threat of absence and the gaping void.

Clearly, silence means much more than the mere absence of sound. What could possibly constellate such polarising experiences of silence as those outlined above? Given the inevitable frequency of silent moments within dramatherapuetic work and the strength and magnitude such moments may evoke within a client's experience, this is a question requiring urgent and thoughtful attention.

In beginning to explore and reflect upon this topic, it quickly becomes clear that far from being simple and straightforward, silence is a deeply complex phenomenon evoking unique and powerful responses in both thought and feeling which are paradoxical, illusive, mystical and extremely difficult to define. Some even come to question its very existence.

The composer and musical theorist John Cage spent considerable time examining the nature of silence and its relationship with sound. Cage believed that the goal of music was to 'sober and quieten the mind, thus rendering it susceptible to divine influences' (Cage, 1973, p. 158). In discussing his most well-known work, the 1932 composition *4'33"*, Cage reflects upon the paradoxical impossibility of actual absolute silence:

> An anechoic chamber is six walls made of special material. A room without echoes. I entered one at Harvard University several years ago and heard two sounds one high and one low. When I described them to the engineer in charge he informed me that the high one was my nervous system in operation, the low one my blood in circulation. Until I die there will be sounds. (Cage, 1973, p. 8)

Here Cage begins to associate sound with living and thus its absence (silence) with death. Therein lies an inescapable reflection of silence as death; that which is still, eternal and extinct. Yet it is the pregnancy of still and silent moments from which all sounds and movements, all births and cessations arise.

It is this paradoxical 'pregnancy' of silence, the expectancy and anticipation held within a 'pregnant pause', which is I think, key in beginning to investigate the role of silence within a therapeutic context.

Silence sounds a specific call to the reflective practitioner. Where does silence sit within our own practice? How are we working with the creative tensions of silence in drama and movement, from which something, in some way, on some level, must emerge?

The artist, author and educationalist John Lane believes the deliberate and conscious act of 'being with silence' is indispensable in all aspects of emotional and creative growth:

> To protect our independence, and to have the confidence to express our native creativity. To be aware that our beliefs, our dreams and opinions, have no need to be other people's second hand notions. It is important to remember the value of thinking for oneself, which is best done in silence. (Lane, 2006, p. 58)

This appears to fly in the face of those prevailing trends fostered and promoted by social network sites, where the idea of being independent is to be no one, in no place. The only realm that matters being the public; the seen, the shared and the liked. The struggle to carve out the possibility of an independent life seems all the more difficult, scary and risky if all you are seen to be is dependent upon your being seen, shared and liked. Just like the sound of that tree, falling in the middle of the forest in which no one has ever ventured. What, where, who are we?

The idea of silence as an artistic imperative is familiar. Writers, musicians and painters have all sought the inspiration of quiet space.

> You don't need to leave your room. Remain sitting at your table and listen. Don't even listen, simply wait. Don't even wait, be quite still and solitary. The world will freely offer itself to you unmasked. (Kafka, 1991, p. 89)

In recent years I have been intrigued by the increasing use of 'silent images' in media and advertising; most notably those small and perfectly balanced towers of smoothly worn pebbles. Perhaps re-evoked in popular consciousness by contemporary land artists such as Andy Goldsworthy, these quiet and natural sculptures reflect archaic forms such as the buddhist stupa: 'structurally analogous to the inner unity reconstituted in the individual by silent meditation' (Rawson, 1991, p. 71).

What promise might these silent structures hold for us today? A sense of balance, a harmony, a modicum of peace and quiet? It would appear that the world of marketing has identified a latent need within us. One which it now seeks to tap into a want, via these silent sentinels.

The function of the buddhist stupa is to turn the mind inwards by outwardly reflecting an unrealised potential already existent within. In the traditions of both art and spirituality we find this shared appreciation of silence an effective tool for development. So I ask: how are we answering the call of silence within a therapeutic context, particularly within dramatherapeutic interventions, where we may often witness a client encountering personal material through the sensation and connection of an unspeaking outer image?

Additionally I wonder: what precisely are these 'silences' we hope, or dread, to encounter? What longings fuel our search? What fears drive our flight?

These strike me as compelling questions that we may do well to ask ourselves. Moreover, that silent experience, both shared and solitary, can provide us with a powerful frame in which we can discover the exacting clarity to see what it is we may be reflecting upon and to what end. I sense that it is only then, through our own unique and individual reflective process, that we can come to intuit and, perhaps in time, gain insight and understanding into the often unspoken needs of our clients.

The Silence of the Shadow

What occurs within us when we enter a silence? There appears much that could be analogous with the experience of stepping into a shadow: a subtle shift, an emergent change and the heightening of senses as we arrive in a less familiar realm.

We enter a transitional space. A smoky threshold between the old and the new, the then and the now, the known and the unknown. By abiding in such spaces, therapeutic interventions may come to unearth many new hitherto unseen and unheard treasures.

In silence we find a rich and authentic place in which to develop the often discussed 'openness to the unknown' (Casement, 2008, p. 26).

However, lacking familiarity, such 'unknowns' may bubble from within the therapist as much as the client:

> Therapists need confidence in the analytical process if they are to be able to tolerate the vicissitudes of being used by their patients in different ways. They need to be able to follow the patient, without feeling too much at sea to function analytically. (Casement, 2008, p. 27)

In his book *In Praise of Shadows* the author Junichiro Tanizaki invites the reader to investigate 'not only the thing itself but the pattern of the shadows, the light and dark which that thing provides ... the uncanny silence of dark places' (Tanizaki, 2001, p. 33). His work is a spare yet detailed encouragement to care intensely about that which is so easily overlooked but if held with mindful appreciation might yield something beyond the reach of neatly packaged formulas. It is in this regard that I believe silence has something of great and real value to offer in therapeutic training and subsequent professional practice.

Tanizaki goes on to praise Japanese food, describing it as 'a kind of silent music' not to be eaten, not to be looked at but to be 'meditated upon'. In particular he settles his attention on the popular confection yokan:

> Is it not indeed a colour to call forth meditation? The cloudy translucence like that of jade; the faint, dreamlike glow that suffuses it, as if it had drunk into its very depths the light of the sun; the complexity and profundity of the colour ... and when yokan is served in a lacquer dish within whose dark recesses its colour is scarcely distinguishable ... you take its cool, smooth substance into your mouth, and it is as if the very darkness of the room were melting on your tongue. (Tanizaki, 2001, p. 26)

Ostensibly Tanizaki is discussing aesthetics but to me his work resounds with much that could be said of a silence within a therapeutic space. His oblique narrative chimes with David Read Johnson's cautionary comment that 'entering the play space can be experienced as entering the client' (Johnson, 1992, p. 119). It certainly captures something of the relative intimacy that can be evoked within a shared silence. A sense that the familiar masks of chatter, small talk and affectation have fallen away, leaving us tender and exposed. This results most typically in a heightened sensation holding sway. Giggling, anticipation, tension and apprehension may ensue. If these can be sat with, allowed to be, until a natural diminishment occurs, then client and therapist may discover they have arrived in an altogether different place.

The entering of 'another place' involves the inevitable traversing of borders. Borders which may have previously functioned to comfort and protect. It is here I believe many of the fears of silence find their footing; the strong societal admonishments of silence as 'mad and bad ... depressive, escapist, weird and anti-social' (Maitland, 2008, p. 25) and thus scary and to be avoided: taboo.

In a recent interview the poet Carol Anne Duffy, commented: 'Poets must be able to listen to silence, poetry being as much about space as it is about words. But there are some silences that one never wants to hear.' (Cooke, 2009).

Duffy may be referring to the silence of absence or loss. She may be evoking a personal encounter akin to 'the silent treatment', that awful and isolating experience of silence used to oppress and punish. Silence as a terrible weapon. In my own childhood I came to learn of the phrase 'the silence' denoting marriages in which husband and wife had not spoken to each other for years. That didn't mean they were not communicating; nothing is more powerful than the silence of an angry person or the silence which sits in a place where the truth is not spoken.

Moreover there is the silence of the politically oppressed, the abandoned, the marginalised, the shamed, the wronged; the finding of one's 'voice' often considered synonymous with the attainments of freedom, liberation and self-determination. All of these associations and more may be fermenting the seeds of one's silence:

> The silent side of history is seen a little in the silent suffering of men and women. But more suffering is lived through than is seen from the outside. It seems that mankind prefers to suffer in silence, prefers to live in the world of silence, even if it be by suffering, than to take its suffering into the loud places of history. (Picard, 1989, p. 48)

That which remains unspoken, unseen, uncertain and unknown within ourselves, our own private underworld, our shadow: how might an exploration of silence enable us to connect with and recover those lost, unknown aspects of ourselves?

Silence is always saying something. If we listen, what might we hear? Silence is a communication.

Silent Transitions

I'm interested here to intrude further on the notion that there is something 'wrong', something 'negative' about silence. I'm also inclined to lean against those often reductive psychotherapeutic interpretations of silence as synonymous with being 'stuck' or 'defended'.

Instead I'm suggesting that silence can function as a therapeutically necessary and an emotionally rich transitional space for reflection, healing and soulful journeying; a secure base for unsticking the stuck:

> The pause, the in-between space indicates unspoken thoughts and feelings … the pause obliges us to look more closely at the sub text and by pausing, by allowing that in-between space, we allow for the possibility of change and the unexpected … Freud emphasizes that in analysis, the analyst should not be taking notes but listening to the tone of voice, listening to the things which are unspoken by the client. (Roose-Evans, 2009)

It is clear that the use and interpretation of silence within a therapeutic relationship must always be carefully considered, especially so when silence sits as a deliberate element of an intervention. Silence will shift in its relevance depending on numerous factors, not least the approach taken by the therapist and the needs of the client. However, in my research I came across several examples in therapeutic literature where silence was denied such latitude. The prevailing voice appeared to be one which casts silence in the negative, so much so that it could easily be considered as anti-therapeutic. This view appears to discover an interestingly loud voice in John Casson's book, *Drama, Psychotherapy and Psychosis: Dramatherapy and Psychodrama with People Who Hear Voices*.

Casson's text doesn't pull punches. Early on in the narrative we encounter the startling quote: 'What makes the patient ill is silence' (Forrester in

Casson, 2004, p. 31). This appears to be used in relation to several accounts involving the traumatic experience of people who had been sexually abused and then forced to remain silent; to not speak of the abuse they had suffered. I would argue that it is the abuse rather than the silence which is at the root of the immediate and subsequent suffering. I initially thought this might be a trivial point to raise given the context and I certainly would not advocate any such form of 'forced silence'. However, on reflection I believe this distinction between an abuse and a silence to be of critical importance in identifying and acknowledging the personal experience of the individual. Having suffered a harrowing, traumatising and intrusive ordeal, might a client not find real benefit in a 'silence supported' experience of space and separateness? One which allows for a gradual regathering and reclamation of their shattered sense of self? The crucial point it seems to me, is not necessarily about working *in* silence but *with* silence.

As I read on, my initial observations clarified in light of Casson's own bold comparisons between silence and suffering: 'Therapy an antidote to silence and isolation, offers people an opportunity to talk, communicate and relate to others.' (Casson, 2004, p. 97) I began to envisage a therapeutic space without silence. A place where only linear logic and explicit expression were held in any worth. In my imagination I mourned the loss of those misty emergent spaces often necessary for the unfolding of difficult narrative and unconscious material:

> Occasionally a group will tolerate a space … sharing or silence … the therapist may well pick up concerns or themes … A long silence will not be helpful and therapists must be willing to model appropriate responses to suggested exercises. (Casson, 2004, p. 180)

Why will a long silence not be helpful? Unhelpful to whom? I imagined the therapist as 'impinging object' (Casement, 2008, p. 55), continually prompting and instigating 'appropriate responses' before judging and prescribing formulaic solutions. In such rushed and inauthentic environments how might one discover those deeper qualities of speech, where we learn to go from talking *about* our felt sense to speaking directly from it? Where we think 'from' is as important as what we think 'about'. The place from which we think exerts a strong affect on the object of our thoughts.

Just as we are highly discerning in selecting where we plant a seed or invest a dollar, because we understand the degree to which that place will shape and determine growth, so too should we be rigorous in our thinking on the quality and effect of the facilitating environments in which we grapple with our therapeutic endeavours.

I found Casson's work especially compelling and challenging. Here was an exhaustive study into a very specific form of 'silent' experience. As I read I found Casson's text to be of great and impressive value. Yet so many of his clearly detailed observations occupied the opposite pole to my own thinking. Nevertheless the contrast which this book offered came to shape and awaken my consideration of the vast spectrum within which my own small thoughts had been constellating. In particular I began to get a clearer appreciation of the tensions (and the relationships) between withdrawing into silence and rushing into speech. The points I have chosen to refute and 'sound off' about provided my silent musings with a genuine and much-needed disruption. However, there was much I chimed in accordance with as well, not least Casson's writings on the nature of good enough therapeutic relationships:

> I believe that whatever method of therapy is used, the prime healing forces are within the client and in the relationship between the client and the therapist: without a safe, empathic relationship there is less likely to be therapeutic benefit for the client. There are non-verbal aspects to this relationship: emotional holding, mirroring, warmth, eye contact, smiles, noticing/witnessing and listening. (Casson, 2004, p. 99)

It is here that I believe the shared experience of transiting in and out of silence can act as an immensely nurturing element in the building of such relationships. In silence we wait for the other. We allow the need some may have for space and separateness. Silence itself can facilitate a clarifying or forgetting process whereby both therapist and client might be empowered to drop the burden of previously held obstructive notions and assumptions of both themselves and one another. A chance to relate to and from a less conditioned, more tenderised sense of self. In these ways silence conjures something akin to a 'liminal space' (Turner, 1974, p. 29); a rite of passage, an initiation, a gateway to the new.

I recall one morning during my training at the Royal Central School of Speech and Drama. I sat in silent meditation with a fellow student on the course. We had both arrived at college via our individual routes and already carried the baggage and accumulations of our day thus far. We shared these briefly before we sat. We both considered ourselves as thoughtful, empathetic individuals, relatively practised in open and attuned listening. Yet mostly our shared stories tumbled out only to lie between us as testimonies to our separateness. Something between us, something in the way.

We stopped talking. We sat. We closed our eyes and grew silent. We came to our senses and then we came to ourselves. Later, opening our eyes, we were at last ready to come to one another. To meet.

In similar ways silence can provide a valuable and containing structure for the development of therapeutic relationships and journeying because it is a process that happens with a client, not for a client. The experience may hold certain tensions, taking some close to the frightening and unbearable, evoking the unwanted and echoing the unspoken. Nevertheless, with a skilled therapist's careful and familial presence, such glimpses of 'how things are' can be gradual and tolerable. Steadily our traveling companions may come to discover another level of the silent mandala – a rich and transformative in-between space brimming with the potential for reflection, resilience building, transformation and growth.

I am not suggesting here that the therapist must always be seeking to inhabit and draw close to the client's experience, nor that there is no value in distance. I merely aim to raise the value of such silent interventions being employed at timely and appropriate intervals. In so doing I am also asking myself: am I sufficiently schooled in the therapy of silence to be able to hear those quiet but urgent needs and can I calibrate a similarly whispered yet effective response?

In returning to the thoughts I opened this chapter with: I want to counter that silence is not an absence but that it is a presence. It is something more than nothing. And that far more can be gained in being with it, holding it and gradually unpacking it, than by simply breaking it.

Dramatherapeutic Silence

How might a grounded familiarity with silence serve, support and enrich the dramatherapist in both their personal journey and their ongoing professional reflective practice?

In some way dramatherapists will typically work to invite their clients to go beyond words and concepts and to enter a world of intuition, imagination and symbol. I believe we may enable our clients' safer access to such potentially silent realms if we ourselves are personally familiar with its topographical curves and contours; silence as an aide to the oblique.

The Sesame Approach to Dramatherapy is also characterised by a reliance on the art forms of drama, movement etc. to deliver appropriate therapeutic benefit 'with no attempt at "interpretation" of personal material, reflecting Jung's emphasis on the importance of symbol' (Pearson, 1996, p. 2). So here again we find something being left to be *as it is*, unspoken, unsaid. It would appear that there are strong currents of silent presence running through the Sesame approach.

Interestingly in recent years, there have been ongoing discussions between drama and movement therapists working with the Sesame approach which have resulted in adding the word 'Sound' to the original term 'Movement with Touch', this being a key strand in the MA training in the Sesame approach. The founder of the Sesame approach, Marian Lindkvist, is clear on the powerful role sound and voice can play within drama and movement interventions and sessions will often be fed by accompanying sound and music. None of this conflicts or disrupts my personal idea of silence within dramatherapy. There may be a line between sound and silence which both divides and unites the two. This interwoven play of silence and sound is similar to the silence found within nature, which achieves a quietness and yet is full of sound. Sounds which don't break up the silence. Silence remaining there, like the stillness of the ground as it is danced upon:

> Silence has both a physical and a psychological impact. Silence acts on the memory and can build up pleasurable feelings of expectancy – when is the

next sound going to come? The imagination can be let loose – what will the next sound be like? (Bunt, 1994, p. 51)

Contemporary dramatherapists will work within communities rich in cultural diversity and alongside professions seeking to quantify and assess. They may encounter many apparently conflicting demands to describe and deliver their work in frames unfamiliar with the metaphorical style of their approach. I have an idea that a familiarity with silence might be of use in supporting the dramatherapist to meet and be with such contrasting working environments while remaining relevant and authentic. A space within which the internal supervisor can 'speak' and be heard. Silence supports listening, allowing the therapist to 'make good use of her knowledge of the dynamics of projective identification' (Casement, 2008, p. 90). The key here is silence's 'space creating power', facilitating mindfulness and enabling the therapist to remain present and discerning. It provides an antidote to the understandable yet often overwhelming urge to prove and present oneself 'perfectly'. A familiarity with silence supports reflection and in time might engender something akin to a 'presence-centred psychotherapy' (Welwood, 2000, p. 105) in which our 'practising therapist self' becomes sufficiently secure and integrated to speak and act from a grounded whole.

The rich and archaic symbolism evoked through the Sesame approach and its ability to transcend and/or bridge cultural difference is, I think, a characteristic of particular note and one which is deserving of special care. Perhaps the reflective practitioner can be supported in this task by an 'intelligent silence, a companion of stillness and hand to shape contemplation' (Climacus, 1959, p. 135), helpful in guiding us confidently through the waves of words, assumption and expectation, where too much attention to conceptual thinking may obstruct and detract from the intuitive language of the symbol and the metaphor:

> for intuition is the more direct way of reaching out to the immediacy of experience here and now. The truth is that life reveals itself most clearly when you do not clutch at it. (Lane, 2006, p. 26)

Concluding Thoughts

The man I meet with is not often so instructive as the silence he breaks (Thoreau, 1995, p. 50).

The therapeutic relationship invariably begins with the breaking of a silence. Who breaks it, and how, may come to influence the nature of the pathway taken, along which both therapist and client(s) will venture. I'm drawing attention here to the fact that this silence is an integral part of the therapeutic venture, not a mere point of departure; even less an obstacle to be overcome! It is in many ways the substance of the pathway and its enduring presence will underscore all else that is encountered en route.

One of the struggles of silence appears to be how to handle it. How much is too little? When does it become too much? A silent ease within the therapist may help to discern and modulate such sensitive calibrations. The question then arises: how might the therapist equip themself with such skills? These may be gained through the personal experience of being a 'reflective practitioner', thus acquiring a good enough familiarity with silent work via a clear and grounded pedagogy-based appreciation.

More classically, the therapist may follow a personal meditation practice. Meditation's time-honoured methods of attention and concentration would appear to provide the therapist with support in honing several essential therapeutic tools. Moreover, some therapists may come to appreciate the broader range of awareness which meditative experience can facilitate.

In discussing the therapist's search for 'better methods to expand and improve therapeutic effectiveness', psychologists C. and A. Simpkins state:

> Influenced by principles of linearity and sequential relationships, rational thought is the most commonly used tool, and tends to follow linear patterns, organising itself with beginning and endings, and by first and last, biggest and smallest and so forth. By contrast, psychological problems engage many levels at once. The emotional, cognitive and behavioural aspects are just part of the problem. Deeper exploration often reveals that there are broader interconnections with cultural, economic, physical and inter-personal levels. (Simpkins and Simpkins, 2009, p. 2)

It strikes me that silence may be an 'effective method' for the bridging of this gap between the linear and the multi-levelled. Offering at least a space where the two might be observed and some moves made towards integration. It also seems relevant to note that, for many, silence does tend to evoke a certain degree of spaciousness and perhaps a more lateral perspective on one's relationship with others and the immediate environment.

Another place where we may find our silence is in the ancient arts of reading and writing. This interface between silence, therapy and writing was explored in an interview with the analyst and author Salley Vickers: 'As an analyst my effort was always to find the place within myself that could communicate with the other person … that experience of finding things within myself has been invaluable.' (O'Kelly, 2009) When asked what she might have learnt as a writer to aid her work as an analyst she replied: 'To say less. I think I have more confidence that sitting very still in a room is what allows people to say what is on their mind, or in their unconscious … I do not push them around. I let them have their own head, or heart.' (O'Kelly, 2009)

My first clinical practice experience took me to an NHS Recovery Centre for Adults with Mental Health Difficulties. The morning community meeting was one hour long and agenda-less. Staff and clients sat in a circle together. There was much silence. It was in one such session, after a significant period of silence, that one of the patients spoke: 'Is there anybody else here who finds this silence utterly unbearable? Why do we sit here like this enduring this excruciating experience?'

This comment and the deep force with which it was conveyed rocked something within me. The patient who voiced those concerns in such a powerful and compelling manner became a regular member of the dramatherapy group I was co-facilitating. During the course of our work together this client came to share an awareness that words had become a comfortable mask behind which he could remain unseen. Conversely silence stood in opposition to this place of active comfort. It held the threat of unmasking; the threat of being seen. Nevertheless, in returning and remaining with these difficulties, even as the work became increasingly non-verbal, something began to grow between us. It wasn't an easy process, especially when the work involved a combination of silence and the added intimacy of close physicality. In the final session a sustained period of silent and close contact movement work was achieved, after which the only sound around the silence was that of deep breathing, the rhythm and depth of which I would associate with a kind of relief. In the closing circle he shared some words. They were few, yet poignant in the way they were placed within the silent space we had created. He said: 'From tiny acorns grow … ' and then the silence returned.

I felt a tremendous affect which I have come to believe carried something of this client's individual dawning appreciation of how dramatherapy and, in particular, non-verbal movement-based work, might be offering therapeutic help and support. I always felt that in that moment of fresh awareness this client held a clearer understanding than I did, and in many ways my written efforts here are part of my ongoing attempt to catch up … or perhaps more appropriately, to let go, and hope that in so doing, I avoid becoming 'the insensitive man who praises silence in a torrent of words' (Climacus, 1959, p. 135).

References

Basho, M. (1996). *The Narrow Road to the Deep North*. London: Penguin Books.

Bunt, L. (1994). *Music Therapy*. London: Routledge.

Cage, J. (1973). *Silence: Lectures and Writings*. London: Marion Boyers Publishers Ltd.

Casement, P. (2008). *On Learning from the Patient*. London: Routledge.

Casson, J. (2004). *Drama, Psychotherapy and Psychosis: Dramatherapy and Psychodrama with People Who Hear Voices*. Hove and New York, NY: Brunner-Routledge.

Climacus, S. J. (1959). *The Ladder of Divine Ascent*. London: Faber.

Cooke, R. (2009). *Interview with Carol Ann Duffy*, The Observer, May 3, 2009.

Johnson, D. R. (1992). The dramatherapist 'in role'. In S. Jennings (Ed.), *Dramatherapy: Theory and Practice 2*. London: Routledge.

Kafka, F. (1991). *The Blue Octavo Notebooks*. New York, NY: Exact Change.

Lane, J. (2006). *The Spirit of Silence*. Totnes: Green Books.

Maitland, S. (2008). *A Book of Silence*. London: Granta.

O'Kelly, L. (2009). *Interview with Salley Vickers*, The Observer Review, 7 May, 2009.

Pearson, J. (1996). *Discovering the Self through Drama and Movement*. London: Jessica Kingsley.

Picard, M. (1989). *The World of Silence*. Chicago, IL: Regnery.

Rawson, P. (1991). *Sacred Tibet*. London: Thames and Hudson.

Roose-Evans, (2009). *Finding Silence*. Gloucestershire: The History Press.

Rowan, C. (1996/97). Silence. *British Journal of Dramatherapy, 18* (3)Winter 1996/97.

Ruskin, J. (2010). *The Works of John Ruskin, Volume 1: Early Writings*. New York, NY: Cambridge University Press.

Simpkins, C. A. & Simpkins, A. M. (2009). *Meditation for Therapists and their Clients*. New York, NY: W.W. Norton.

Tanizaki, J. (2001). *In Praise of Shadows*. London: Vintage.

Thoreau, H. D. (1995). *Walden*. New York, NY: Dover.

Turner, V. (1974). *Dramas, Fields and Metaphors: Symbolic Action in Human Society*. New York, NY: Cornell University Press.

Welwood, J. (2000). *Toward a Psychology of Awakening*. Boston: Shambala.

6

The Gaze

Alanah Garrard

How does one human connect with another? What allows us to understand each other and ourselves? Where does change happen, and the implicit become explicit? There is a quality, a feeling that is hard to identify and verbalise, that allows one to perceive another in a way that goes beyond the normal senses of seeing or listening. This chapter is entitled 'The Gaze', but this does not simply refer to observation, or fixing someone with a look. It is a choice of words that represents a way in which one person can perceive and experience another, not simply through their eyes but with a certain quality that includes their body and mind. The Sesame Approach to Drama and Movement Therapy, although firmly grounded in Jungian theory, is fluid in its continued development and understanding of the possibilities of intersubjective contact with another.

The Ancient Greeks referred to *kairos*; a moment that is qualitatively different and unpredicted, a moment that pulls two people fully into the present. So for the purpose of this chapter, how does drama-therapy enable us to connect with our clients, to be able to see them beyond the everyday and provide something that would be considered therapeutic? The French philosopher Merleau-Ponty examines the relation between the mind and body, or rather, in overcoming their duality, working with the concept of a body-subject through the practice of phenomenology. Our experience and understanding of others and ourselves are shaped through our perceptions and bodily responses:

> the view is of the body-subject and its lived experience before it is abstracted into separate paths – mind and matter, knower and known, the invisible and the visible ... by travelling along it one sees more than what has been seen before and deepens his or her understanding of self, other, and the world. (Polkinghorne, 1994, p. 129)

Below I will consider Merleau-Ponty's writings alongside examples of therapeutic practice in which challenges to individuals' perceptions have had an impact on work and relationships.

Dramatherapy allows a client the opportunity to move away from cognitive processing; not entirely, as the mind and body are intrinsically linked, but with the involvement of the body in a physical capacity there is the prospect of an exploration beyond the mind, and a recognition or understanding of an experience physically as well as emotionally and mentally. In his essay 'The Transcendent Function', Jung writes on the union of conscious and unconscious content and that imaginative work can be liberating: 'emotional disturbance can also be dealt with in another way, not by clarifying it intellectually but by giving it visible shape.' (1997, p. 54) Communication, both verbal and non-verbal, can allow for a rich illumination of phenomena between the client and therapist, and what is occurring between them if attention is given not just to the words that are spoken and not just to the body in front of us, but to something deeper.

The writing of Eugene Gendlin considers the importance of the body therapeutically, but within our bodily experience he also considers the role of perception. For Gendlin, the idea of perception is not a shared experience. Within the dialogical encounter he splits perception into the percept and the perceiver, and he puts the perceiver behind the percept, rendering in his eyes, he believes, the body as merely a perceiver (Gendlin 1992). Gendlin's view defines the roles of perceiver and percept in a distinct way. This may not necessarily be the case, nor is it a position when considering perception that everyone agrees with, as Merleau-Ponty makes clear: 'he who sees cannot possess the visible unless he is possessed by it.' (1968, p. 134) However, Gendlin wants to go beyond perception into a deeper experience, into what he defines as a felt sense:

> the ' ... ' is not just a perception, although it certainly includes many perceptions. Is it then a feeling? It is certainly felt, but 'feeling' usually means emotion. The ' ... ' includes emotions, but also so much else ... So there is no common word for this utterly familiar bodily sense of the intricacy of our situations along with the rapid weighing of more alternatives than we can think of separately. In therapy we now call it a 'felt sense'. (1992, pp. 346–347)

There is awareness that we may well have our perceptions of each other which are between us but that we also affect each other in our situations, and our situation is also not separate from our bodily sense; they are not simply a mixture of two things but intrinsically linked. There is not one without the other. For Gendlin this interactional bodily intricacy comes first; it is 'the body of interactional living in its environment' (ibid., p. 352) that is elaborated by language and language, for Gendlin, has its limitations: 'there is no language in which to discuss what is more than language.' (ibid., p. 350)

This felt sense can then be utilised by the therapist through their body to gain a deeper knowledge of what is happening for both therapist and client. Gendlin writes extensively (1992, 2000) about the choices and the next steps that one takes. He writes of a bodily life-process (2000) in which something happens and has certain results. For the next step to happen the bodily life-process takes in many factors such as a smile, a move, often automatically and then produces the next step. This bodily knowing, Gendlin believes, works implicitly but if attention is given at this bodily level one can arrive at new steps that do not come automatically. When working with clients, this attention to the body can allow for a deeper understanding of the choices that we make as therapists in terms of what we ask, our next steps and the information our bodies are telling us. How this information is used, however, differs depending on how the therapist chooses to work.

In the Cartesian view, knowledge is acquired through abstract reflection and objectifying our cognitive enquiry. This is in direct opposition to the idea of embodiment in which thought and body are intertwined. Phenomenology was a move away from Descartes' split of the mind and body as separate entities and its aim was to embrace a more reflexive attitude to our everyday experience. Husserl's phenomenology called for one to step outside of our natural attitude, our everyday experience, and to adopt a phenomenological attitude, of epoche, an attempt to suspend our preconceptions and explanations for description and experience. In Husserl's description of phenomenology for the *Encyclopaedia Britannica,* he writes, 'Through reflection, instead of grasping simply the matter straight-out – the values, goals, and instrumentalities – we grasp the corresponding subjective experiences in which we become "conscious" of them.' (Husserl, 1927, para 2 quoted in Smith et al., 2009, pp. 12–13) Husserl's aim was to ascertain what was at the core of a subjective experience; his objective was to reach the content of conscious experience by focusing on experience itself (Smith et al., 2009).

Merleau-Ponty's phenomenology has been described as, 'a thinking thinking about what is itself un-thought, even unthinkable, a thinking which thinks about what *must* happen, or rather, must *already have happened*' (Macann, 1993). For Merleau-Ponty there is a unity between body, space and time. The body and its actions are not mechanical processes but are forms of knowledge. What happens physiologically within the therapeutic space is as informative as any words that are uttered. For Merleau-Ponty there was a desire to investigate the connectedness of the experiential world. Throughout his most well-known work, *Phenomenology of Perception,* Merleau-Ponty considers his investigations within the realms of intellectualism, which in philosophical terms is the doctrine that all knowledge is derived from reason, and empiricism, in which all knowledge is derived from sense experience. Both of these approaches were flawed for Merleau-Ponty and he introduced the concept of 'attention' as a means by which to balance the two. He believed that both intellectualism and empiricism took the objective world for granted. This new form of attention would take questioning back to the pre-objective realm, its purpose to break away from objective thought in order to learn how to live. The pre-objective realm is instinctive, how we begin our existence in the world and one that we separate from in order to develop (Macann, 1993). Merleau-Ponty focused on the lived experience of human existence, to retrace through description the immediacy of an experience before it had been transformed by science and common sense. He sought to accredit concepts of subjectivity, intentionality and mentality to the lived body. He believed the body to be composed of both physical and intentional dimensions, and that we are never spectators of experience but remain within it. Our reflective knowledge occurs as we are bodily engaged with the world. Dramatherapy, I would suggest, is an embodied phenomenological practice. In all of its aspects, storytelling, re-enacting, role playing, free movement and improvisation, there is an uncovering from within, an uncertainty of direction, an unknowing of what can happen next and a need for the therapist and client to engage bodily with the experience, to stay within the present moment. Jung, too, like Descartes, considered the idea of a split, but in his view it was between the conscious and the unconscious, believing that life demanded directed conscious functioning which risked considerable disassociation from our unconscious. Through working creatively, 'a product is created which is influenced by both conscious and unconscious, embodying the striving of the unconscious for the light and the striving of the conscious for substance' (Jung, 1997, p. 54). This concept is held in mind when working within the Sesame approach, that although we are in a fully conscious state, a space is given for unconscious material to manifest itself bodily and into our awareness. In Darren Langridge's article on therapy and embodiment (2005) he talks about Merleau-Ponty's views on acting: how through allowing a new creativity in which the actor takes on the role of someone else, they may recognise aspects of their embodied selves that had previously been obscured, and how through enactment they may realise previously disavowed experiences and be able to give them a voice. The exploration of a new role, whether it is through a character of a story, an improvised scene or an archetypal fairy tale character, can allow an opportunity to experience oneself in an altered way. It is not simply the client that engages with the session in this way. The therapist, too, has a role to play: 'the recognition that one is an embodied being includes the acknowledgement that even in a situation of being an observer one is an involved observer – someone who is being affected by and is affecting what is taking place.' (Finlay, 2006) So within the therapeutic endeavour each person is the observer and the observed, the perceiver and the perceived: 'he who sees cannot possess the visible unless he is possessed by it.' (Merleau-Ponty, 1968, p. 134)

Traditionally, in Freudian terms, one would term the unconscious experience of transferring effects from patients to therapist as transference. The patient's love, hate, and other emotions usually related to a figure of importance in their early years, are re-experienced and transferred onto the therapist. It is a type of displacement that functions as a defence as a means to conceal the origin or true wish of the patient (Holmes, 2005). At the root of the classical concept of transference is the notion that the way we respond to people in the present is directly linked to experiences in the past. As individuals we have developed habitual reactions to people and situations and these are triggered depending on our experiences. This unconscious transferring of effects can be both negative and positive and given that therapy is a relational experience the patient too can be the object of transference for the therapist which is termed as countertransference. Whereas, classically, Freud felt that the countertransference needed to be excluded from analysis as quickly as possible, in more contemporary views this response by the therapist is seen as a way of understanding the client's unconscious communications, acting as a guide for interpretations (Lemma, 2007).

Nicola Diamond (2001) considers how in therapy many clients express their emotional pain through physical ailments with the body acting as a conduit for expressing feelings. Traditionally psychoanalysis viewed bodily impulses and feelings as coming from internal sources. Diamond goes on to explore the concept of 'bodily countertransference', connecting the therapist and client with shared feeling that the therapist experiences as a physical sensation; emotional pain communicated somatically between therapist and client. Freud believed that bodily identification (the taking on of another's bodily demeanour) is not a phenomenon exclusive to babies. By identifying with someone's position, his or her physical ailment was adopted, as seen in Freud's case of Dora who adopted her mother's cough. Diamond points out that Freud never explained how these phenomena took place but she endeavours, through looking at the development process, to reveal how this may come about:

'when I enter the world, my body is not cut off from another person's body. Rather, I enter a shared world in which, initially, I experience my body with the others' bodies and I discover my own gestures in theirs.' (2001, p. 51) Therefore the body is not located in an isolated space and experiences are inhabited in a shared interpersonal bodily situation. As adults, we revive boundaries that help define me from you. However, according to Diamond, one can temporarily slip across the boundary and affect one another in a bodily way. With further exploration and the inclusion of the theories of Trevarthen, a researcher in developmental psychology and biology, on theories of primary intersubjectivity, the link between development and the transfer of emotions to physical sensations as adults becomes clearer: 'it is the primacy of relation, the coexisting space and the fact that interaction is the outcome of what happens in the interweaving of intentions in a shared body space that define the inter-personal experience.' (ibid., p. 53) Trevarthen also points out that the emotional and non-verbal primary form of communication is the basis of interpersonal knowing, with sensory and affective exchanges provid-ing the foundation for the emergence of sense, meaning and language. So here we have considered the concept of transference and countertransfer-ence that can be communicated through the body somatically without language. Once we have received that information and attempted to define where it has come from, how can this help the therapeutic process? How does one describe a moment of meeting another therapeutically in which something happens but struggles to be verbalised? 'Meaning-making is thus a bodily inclusive hermeneutic cycle.' (Todres, 2004, p. 41) It is a space that allows for the interpretation of the possibility of understanding of both verbal and non-verbal expressions. It is an unfixed state of becoming.

Daniel Stern uses the term 'a moment-of-meeting' (1998). 'A "moment" is conceived of as a short subject unit of time in which some-thing of importance, bearing on the future, is happening.' (p. 302) During one of these 'moments' the implicit knowledge of each person is altered through the intersubjective context between two people. The relationship has changed. It does not need to be made verbally explicit. We perceive ourselves and see ourselves through others' eyes: 'we rec-ognise our own actions through others' recognition of them so that we experience ourselves through others.' (Ramsland and Ramsland, 1989, p. 26) Stern believes that a moment-of-meeting requires each individual to respond to the moment in a unique, authentic way that has to be mutually recognised for a new intersubjective state to come into being. This moment-of-meeting will catapult their implicit knowledge into consciousness, therefore changing their relational knowing. In his book *The Present Moment* (2004), Stern develops the idea of this moment-of-meeting. In the preface he explains that the book is about subjective experience that brings about change in psychotherapy; that verbally explaining or narrating is not enough but an actual experience, 'a subjectively lived happening' (p. xiii) is required. Stern talks about leaning towards a next action.

In his chapter entitled 'The Intersubjective Matrix', Stern (2004) describes a kind of mental contact, an intersubjective contact in which two people see and feel the same mental landscape for a least a moment, a moment that is co-created and shared with someone. Stern considers intuition, a person's understanding of what might be about to happen through a series of messages, for example visual prompts. When someone reaches to scratch their head we will anticipate that is what they are about to do. Expressions will alert someone to how we may be feeling or thinking. As we recognise ourselves in others, the boundaries between us remain intact but permeable. We are surrounded by others' intentions, thoughts and feelings and we are in a shifting dialogue with the felt intentions of others. Our feelings shaped by others and our thoughts are concreted in dialogue even if it is with ourselves. According to Stern, 'two minds create intersubjectivity. But equally, intersubjectivity shapes the two minds. The centre of gravity has shifted from the intrapsychic to the intersubjective' (2004, p. 78).

In his later writings, Merleau-Ponty uses and considers the concept of 'chiasm', through which he investigates experience. According to Gasche, the chiasm 'is a form that makes it possible to determine differences with respect to an underlying unity' (as quoted in Toadvine, 2012, p. 337). There will always be more than one point of view in relationship. I cannot see myself as the other sees me, and that is the same in reverse. There are limitations to what we can really know of each other for we only ever see from our own position; however, experience can be shared and recognised. Through our senses one can perceive another's perspective:

> it suffices that I look at a landscape, that I speak of it with someone. Then, through the concordant operation of his body and my own, what I see passes into him, this individual green of the meadow under my eyes invades his vision without quitting my own, I recognize in my green, his green. (Merleau-Ponty, 1968, p. 142)

The term 'chiasm' draws on both the physiological and rhetorical senses. It is a figure for thinking through the relationship between the body and the mind, the factual and the ideal (Toadvine, 2012). 'There is a body of the mind and a mind of the body and a chiasm between them' (Merleau-Ponty, 1968, p. 259). As an example of this, Merleau-Ponty describes the relationship between hands touching and how the hand may exchange roles: when one is the agent of touch, the other slips into the role of object, but with a change of attention the roles are reversed. This can be transposed to all of the senses. As one feels they are being observed, with a change of focus and attention one can just as quickly become the observer. Through perception there is an introduction into an inter-subjective realm where the four eyes of the two caught in a reciprocal relationship converge. There is an exchange where the boundaries can be crossed, so the touch becomes touched, the passive becomes active, the self ends and the other person begins. Working within an intersubjec-tive plain of relatedness, the individual subject is required to see others no longer as objects but as other subjects; there is a need for mutual recognition.

During my training as a Sesame dramatherapist I was working with a group in a mental health day care centre. The group had been working together for a number of weeks and relationships and dynamics had been formed, not only during the weekly sessions but also amongst those clients that saw each other regularly at the centre. One member of the group was a domineering male, I will call him C, who was experienc-ing psychotic episodes and had on a number of occasions attended the sessions with a very frenetic and chaotic energy, quite often dominating the sessions both physically and verbally. Another member of the group was a female, I will refer to her as E, who was neither overly quiet nor demanded attention, but she appeared quite self-conscious in warm-up games and in previous sessions, although seemed to enjoy the sessions as a whole. In this particular session, we had begun with a warm-up of a sound and gesture circle where members had reflected back the movement and sound of the person who had stepped into the centre. Each member was then asked to take their own space and think about an animal that they would like to work on. They spent a period of time thinking about the animal, imagining its physicality, gestures, movements and surroundings, and then were asked to move about as that animal in their own space, to embody it. As I was running the session I was observing what each member of the group was doing and what animal they were representing. E appeared to be taking on the mannerisms of a lion and C a mouse. The group was absorbed in the work, each working within their own space and, once it felt right, I asked the group to start moving about the room as their animals and interacting with each other.

What do I mean by 'once it felt right'? Here is where my role as the therapist needs not to be simply observational, but engaged bodily in what is happening in the session; a need to pay attention to the responses I am having both as someone running the session and containing the space but also physically to what I am observing and sensing; to be aware that although I am observing and not, for all practical purposes, joining in, my presence in the room is influential to what is going on, to the notion that the group members know I am watching but I too am being observed. It is a contrived situation where we are all working on different levels of involvement. There is a balance for all with how engaged they become in the exercise and whether they are able to allow themselves to become absorbed. In Merleau-Ponty's terms the question is the degree to which they can move from the objective to the pre-objective where instincts take over.

It struck me that C's choice to be a mouse was an interesting one but it was not until C and E interacted with each other, C as the mouse and E as the lion, that the significance of their choices became apparent. Their traditional roles and dynamics that I had noted previously in the sessions were entirely switched as I saw them approach each other in their animal roles, E bold and aggressive, C cowering and frightened. They experienced each other and themselves in a totally different way, allowing for a new mutual understanding that each can be different. Not only were they witness to their experience but I was too. There was a connection, an understanding that was not just twofold. Their experience was their own but it was held within the limits of the session. In my view they had lost themselves within an intersubjective moment where their perceptions of each other were altered and their relationship changed. By somehow identifying it from an observational standpoint, it transformed the event from a passing moment, that could have almost not existed except between the two of them, to something far more significant. So what I bore witness to was a meaningful moment, a moment of *kairos,* as I mentioned above, in which everything happens and is of a qualitative permanent nature. It has an emergent property, a new intersubjective context. This intersubjective state is largely a non-verbal aspect in the relationship between two people. It is a shared implicit relational knowledge concerning how the two are with each other and how they work together. Merleau-Ponty classed it as one system with two terms: 'my behaviour and the other's behaviour which functions as a whole … in perceiving the other my body and his are coupled resulting in an action that pairs them.' (1964, p. 118) Through their interconnectedness they gained knowledge of themselves and each other.

In his lecture 'Art and the World of Perception', Merleau-Ponty writes: 'no attempt to define or analyse it, however valuable that may be afterwards as a way of taking stock of this experience, can ever stand in place of the direct perceptual experience.' (2008, p. 72) No matter how much we try and use language as a descriptive tool, it is experientially based. Of course it is important to try and understand the process by which change occurs – research is fundamental to learning – but how do you put language to an experience that goes beyond it? Are we able to fully express our experience and ourselves through language? Is verbal communication a linguistic abstraction away from the immediate experiencing of a client? Ramsland and Ramsland (1989), in their paper on indirect communication within therapy, consider the order of thought, reflection and words. Words are formed from a thought and then there is the inward subjective experiencing of what it means to speak those words and whether those words represent fully what is required. Are we ever fully able to express ourselves? Although Merleau-Ponty realised that language was an obvious demonstration of expression, he believed that this was not the only form in which meaning could be represented.

As a dramatherapist, I worked for a number of months with a client whom I will call F. She was born with severe cerebral palsy and was both physically and mentally disabled. She was unable to speak and we would work each week in the music room of the residential home that she lived in. The room was spacious and bright and I would lift F out of her chair and place her on the cushioned mats. The work we did focused on using the senses: seeing, hearing, touching. We worked with the imagination using music and imagery as a way of transporting ourselves somewhere else and slowly over weeks a relationship was formed. We experienced each other; as we worked together we learned how to respond to each other without deliberation, we became symbiotic in our movements and at times it was unclear as I was resting her arm on my hand, or we were palm to palm, who was leading and who was following. One of Merleau-Ponty's designs was to teach us to relearn what perception means against the mental constructions that we impose on ourselves (Macann, 1993): 'we simply have to set aside the prejudices of science and common sense and let ourselves be carried along by the current of existence, attending carefully to what reveals ourselves when we remain open to the richness and variety of sensory perception.' (ibid., p. 182)

On one occasion I went to collect F from her house and, on entering, all the residents were lined with their wheelchairs in a row so they could only see the back of the chair in front. On enquiring I was told that the carpets were being cleaned and they had been in this position for a number of hours. F and I left to go to the music room and I was carrying great sadness about what I had seen. We started the session as usual and I sat with her on the mats and took her hand. F looked at me, our eyes met, and in that moment our relationship changed. What was in that look was all the time that we had spent together, everything that we had learnt of each other. I think she felt my sadness, my care and my respect for her. To feel a certain way about something is to perceive it in that way. The affective content of perception contributes to the perceiver's sense of what action is required (Ramdenh-Romluc, 2012) and in that moment there was no action to be taken, nothing to be said, just a look to be shared.

'As soon as our glances meet, we are no longer wholly two, and it is hard to remain alone.' (Merleau-Ponty, 1964, p. 231) We finished working together a few months later but that look that we shared has always stayed with me due to the depth of feeling exchanged in such an unspoken way, but also because I have always wondered how and why it was so impactful which has led me to try and uncover what these moments actually are.

In his preface to *Phenomenology of Perception*, Merleau-Ponty writes: 'we are through and through compounded of relationships with the world.' (2002, p. xiv) This is true. We are always in the world with others which is what makes the exploration of what joins us so vital, and what makes it so interesting is that although we are beings in the world with other beings each of us is fundamentally unique and yet connected. We are both the perceiver and the perceived, we are not independent of each other nor are we identical: 'Fundamentally it is neither thing seen only nor seer only, it is Visibility sometimes wandering and sometimes reassembled.' (Merleau-Ponty, 1968, pp. 137–138)

The Sesame practitioner of today is working with the knowledge of combining tradition and practice long established, alongside a growing and exciting time of research in which developing therapeutic concepts are becoming internalised within the practice, with an exploration of what it means to be with another physically, emotionally, mentally and in the space in between. Jung's aspirations of allowing for a union of unconscious and conscious content was 'a way of attaining liberation by one's own efforts and of finding the courage to be oneself' (1997, p. 60) and this can be said, too, of the therapist that can risk not knowing and allowing the unexpected to emerge and to be in that moment alongside the other.

References

Diamond, N. (2001). Towards an interpersonal understanding of bodily experience. *Psychodynamic Counselling, 7*(1), 41–62.

Finlay, L. (2006). The body's disclosure in phenomenological research. *Qualitative Research in Psychology, 3*, 19–30.

Gendlin, E. (1992). The primacy of the body, not the primacy of perception. *Man and World, 25*, 341–353.

Gendlin, E. (2000). When you feel the body from inside, there is a door. www.focusing.org/gendlin/docs/gol_2232.html

Holmes, C. (2005). *The Paradox of Countertransference*. Hampshire: Palgrave Macmillan.

Jung, C. G. (1997). *Jung on Active Imagination*. London: Routledge.

Langdridge, D. (2005). 'The childs relations with others' Merleau-Ponty, embodiment and psychotherapy. *Journal of the Society of Existential Analysis, 16*(1), 87–99.

Lemma, A. (2007). Psychodynamic therapy: The Freudian approach. In W. Dryden (Ed.), *Dryden's Handbook of Individual Therapy* (5th ed.). London: Sage Publications Ltd.

Macann, C. (1993). *Four Phenomenological Philosophers*. London and New York, NY: Routledge.

Merleau-Ponty, M. (1964). *The Primacy of Perception*. Evanston, IL: Northwestern University Press.

Merleau-Ponty, M. (1968). *The Visible and the Invisible* (Trans. Lingis, A.). Evanston, IL: Northwestern University Press.

Merleau-Ponty, M. (2002). *The Phenomenology of Perception* (Trans. Smith, C.). Oxon and New York, NY: Routledge.

Merleau-Ponty, M. (2008). *The World of Perception* (Trans. Davis, O.). Oxon: Routledge Classics.

Polkinghorne, D. (1994). A path for understanding psychology. *Journal of Theoretical and Philisophical Psychology, 14*(2), 128–145.

Romdenh-Romluc, K. (2012). Merleau-Ponty. In S. Luft & S. Overgaard (Eds.), *The Routledge Companion to Phenomenology*. Oxon and New York, NY: Routledge.

Ramsland, K. & Ramsland, S. (1989). Erickson and Kierkegaard: Indirect communication in psychotherapy. *Theoretical & Philosophical Psychology, 9*(1), 19–29.

Smith, J. A., Flowers, P. & Larkin, M. (2009). *Interpretative Phenomenological Analysis: Theory, Method and Research*. London: Sage.

Stern, D. (1998). The process of therapeutic change involving implicit knowledge: Some implications of developmental observations for adult psychotherapy. *Infant Mental Health Journal, 19*(3), 300–308.

Stern, D. N. (2004). *The Present Moment*. New York, NY: W.W. Norton.

Toadvine, T. (2012). The Chiasm. In S. Luft & S. Overgaard (Eds.), *The Routledge Companion to Phenomenology*. Oxon and New York, NY: Routledge.

Todres, L. (2004). The meaning of understanding and the open body. *Journal of the Society for Existential Analysis, 15*(1), 38–54.

7

Neurodevelopmental Approaches

Jo Godsal

Introduction

As Sam and I settled into the therapy room for the start of our first session, I began to talk, explaining a little about what we might be doing here, about what dramatherapy might be, about who I was. After a few moments she got up from the floor where we were sitting and rummaged through a box on the side. She picked out two kazoos, handed one to me, put the other in her mouth, and only then would she talk to me. For the rest of that first 50-minute session we communicated entirely through the muffled rasping of the kazoo. She was willing to communicate, and was quite animated and strangely eloquent, but she made the point loud and clear: we would not be using words here. I was a therapist without words. Which was, of course, absolutely the right place for us to start.

Over two-and-a-half years we slowly worked towards words. By this I don't mean she could not or would not speak, simply that it took a long time for the important communication to be verbal. Eventually we did finish up in a place in which verbal thought and reflection were possible. But we had to start in a place before words, before cognition, and slowly develop an ability to communicate, to relate, to symbolise and play, before finally we reached a place of thought. Our first language is not verbal, and its structures are not cognitive. This is a developmental process which we all go through, within the differing environments of our early years. Sam's earliest experiences were neglectful and chaotic. For Sam, that developmental process had been interrupted through early trauma, which coloured and undermined all the good enough care she would receive in later childhood. It was a process she had missed out on and one in which I had to meet her at the beginning. And it is also a process which dramatherapy is particularly well placed to facilitate.

I worked with Sam at the Mulberry Bush School, a residential therapeutic community for children who have experienced high levels of trauma and neglect. In this chapter I want to look at the ideas behind a therapeutic community and the work of the school. I will look into the neuroscientific theory that brought dramatherapy to the school and how this has been played out in practice. While I was at the Mulberry Bush School we used the residential community and neurosequential approach to form a developmentally sensitive model. I want to look at this model and how it has informed my practice, and how it can help in thinking about ways in which to work with different children. Why did Sam need me to begin the work without words? And how does the therapeutic journey we went on synthesise these differing areas of theory and practice into a dramatherapeutic approach?

The Mulberry Bush

The Mulberry Bush, a residential therapeutic community for children who have experienced severe trauma and neglect, was established in 1948 and has a reputation for excellence and leadership in the field of therapeutic child care. It had a team of psychotherapists and was founded on psychodynamic principles by Barbara Dockar-Drysdale, who trained under, and was supported by, D. W. Winnicott. The school's practice, as well as the wider field of therapeutic child care, has developed over the years since, but remains based on psychodynamic principles. These might be best summed up as an understanding that behaviour is communication, a culture of reflective practice, and the importance of relationships. The main work with the children takes place in what is called Milieu Therapy (see Gunter, 2005; Kornerup, 2009), whereby the lived experience of relationships and groups provides a holding, reflective and reparative experience.

In April 2010 I started work at the Mulberry Bush alongside a music therapist, because the then psychotherapy team believed that we would enable them to better meet the needs of the children. Caryn Onions, Consultant Child and Adolescent Psychotherapist at the Mulberry Bush, has written about how, prior to bringing us in, she had identified three groups of children. These were 'a limited group of children who seemed to benefit from psychotherapy, a larger group who managed psychotherapy to start with but then had difficulty attending and often dropped out, and another group who were unable to access it at all' (Onions, 2013, pp. 141–142). She was interested in that middle group, those who seemed as if they should benefit, but for whom psychotherapy was not working. She goes on to say that 'they tended to be the more aggressive and violent children, who showed little capacity to think or reflect' (p. 142).

Onions identified that while psychotherapy engages that capacity to reflect and think, music therapy and dramatherapy are ways of working more indirectly, and through using less cognitive approaches. She was clear that the dramatherapist should be Sesame trained due to the focus on movement and the body, to complement the less body-based psychotherapy already in place. Onions was interested in how the arts therapies work with children at pre-verbal, or pre-cognitive, levels where so much of these children's trauma has taken place. The particular consideration of the developmental stage at which a child has experienced trauma is key to understanding how they can best be supported, and the range of developmental approaches within dramatherapy enables the work to be adapted to the needs of the child.

It is hard to describe a typical child at the Mulberry Bush as they all bring unique histories and unique responses to those histories. Children at the Mulberry Bush are between 6 and 12 years old, coming usually for three years, from all over the UK. Most, but by no means all, are in foster care or have been adopted. Almost always their home placements, no matter the type, are in crisis as the child is likely to be unmanageable. They are often excluded from school or accessing it in a very limited way. It is not unusual for those children in foster care to have been through a great many placements and be stuck in a cycle of placement breakdown.

I remember reading the file of a child who had had 15 placements in 18 months prior to starting at the Mulberry Bush.

These children have experienced early trauma. Sometimes this is physical, sometimes sexual, but most commonly there has been an ongoing experience of neglect. The Mulberry Bush approach is not focused on the impact of a single trauma; rather it is to work with environmental failure, or what van der Kolk would call developmental trauma (2005), or Courtois and Ford describe as complex trauma. Courtois and Ford (2009) define complex trauma as:

> Resulting from exposure to severe stressors that (1) are repetitive or prolonged, (2) involve harm and abandonment by caregivers or other ostensibly responsible adults and (3) occur at developmentally vulnerable times in the victim's life, such as early childhood … when critical periods of brain development are rapidly occurring or being consolidated. (p. 13)

As I have written about my work at the Mulberry Bush elsewhere, the school is dealing with 'an inheritance of abuse and betrayed attachments that have impacted on the children's development, and have often been experienced pre-verbally' (Cropper and Godsal, 2016, p. 13). As I will explain later when looking at the neuroscientific ideas around early trauma, that repetition during brain development and the toxic nature of those early attachment relationships have the effect of writing these experiences into the brain. They become the primary narrative of what to expect from relationships, and therefore of how these children react to the world and those around them.

Therapeutic Community – A Reparative Foundation

The Mulberry Bush is a therapeutic community which has been written about extensively – John Diamond's article, 'The Mulberry Bush as a Therapeutic Community: Context and Culture 1948–2008' (2009) gives a useful overview of the history and development of some of the key concepts. There are a number of therapeutic communities across the UK and worldwide, ranging from those which work with children to prisons and a range of mental health settings. In his article 'The Quintessence of a Therapeutic Environment' (2013) Haigh acknowledges that the many different therapeutic communities have a wide range of practices, settings, even aims. The residential setting for children aged 6–13 at the Mulberry Bush will have marked differences from an adult psychiatric day centre or a therapeutic prison. However, despite these variations there is a recognisable core to these therapeutic communities and he has identified five common key features and the cultures necessary to provide them:

- Attachment – a culture of belonging;
- Containment – a culture of safety;
- Communication – a culture of openness;
- Involvement and inclusion – a culture of participation and citizenship;
- Agency – a culture of empowerment. (pp. 6–16)

These certainly ring true to my experience at the Mulberry Bush, though with a strong bias to the first three. This is unsurprising as this is a developmental process and Mulberry Bush children are both chronologically and, more particularly, developmentally very young. The children at the Mulberry Bush are between 6 and 13 years old, but their earliest experiences tend to be of trauma and neglect.

Haigh sees the therapeutic community as a place which can provide clients with the experiences that have been missed out. As Haigh sees it, the therapeutic community is reparative, providing the opportunity to return to the early relationships within a wider community. He points out that his stages are 'a simplified sequence of the fundamental requirements for reasonable emotional health in anybody – through the process of primary emotional development' (p. 14), so the work of the therapeutic community is to provide an experience of 'secondary emotional development' (p. 14).

This secondary emotional development is very much in line with the history of the Mulberry Bush. Dockar-Drysdale described the focus of the work of the Mulberry Bush as 'The Provision of Primary Experience' (1966), which Haigh would recognise as this secondary development – providing in a new setting the relationships and experiences of attunement and psychological holding that were denied first time round. For Dockar-Drysdale, the work is to enable that to happen again, through providing that same level of adaptation, preoccupation and regressed holding to those who did not receive it. 'My thesis is that all these group of children require the provision of primary experience which has, so far, been missing from their lives.' (p. 101)

Dockar-Drysdale differentiates the children according to the point at which they have experienced the failure of primary provision. Those who have experienced this at the earliest stage she calls 'frozen children'. She describes these children as 'without boundaries to personality, merged with their environment, and unable to make any real object relationships or to feel the need for them' (p. 99). She makes the point that these children need to experience the primary provision that they never had, made possible within a carefully managed therapeutic lived experience. This is less a regression than a progression from the start: 'Such a child must be provided with actual emotional experiences of progression to separating out; thereby establishing identity, accepting boundaries, and finally reaching a state of dependence on the therapist.' (p. 99)

Those who have received some primary provision and begun the process of healthy separation from the mother, but for whom this has been interrupted, she calls 'archipelago children', those who:

> have achieved the first steps towards integration; so that one could describe them as made up of ego-islets which have never fused into a continent – a total person ... they are either wildly aggressive, destructive, and out of touch in states of panic-rage or terror; or they are gentle, dependent and concerned. (p. 99)

These children need to regress to that primary experience and recommence the process of integration through the care of the residential therapeutic community.

Those who have formed a self through separation but then need to protect it she calls, using Winnicott's terms, those with a 'caretaker' or 'false' self. For these children she describes a regressive holding experience that eventually enables the child to hand over the caretaker role to the therapist.

When we look at Haigh's developmental model and Dockar-Drysdale's focus on returning psychologically to the point when the child's primary provision has failed in order to progress again, we see a clear need for a developmental and reparative approach to therapy with those who have experienced this early, complex trauma. These two models can be helpful in providing a sense of what that approach might use as guide-posts, from the basic overall model that Haigh suggests to the focus on early experience and the impact on development of the self that Dockar-Drysdale offers.

The Mulberry Bush has these two models as its foundation, as the theoretical underpinning of the environment in which the work takes place. In Haigh's terms there is a culture of belonging in which children can develop therapeutic relationships. There is a culture of safety which enables a child to feel held in a way they were unable to in home place-ments and schools, and of course historically due to trauma and neglect. A culture of openness enables a supported, psychodynamic and reflective experience of psychological development. To put it in Dockar-Drysdale's terms, primary experiences are provided through care which meets the earliest needs and responds to their gradual development. This is the ther-apeutic milieu in which dramatherapy takes place, and it is this reparative developmental focus that my dramatherapy practice took on during my time working at the Mulberry Bush.

Dramatherapy in a Therapeutic Community

But how do these models effect the way I, as a dramatherapist, have worked? The reparative developmental approach with children who have experienced early trauma and neglect requires working with those early experiences by returning to that stage. By this I certainly do not mean enacting early experiences, which is likely to be re-traumatising. Nor am I suggesting talking directly about those early experiences – this is both unrealistic and unhelpful. Can we really expect a child to be able to artic-ulate their earliest experiences? When trauma happens at a pre-verbal stage, it is remembered in pre-verbal ways (Rothschild, 2000). Van der

Kolk and Saporta (1991) point out that, when dealing with experiences from those early stages, the brain is immature, and so those early experiences 'cannot be easily translated into the symbolic language necessary for linguistic retrieval' (p. 206). This is why the arts therapies are particularly suitable for working with early trauma, because they are not reliant on language, but are able to find ways to express the unspeakable. There may be an assumption that dramatherapy is a verbal process, but the reality is that the Sesame approach gives equal weighting to play and movement that is non-verbal. As Sam let me know in our first session, sound can be as eloquent as words.

In our first sessions together, Sam and I met through sound rather than speech. We used the kazoos to communicate, and also percussion instruments. We would take it in turns to play a rhythm and the other would then have to copy it. As we went on these would become increasingly complicated, until they were impossible for me to follow. I felt like she wanted to know if I would stay with her, if I would keep trying to understand this language that she was creating, rather than imposing a language of my own. The early turn-taking had echoes of a mother playing with and echoing the sounds of the infant, developing a language together. It did not matter when I failed to recreate the sounds exactly; instead she seemed to have understood, and was satisfied that I was willing to follow, and to try.

Winnicott described the importance of primary maternal preoccupation, that state of perfect attunement (1958) at the earliest stages. After that the importance becomes the response to failures – 'It is the innumerable failures followed by the sort of care that mends that build up into a communication of love, of the fact that there is a human being there who cares.' (1968, p. 98) My failures, and the adaptations in the wake of those failures, became part of the process of creating a meaningful connection between us through non-verbal experience, an experience she was denied at the pre-verbal level. Sam was neglected in her first year, her mother was unable to adapt and respond to failures, and instead left her without that lived experience of care. I could try and tell Sam verbally that I care, but her early experience tells her that is not true. It takes that recreation of the earliest experiences, and their ongoing repetition, for it to be real for her. This then fits with the therapeutic community ethos, a reparative model in which we go back to the beginning and provide the missed experience. And dramatherapy is able to provide that experience non-verbally.

Working verbally at this stage would miss the point, as we are working with those pre-verbal experiences, and ones which cannot be communicated with words, but it also can be unhelpful. In these cases, words are experienced as nullifying or denying the felt experience. Bradley (1999) makes the point that:

> Children who have suffered severe emotional trauma have rarely felt that they have been heard or understood by another person who they could trust to bear the pain of what they have to say. Words spoken to them can be experienced as annihilating as the original trauma. (pp. 25–26)

So I responded to Sam in the medium she suggested: sound. Responding to the client in kind is the least we would expect from a therapist. So how do we then decide what to do next? A developmental approach starts with that primary experience that was denied, but it must also move forward. Within dramatherapy there are some very useful models for this, such as Jennings's Embodiment-Projection-Role scheme (1999), Landy's Role Theory (2010) and Bannister's Regenerative Model (2003). In my work at the Mulberry Bush I have found Bruce Perry and his Neurosequential Model of Therapeutics (2006) a particularly useful framework for understanding where a child is at, and how to move forwards with them.

The Neurosequential Model and Dramatherapy

Over recent years there has been a growing wealth of neuroscience research and increased understanding of the brain-based impact of what we do. Ideas about the brain are becoming part of the culture, not just in the scientific community. Phrases such as 'reptilian brain' to reflect the idea of a more emotional, non-verbal part of the brain have become commonplace. Neuroscience is part of policymaking in the UK: in 2008 Graham Allen MP and Iain Duncan Smith MP declared that 'Neuroscience can now explain why early conditions are so crucial' (2008, p. 57). Increasingly this is seen as the gold standard, perhaps because of the appeal of attaching something so scientific to the sometimes more nebulous or theoretical realms of therapy. While we must pay attention to these developments, we also need to remain aware that neuroscience is still in the early stages of our understanding, there will undoubtedly be new and surprising developments down the road, and that there have been plenty of debates about whether it is always used correctly.

That said, I do believe that these new findings can help us understand and shed light on what we already know, and that the challenge is finding the meeting points between therapy and neuroscience. There are a number of writers looking at these overlaps and how they can illuminate our current thinking (see Schore, 2001; Gerhardt, 2004; Music, 2011;). Van der Kolk (2005) has written extensively on the neurodevelopmental impact of trauma, even arguing for a new diagnosis of developmental trauma which echoes the definition above of complex trauma with a focus on the physiological and neurological impact of early trauma. The Mulberry Bush approach has been particularly influenced by the work of Bruce Perry (2006, 2009 and others), and specifically his Neurosequential Model (2006). This gives a useful framework through which I want to look at my work with Sam, and how thinking about the work in neurosequential terms can help understand the developmental process at work over nearly three years as the sessions moved from sound into narrative, play and language. But first I want to give a brief introduction to the Neurosequential Model through looking at Perry's first three principles of neurodevelopment.

Perry's First Principle of Neurodevelopment

The brain is organised in hierarchical fashion, such that all incoming sensory input first enters the lower parts of the brain. (2006, p. 30)

We like to think that our brains receive information, we process it and then we react. But, as Perry points out, we first process the information in the lower parts of the brain, which are pre-verbal. This means that for something to reach our thoughtful consideration in the cortex, it has to have passed through the lower parts without leading to a pre-verbal, or unconscious, response. Generally, these are responses to threat as we have evolved to respond to threat without wasting time and energy on thinking about it, the so-called flight-or-fight response. The children we work with have grown up with threat and become hyper-vigilant, so that, at an unconscious level, all sorts of things that might seem innocuous become associated with threat.

The child is then likely, when anything triggers strong feelings, to react in a way that is out of context, out of proportion and out of control. The child becomes highly unregulated and unreachable – 'The individual will think and act in very primitive ways, and therefore will be less accessible to academic or therapeutic interventions using words or therapeutic relationships as the mutative agents of change.' (p. 34) Perry links this to transference and attachment, making the point that for the 'brainstem'-driven child (i.e. the child whose anxiety or upset is causing them to regress to behaving in a way that is only using those early non-verbal parts of the brain) the disorganised attachment model or negative transference projection is a primitive and powerful neurological experience of reality. As Perry says, 'these pre-cortical associations can profoundly interfere with therapeutic work' (p. 34) as trauma means a child soon becomes unregulated, and the unregulated child cannot access words to process or unpick this. We and our client cannot access the thoughtful higher parts of the brain, so we must find ways to help our clients to regulate and to process the feelings in therapy in ways that are more accessible to the part of the brain they will actually be using.

In clinical terms the implications of this are clear – we need to create an environment that is safe and secure for therapy, and we need to be able to work with the early brain. Sam was hyper-vigilant, primed to respond to the slightest perceived threat. The brainstem triggers what is often called the fight-or-flight response, and the moment Sam became agitated or stressed this brainstem-led response was clear in her behaviour – she would run, or she would attack. We had a trusted adult outside the room to support her. She never actually did run, but some of that trust was able to be transferred over to me. I had a good, friendly, relaxed and genuine relationship with the therapeutic care worker supporting outside the room and we would chat as he handed Sam over or took her away. This less-than-clinical interaction seemed to establish something useful for Sam, and she soon started to use this support to help her with the session endings. For the first six months we would end the play five minutes early and go out into the corridor and play a percussion-copying game with the support worker. Sam was clear that she needed these layers of safety to be able to engage, and it worked. The support worker was always game, but never comfortable with this peculiar ritual, and perhaps this shared experience of the strangeness of what we do in dramatherapy also helped reduce any potential worry or stress.

Safety was an early theme in the work inside the sessions too – once we moved on from percussion we played with small animal figures and she set up zoos or farms. For weeks on end the animals would escape, the lions would attack or the elephant would stampede. I was the farmer or zoo keeper, and on the whole I was useless. I was never allowed to build walls strong enough; when I tried to stop the animals they overwhelmed me. I have written elsewhere (Cropper and Godsal, 2016) about the importance for these children to make the therapist feel useless as the key early transferential relationship in therapy. As well as that need for us to taste something of their experience of despair and helplessness, in this case, and in most others I worked with, there was a simple need to see what was safe and to play around with these themes of un-safeness. Once again, telling my client that the room is safe, that I can contain or manage what they bring, is not enough. Their experience is that they are unmanageable, and that feelings are overwhelming, so the containment and safety the therapist is offering must be played out and experienced before it can be believed.

Finally, if I was to tackle her experience of early trauma head on, by asking her to talk about it, or steering the play into a direct reflection of early experiences, this would, at this point, be too much. As Perry says, to trigger early memories or high emotional states is to dysregulate the child and ultimately to make them inaccessible – as Onions says, these types of children 'showed little capacity to think or reflect' (2013, p. 142).

Perry's Second Principle of Neurodevelopment

Neurons and neural systems are designed to change in a 'use-dependent' fashion. (2006, p. 34)

This principle explains how neural systems change according to use, especially in early development, but not exclusively. This means that, if there is a problem in development through trauma, then this becomes written in the brain, and then in the presenting behaviours. He points out that 'neuropsychiatric symptoms and signs present in maltreated or traumatised children are related to the nature, timing, pattern, and duration of their developmental experiences' (p. 36). In other words, the presenting symptoms can be understood as representative of the missing or dysfunctional experiences, and that these are what we need to work with. This is in line with Dockar-Drysdale's assertion that 'the point at which traumatic interruption has taken place determines the nature of the survival mechanisms used by the child' (1966, p. 98).

Perry believes that 'children with brainstem mediated hyper-vigilance, impulsivity and anxiety [which is a good generalisation of the children at the Mulberry Bush with their history of early trauma and chaotic present behaviour] require patterned, repetitive brainstem activities to begin to regulate these brainstem systems' (2006, p. 38). He stresses the need for repetitive experiences that use the parts of the brain that have been neglected. One example of this at the Mulberry Bush would be the regular drumming work with children, which is used as a way of helping them to regulate themselves. Rhythm is a key part of early experience, from hearing the mother's heartbeat when held close, to the more general rhythms of regular, predictable care. Through drumming groups they have that repetitive experience of regular, rhythmic holding, and learn to join it and play around with it. Perry's Neurosequential Model would suggest an entire programme based around regular and repetitive experiences aimed at meeting neglected areas. This is where the therapeutic community model is so useful, so the children I saw at the Mulberry Bush were experiencing this kind of planned therapeutic environment.

Dramatherapy sessions are unlikely to be as regular and repetitive as these experiences Perry is talking about, but there are important clinical implications. Firstly, we cannot underestimate the importance of repetition and ritual in the work. Change is slow, and for a child to internalise the positive holding provided in therapy, that reparative return to the missed early experience of parental attunement, it may well need to be experienced a great many times. We know this from experience, and we can also understand this in terms of the need to establish the neural pathways that create what Bowlby might think of as an internal working model.

Perry then makes the following point:

> talking, or even therapeutic relational interactions, are not particularly effective at providing brainstem altering experiences. Dance, drumming, music, massage – patterned, repetitive sensory input will begin to provide the kinds of experiences that may influence brainstem neurobiology to reorganise in ways that will lead to smoother functional regulation. (2006, p. 38)

In other words, talking about it does not change it, when we are looking at early experience. Rather, change comes through a lived experience.

As we learnt above, the presenting symptoms are an indicator of the timing of trauma or abuse, so for those 'brainstem mediated' clients we can assume early trauma. For those who have experienced the earliest trauma or neglect, words are not helpful. As dramatherapists we have ways of working with these children that use that earlier, pre-verbal, sensory experience. In addition, our use of structure and ritual can be thought about in these terms of regulation, that enable our clients to regulate themselves, in their bodies as much as in the more advanced terms of abstract cognition of thoughts or feelings, and so access therapy at the developmental level they require.

For Sam, the pattern of the rituals was an important part of establishing her feeling of security, but also of developing those rhythms of reliable care. We worked not through dance as such, but through movement. I was able to meet that flighty energy in play. The overwhelmed zookeeper was in stark contrast to the way I was able to play with the movement that she at times found overwhelming in herself. Sam was able to use the sessions to play with those ungrounded feelings, clambering around the room, moving at speed, and being met in that play. As a Sesame Drama and Movement therapist, I had the tools to work with movement, and I was able to help her to develop these experiences, transforming these heightened sensations in her body into feeling grounded and more in control through movement-based play. Early trauma often manifests physically in the hyper-vigilant child's movement, and through movement work they can be helped to become more regulated and grounded.

Perry's Third Principle of Neurodevelopment

The brain develops in a sequential fashion. (2006, p. 38)

Perry points out that at birth the brain is undeveloped and that it gradually develops, starting with the more regulatory regions through to the more complex parts. As he points out: '*The key to therapeutic intervention is to remember that the stress response systems originate in the brainstem and diencephalon.* As long as these systems are poorly regulated and dysfunctional, they will disrupt and dysregulate the higher parts of the brain' (pp. 38–39, emphasis in the original). The point he stresses is that the impact on the earliest, regulatory aspects of the brain must be worked with first, and that therapeutic input should reflect that sequential development.

> All the best cognitive-behavioural, insight-oriented, or even affect-based interventions will fail if the brainstem is poorly regulated … Once state regulation has improved, the child can begin to benefit from more traditional therapy. The sequence of providing therapeutic experience matters. Just as healthy development does, healing following childhood trauma starts from the bottom up. (p. 39)

We have clear echoes of Haigh's developmental journey through the therapeutic community and how the work of modern neuroscience can build on these more traditional foundations.

Perry illustrates the 'normal' timings of brain development for the four main areas – the brainstem, diencephalon, limbic and cortex. For each stage he summarises the critical functions being organised and the primary developmental goal. He then suggests some examples of optimising experiences that can stimulate and meet the needs of that part of the brain, as well as therapeutic and enrichment activities (p. 41). The bottom-up approach Perry is suggesting makes it clear that to start with 'abstract cognitive functions', something being organised in the cortex during the later stage of development, is pointless if a child has deficits in the building blocks that came before. It is also worth remembering at this point that early experiences of trauma, if experienced pre-verbally, will be remembered pre-verbally. Instead we need to return to the language that the child will understand first, and Perry provides us with a fantastic tool for understanding what languages we have at our disposal.

Combining the Therapeutic Community and Neurodevelopment

Perry's work is very sympathetic to the foundations that Haigh has laid out within the therapeutic community. This work led to some changes in the way the Mulberry Bush works, particularly a real focus within the school on regulation, helping a child to be in a fit state to think before starting to talk. This might mean a child will spend time on a swing, or might respond well to wrapping themselves up in a blanket, or whatever has been identified as something that helps them feel contained once more. This raised a question for some in the school as to whether this was taking the focus away from its psychodynamic principles. Ultimately the therapeutic community is what Perry might call a therapeutic web (2006, p. 46), with relationship as the primary tool, within a framework of reflective and psychodynamic thinking. The regulatory work is focused on making this tool accessible to the children – it was soon understood that it is a precursor to psychodynamic thinking rather than a replacement for it.

At the Mulberry Bush the child's needs are assessed and they are referred for different therapies (see Onions, 2013 for a more in-depth look at how this assessment process works in practice and more on psychotherapy within this setting). Music therapy is offered for those at the earliest stages in terms of neurodevelopment, working non-verbally and using the instruments as a therapeutic container for a relationship which might otherwise be too complex and threatening for the child. Those able to access thought and emotion work with the psychotherapists, who work in a developmentally sensitive way. Dramatherapy covers the space in between – children able to make some use of relationship, some use of play, but for whom psychotherapy would be overwhelming. Usually these children have experienced neglect or trauma at a pre-verbal stage and need the therapy to be able to work at this pre-verbal level.

Onions (2013) connects these therapies broadly to Perry's stages of neurodevelopment – music therapy for the first stages, the brainstem and diencephalon, dramatherapy for the diencephalon and the more relational, limbic stage, and psychotherapy for the cortex. Perry suggests creative arts and therapies to meet the limbic developmental needs, as well as use of rhythm, narrative, movement and story for the stages either side (2006, p. 41) – things we most certainly find in our dramatherapist's toolbox. Dramatherapy, therefore, is a particularly useful intervention with children who have suffered early trauma because of its ability to meet a range of developmental needs, and to move with the child as they work with these stages of development. We can straddle the range of needs from the pre-verbal movement work, to the early movement and beginnings of symbolic processing, through the relational connections and increasing complexities of narratives, through to the stage of abstract thought and reflection. Dramatherapy in this setting is used to cover that middle ground, but as a modality it is an ideal developmental therapy to meet the needs of children who have experienced complex or developmental trauma.

Neurosequentially Influenced Dramatherapy – Working from the Bottom Up

As dramatherapists I think we are perfectly placed to be able to move along the neurodevelopmental spectrum that Perry has identified, and able to provide the pre-verbal regulation of the earliest stages, through the growing complexities of narratives and play in the diencephalon and the relationships of the limbic, and into the more abstract and cognitive arena of the cortex. This is not a new concept in dramatherapy – David Read Johnson's chapter, 'Developmental Approaches in Drama Therapy' (1982), calls for:

> Treatment [which] first involves an assessment of where in the developmental sequence the person has stopped him/herself, and then starting the journey again with the therapist as a companion and guide. (p. 184)

What I find in Perry's work is a guide for the therapist on that journey.

Perry's scheme, with its 'Optimising experiences' and 'Therapeutic and enrichment activities' (2006, p. 41), gives clear suggestions on the sorts of ways we can work to meet the needs of the child in terms of the different brain developmental needs – the brainstem, diencephalon, limbic and cortex. While I am saying we need to pay attention to and be guided by these, this is not a process to be applied to the child. I am not suggesting a rigid scheme of work – the work can never be as linear as it might appear on paper, and Perry and Haigh make that point about their own schema. Clients regress and progress, work takes steps back and forward. We also must be humble about what we can achieve – Perry may point out the usefulness of touch in helping regulation and meeting the developmental needs of the brainstem, but a few sessions involving touch does not mean we can tick that off as rewired, damage repaired. To truly apply his approach would require many more repetitions on a much more regular basis than the dramatherapist is ever likely to provide. Anything we do takes place within the relationship, and it is the child who guides us.

What we can take from this, though, is an understanding of how the different aspects of the dramatherapist's work, from touch to drama, movement to myth, can meet different levels of a client's development. It can help our practice if we consider the child's history when deciding which of these tools from the dramatherapist's toolkit will best meet the needs of the child.

Perry has a table showing 'Sequential Neurodevelopment and Therapeutic Activity' (2006, p. 41) which shows the ages at which the different brain areas are thought to develop, and this can give us an indication of the brain-based approach we might use for each child. Perry suggests that the 'age of most active growth' for the brainstem is

0–9 months, the diencephalon 6 months to 2 years, the limbic 1–4 years and the cortex between 2 and 6 years old.

I recently worked in a mainstream school with a girl, Zoe, who witnessed her father destroy all the family belongings in a rage before he was taken away in an ambulance to be sectioned. She then lived for a period in refuges. She apparently was coping with this all remarkably well, until, a year on, she became highly anxious and violent towards her mother. In many ways this is a story that would seem familiar to the children at the Mulberry Bush, but the major difference is that this all took place when she was 5 years old. Zoe did not need me to play in those early ways that Sam needed. She was reluctant to talk directly about the experience as it was too upsetting; instead the work took place in stories and symbols, but these were symbols expressed verbally and cognitively, as well as through the psychodynamic unconscious processes. She made keys and castles and told stories about a monster who was able to steal the key and break into the castle. Over time she was able to talk about her experience, but largely she used the sessions to make more containers and holders, and to build up again that sense of strength and security. Before we finished she told another story about that monster and how the children in the story were able to get the birds to carry him off and deposit him on Mars.

Perry's model of brain development shows us that at the age of Zoe's traumatic experience the more complex parts of the brain were developing, so working with the cortex was a viable way to understand the experience. Narrative, symbol, and words, through relationship and play, were the natural language of her experiences and her way of processing them. What happened was remembered in feelings, words and thoughts, so the traumatic experience could also be processed in feelings, words and thoughts. Not too directly, but through stories and the therapeutic relationship.

Sam, on the other hand, needed my work with her to start at the beginning. Her trauma took place in her first months, when, as Perry suggests, it was the brainstem that was developing. Therefore, she needed me to start with that language – regulation, rhythm and touch are the ways to attune to this type of child.

This was not the end of the work though. This was a child who went into care at a year old, so she was removed from this neglectful environment. Often children we work with will appear to have split in their presentation – at times they can appear to be mature, functioning products of the years of good enough care they have received. Then in a moment they can become toddlers or even infants, unregulated, unreachable, and certainly unthinking. We work with both parts, the traumatised infant and the 10 year old, and we work to bridge that gap.

Over the following years my work with Sam moved through the stages that Perry identifies. From that beginning of working with the brainstem, non-verbally, through repetition, regulation, rhythm, we moved into increasingly complex areas. The primary developmental goals during the development of the diencephalon, Perry argues, are sensory integration, motor control, relational flexibility and attunement (2006, p. 41). We start to move into a world of early relationships, simple narratives, and multi-sensory input. For Sam this was through the use of toy figures and the creation of a strange family of toys. In the beginning they were simply infants, and I had to try and meet their needs. We moved through the cycles of attunement, mis-attunement and re-attunement, when I would try to understand what they needed. Sometimes I would be right, but more often I would not, she would let me know, and I would then correct my actions. The key for Sam, though, was that I kept on trying, giving her the experience of the world adapting to her rather than of needs being ignored. I was meeting her need to experience attunement on a practical level.

According to Perry, the limbic part of the brain is the next part to develop and it is at this stage, from 1 to 4 years, that the child develops more complex relationships and interaction, emotional states, and understanding of others, such as empathy (2006, p. 41). Perry identifies the optimising experiences that can help meet this developmental need as increasing sophistication of narrative, complex movement and social interaction. This was reflected in the following stage of the therapy which became focused on relationships, between Sam and me, but particularly between the characters in her increasingly complex stories. She no longer needed me to play out this reparative dance of early nurture and attunement; instead she needed to explore relationships through play. So instead of my having to be the carer, we met together in the play. Initially this was using the figures, but soon enough Sam and I became characters in a longer tale. In fact, we were these characters for a-year-and-a-half, each week playing out a new version. Themes came and went, locations played out, and slowly the narratives spread over weeks instead of just sessions. Together we explored an internal world that was able to develop in complexity and richness. Perry recommends play and play therapies for the limbic stage (2006, p. 41) as this is an ideal way to explore relationships. It is worth remembering that this part of the brain develops, typically, between 1 and 4 years old, so that play is the natural language of this stage.

The next stage that Perry identifies is the cortex, when abstract cognitive functions are the critical functions being organised (2006, p. 41). In other words, thought and ideas. So often therapists expect a client to be able to think or reflect, but for a child like Sam, whose traumatic experiences happened way before the cortex developed between 3 and 6 years old, thought and reflection were meaningless. She never did use me to talk directly about her experiences, but I began to put more words to the experiences in the sessions, commenting in character on the feelings, giving her a new vocabulary for her experience. As we moved towards an ending we spoke a little about our time together, remembering what we had done over the years, the places we had been, the people we had met. Her earliest experiences were still inaccessible through talk, but the experiences in therapy that reflected the missed needs and worked with the neglected parts of her were able to be thought about.

We can think about this time with Sam in terms of Perry's working with specific parts of the brain, or as a response to attachment needs and working with the internal working model, or in terms of transference and projection. We could think along the developmental model of Haigh or use the ideas of Dockar-Drysdale. We could apply developmental models specific to dramatherapy as mentioned above. For me the important thing is that we can use these models to help guide our practice. I have heard many therapists speak about 'meeting the client where they are' and I think that the Neurosequential Model is useful for helping us do that. It provides us with a guide to how we might work with a child, and a reminder that we must find a language that is meaningful because it is the one in which those traumatic experiences are remembered. It also helps us to navigate our way through the slow process of change.

Conclusion

My six years at the Mulberry Bush has had an enormous impact on my work. It may be that I would have worked with Sam in the same way in any other setting – the work was client led after all. But my work is now much more focused on providing a reparative experience through meeting the child at the right developmental level. The work of the therapeutic community has given me an understanding of how we can provide these healthy early experiences that traumatised children are denied. The neurosequential work of Bruce Perry has given me a framework for understanding the ways to work with a child to meet those developmental stages. And my own dramatherapy work with children has shown me the range of ways we are able to work as dramatherapists to meet early needs, as well as current ones, and to follow our clients on their developmental journeys. Touch, movement, play, story, role. These different tools of our trade are the things that enable us to meet children where they are at, and to provide the holding, the relationship, and the attunement that enable change.

References

Allen, G. & Duncan-Smith, I. (2008). *Early Intervention: Good Parents, Great Kids, Better Citizens*. London: Centre for Social Justice and The Smith Institute.

Bannister, A. (2003). *Creative Therapies with Traumatised Children*. London: Jessica Kingsley Publisher.

Boston, M. & Szur, R. (1983). *Psychotherapy with Severely Deprived Children*. London: Karnac Books.

Bowlby, J. (1973). *Attachment and Loss, Vol. 2 Separation*. London: Hogarth Press.

Bradley, C. (1999). Making sense of symbolic communication. In A. Hardwick & J. Wrodhead (Eds.), *Loving, Hating and Survival: A Handbook for All Who Work with Troubled Children and Young People* (pp. 23–37). Arena: Ashgate.

Courtois, C. A. & Ford, J. D. (2009) Defining and understanding complex trauma and complex traumatic stress disorders. In C. A. Courtois & J. D. Ford (Eds.), *Treating Complex Traumatic Stress Disorders: An Evidence Based Guide* (pp. 13–30). New York, NY: The Guilford Press.

Cropper, K. & Godsal, J. (2016). The useless therapist: Music therapy and dramatherapy with traumatised children. *Journal of Therapeutic Communities, 37*(1), 12–17.

Diamond, J. (2009). The Mulberry Bush as a therapeutic community: Context and culture. *Therapeutic Communities, 30*(2), 217–228.

Dockar-Drysdale, B. (1966). The provision of primary experience in a therapeutic school. In B. Dockar-Drysdale (Ed.), *Therapy and Consultation in Child Care* (pp. 97–116). London: Free Association Books.

Dockar-Drysdale, B. (1993). *Therapy and Consultation in Child Care.* London: Free Association Books.

Gerhardt, S. (2004), *Why Love Matters.* Hove: Routledge.

Gunter, M. (2005). Individual psychotherapy versus milieu therapy in childhood and adolescence. *Therapeutic Communities, 26*(2), 163–173.

Haigh, R. (2013). The quintessence of a therapeutic environment. *Journal of Therapeutic Communities, 34*(1), 6–16.

Jennings, S. (1999). *Introduction to Developmental Playtherapy: Playing and Health – Persephone's Journey.* London: Jessica Kingsley.

Kennard, D. (1998). *An Introduction to Therapeutic Communities.* London: Jessica Kingsley Publisher.

Kornerup, H. (2009). *Milieu-Therapy with Children: Planned Environment Therapy in Scandinavia.* Lejre: Perikon Books.

Landy, R. J. (2010). Role theory and the role method of drama therapy. In D. R. Johnson & R. Emunah (Eds.), *Current Approaches in Drama Therapy* (2nd ed., pp. 65–88). Springfield, IL: Charles C. Thomas.

Music, G. (2011). *Nurturing Natures.* Hove: Psychology Press.

Nicholson, C., Irwin, M. & Dwivedi, K. N. (Eds.). (2010). *Children and Adolescents in Trauma: Creative Therapeutic Approaches.* London: Jessica Kingsley Publisher.

Onions, C. (2013). Making meaningful connections: Assessing for clinical work in a child residential setting. *Journal of Therapeutic Communities, 34*(4), 141–151.

Perry, B. D. (2006). Applying principles of neurodevelopment to clinical work with maltreated and traumatized children: The neurosequential model of therapeutics. In N. Boyd Webb (Ed.), *Working with Traumatized Youth in Child Welfare* (pp. 27–52). New York, NY: The Guilford Press.

Perry, B. (2009). Examining child maltreatment through a neurodevelopmental lens: Clinical applications of the neurosequential model of therapeutics. *Journal of Loss and Trauma, 14,* 240–255.

Perry, B. & Szalavitz, M. (2006). *The Boy Who was Raised as a Dog*. New York, NY: Basic Books.

Read Johnson, D. (1982). Developmental approaches in dramatherapy. *The Arts in Psychotherapy, 9*, 183–189.

Rothschild, B. (2000). *The Body Remembers: The Pyschophysiology of Trauma and Trauma Treatment*. New York, NY: W.W. Norton.

Schore, A. N. (2001). The effect of early relational trauma on right brain development, affect regulation and infant mental health. *Infant Mental Health Journal, 22*(1–2), 201–269.

van der Kolk, B. (2005), Developmental trauma disorder. *Psychiatric Annals, 35*(5), 401–408.

van der Kolk, B. A. & Saporta, J. (1991). The biological response to psychic trauma: mechanisms and treatment of intrusion and numbing. *Anxiety Research, 4*, 199–212 (cited in Saotome, J. (2010). Being speechless: Art therapy with self harming adolescents. In C. Nicholson, M. Irwin & K. N. Dwivedi (Eds.), *Children and Adolescents in Trauma: Creative Therapeutic Approaches* (pp. 180–96). London: Jessica Kingsley.

Ward, A., Kasinski, K., Pooley, J. & Worthington, A. (2003). *Therapeutic Communities for Children and Young People*. London: Jessica Kingsley.

Winnicott, D. W. (1958). Primary maternal preoccupation. In *Through Paediatrics to Psycho-Analysis* (pp. 300–305). London: Tavistock.

Winnicott, D. W. (1968). Communication between infant and mother, and mother and infant, compared and contrasted. In W. G. Joffe (Ed.), *What is Psychoanalysis* (pp. 89–103). London: Balliere, Tindall and Cassel.

8

Two to One

Alyson Coleman and Alison Kelly

Introduction

This chapter introduces and explores our experience of 16 years working together as co-facilitating dramatherapists. Co-facilitation is a therapeutic approach in which two dramatherapists run a dramatherapy session together, jointly taking responsibility for all therapeutic aspects. It is used in dramatherapists' work both with individual clients and with groups. Co-facilitation incorporates the many elements of dramatherapy but with double the therapeutic and theatrical tools. Sessions are fluid as we move in and out of role within improvisations and story enactment. In our clinical work the drama and the bereavement praxis are intertwined within the intervention. Spontaneous play often fuels the process, as we think and work on our feet.

In this chapter we will examine the co-facilitation framework we have developed within an NHS bereavement service.

Our co-facilitation relationship didn't just 'happen' but grew from our training on the Sesame Drama and Movement Therapy training at the Royal Central School of Speech and Drama, University of London. The fabric of the course introduces students to client settings by working in small teams on clinical placements as part of the MA Group Apprenticeship Model. Within this model, the lead therapist role is rotated among the students, with their peers taking a 'co-facilitating' role. An experienced clinical supervisor is a fundamental part of this team, modelling the method and passing on tacit knowledge to trainees. The supervisor also embodies the student's own emergent, inner supervisor and ensures a safe process of work for, primarily, the client but also the trainee. Students immediately enter into their own supervision after the session, therefore developing a 'supervision in action' element and the opportunity for a deeper understanding of reflective practice. This concept has evolved in our practice to the point at which there is an equality of facilitation.

There is little academic research involving two therapists co-working in the same modality with one client. Co-working is more frequently referred to in relation to groups such as psychotherapy groups (Yalom, 2005, p. 443), family therapy (Burnham, 1986, p. 71) and cross-disciplinary work – for example that of a play therapist and social worker (Cattanach, 2005, p. 227). Dramatherapists, however, have a history of co-facilitation – as demonstrated by groups such as Roundabout, a registered charity who have been pioneering drama and movement therapy across London for the past 30 years (Haythorne and Cedar, 1996, p. 251).

The co-facilitation model takes an idiographic approach in that it is concerned with facilitating or holding the client while they focus on the detail of their personal world. This is made possible by the texture and depth of attention that can be offered by two therapists who are constantly reviewing their own conceptions and processes, enabling accuracy of responsiveness from the therapists to the client and between each other. This is then channeled or routed through the 'involvement in drama with a healing intention' (Jones, 1996, p. 6).

Timeline

Our professional relationship started in 2000 when we were both members of the arts therapy team in a Pupil Referral Unit (PRU) for children with emotional and behavioural difficulties, where we co-ran a dramatherapy group for children who were experiencing loss and change in their lives. This work coincided with our own recent personal bereavements. We had each experienced the death of a parent: one very suddenly in 2000, the other in 2001 following a lengthy period of treatment. These bereavements inevitably had an impact on our personal and professional lives; our experiences informed our thinking about our work in the PRU and we were alive to the connections around early loss and bereavement for our young clients.

By 2003, in addition to the PRU, we were asked by educational, social and health services – who had heard about our specialist co-facilitated therapy – to work with complex bereavement cases as there was no other suitable service available. This highlighted a gap in provision and was a significant phase in the development of our style of co-working. The types of bereavement were varied and differed from our previous PRU cases. For example, working with clients who had experienced death of a relative by suicide, murder or criminal activity, which all expanded our knowledge base and advanced our way of working.

In 2004 we were offered a part-time job-share role within an NHS community paediatric palliative care nursing team. Our new post had previously been held by a lone counsellor whose work had comprised the management of a complex pre- and post-bereavement caseload. As the sole psychological professional in a team of nurses, this role had presented significant challenges for the previous individual post holder. Ultimately it became untenable and led to the loss of the post. In light of this experience the community service senior managers welcomed and encouraged our proposal as a job-share position. Learning from the experience of our predecessor, we evolved a co-facilitated approach for all pre-bereavement cases. It was our belief that children with a life-limiting diagnosis are more likely to experience complex emotional issues requiring specific therapeutic intervention and the robust containment of two therapists.

In 2005 we completed a postgraduate diploma in childhood bereavement. The cohort was made up of social workers, hospice staff and police liaison officers. The multi-disciplinary nature of the student group inevitably prompted our further reflection on dramatherapy's contrasting creative psychodynamic methods.

Alongside this training we were well supported with individual supervision and joint consultation. This gave us the space to share in detail our own bereavement histories and associated stories. We began to develop our post into a clearly defined dramatherapeutic therapy service.

Building the Foundations

We appointed an experienced consultant who helped us to understand the value of rigour in the start-up process. We also received her invaluable support as we encountered the many challenges involved in creating a shared history for the service. We visited faith groups to educate ourselves in the diverse range of death rituals and beliefs; building a relationship with the local imam helped enormously in terms of spiritual and practical involvement with Muslim families. One of the tasks we set ourselves was to take a guided tour of a wide range of settings associated with death rituals, such as a crematorium, funeral directors and a temple.

Little did we realise quite how 'behind-the-scenes' the team at the crematorium would take us: perhaps they assumed, quite wrongly, that we would take the more graphic side of cremation in our stride. Our somatic response was one of shock which contrasted with the dignity and pride of the crematorium attendant, to whom all of this appeared everyday.

The hospital chaplain put us in touch with a funeral director for our next visit. As we sometimes use a sand tray and small objects within dramatherapy sessions, we had phoned ahead to ask whether they could suggest somewhere we could buy a small coffin for our work. We imagined some type of Lego or Playmobil model but the undertaker very kindly suggested it would be no trouble for his carpenter to make us one. Upon arrival at the funeral directors, we were warmly welcomed and ushered through the public reception area, again stepping 'behind the scenes'. We were taken into a chapel of rest and there, to our surprise, was a full-sized child's coffin complete with a far-too-realistic baby doll inside. The carpenter had skilfully made us a real coffin. Ali was lost for words and tearful: seeing the coffin there, so realistic, took her back to a childhood memory of the death of her infant brother, whose funeral she did not attend owing to the culture of the time. Meanwhile Alyson was caught between wanting to express sincere gratitude and wondering what on earth they would do with it. It was bigger than any sand tray! It still sits in our office cupboard; we've never quite been able to bring it out, some 12 years later. Perhaps the coffin is symbolic of part of our personal response to the death of clients. It remains unseen, safely contained at work, enabling us to leave it there and go home at the end of the day.

The unsettling nature of this experience highlighted the way in which memories can be triggered (Rothschild, 2000) without obvious warning. Furthermore, experiencing these encounters together while witnessing one another's individual and unique response, led us to recall a poignant image: of two birds flying within a flock, where the stronger one can fly at the front, allowing the other to rest or be out of the direct wind current. These rich collaborative spaces and experiences fed our early work together and enabled us to explore and develop the dynamic of our professional and personal relationship 'to sustain the heartbeat and make it thrive' (Gersie, 2012).

Same but Different

Joint consultancy has always encouraged challenge, support, questioning, exploration and creativity. Within this space we have reflected upon our differing faiths and cultures. We inevitably bring something of our own spiritual beliefs into the therapy space and frequently ponder on our quite different viewpoints such as those concerning life after death. For example, it soon became apparent that Alyson was more familiar with Christian rituals, coming from a small village where several generations of her relatives are buried in the local churchyard. In contrast, Ali's experience of growing up in London was of her relatives being cremated. During consultation we realised that we both had a childlike assumption that living in the countryside meant burial and in the town meant cremation. One unifying spiritual aspect that we share is our love of our gardens. We both find the cycle of nature, literally being in touch with the ground, the changes with the passing of seasons and time, allowing ourselves to just 'be' to be a source of joy; the difficult feelings returning to the earth, a garden spade being an invaluable tool to make sense of the work. On waste ground behind our NHS base our team has made a beautiful garden. We often return to its beauty and simplicity at the end of a day, a different form of co-working – tending our shared section of the plot.

Although we are similar in many ways we inevitably find ourselves responding differently to situations. We were both nervous about our first NHS referral, as on paper the circumstances of the family struck us both as shocking and upsetting. In the car on the way to meet the family, Ali asked Alyson to slow down, and then to pull over, and was sick at the side of the road. Alyson responded by becoming disorientated and feeling panicked. Despite these strong responses, it seemed we had no choice but to care for each other and carry on to the visit. Although shocking, the solid support we offered each other enabled a containment of these feelings in order to continue on to work with the family.

Another striking difference is our emotional response expressed through food. After one particularly harrowing hospital visit with a client, we came out onto a busy London street where Ali's request to find the nearest café for a cream cake left Alyson repeating over and over, 'Oh no, I couldn't, I couldn't. Not now.' This tends to be our usual pattern of response: Ali being hungry after difficult work and Alyson not being able to eat at all. These somatic countertransferences have become part of our working culture – the comfort of the shared relationship and experience, to be drawn upon in times of stress, and the security of our intimate knowledge of each other which needs no explanation in the moment. They are our predictable friends; we welcome them and listen to their wisdom.

We truly value each other's playfulness and sense of humour. Tensions can be broken, energy changed and situations seen from a different perspective through laughing – mostly at ourselves or each other. We still chuckle at a particular incident when, during an opening ritual with a young person, each of us took a turn to say hello or open the session with a turn on a large, shared drum. This evolved into several rounds of louder and bigger explosions of expression from the client. We played with rhythms and volume, his loud or slow to our soft or fast, etc. When Ali spontaneously added the word 'fuck' to her rhythm, Alyson's jaw dropped; she was completely shocked at Ali's use of the word in that context. Ali continued with the rhythm, building to a whole-hearted shouting and repetition of 'Fuck! Fuck! Fuck!'. It was only as the session progressed that Alyson noticed the young person had the word 'FUCK' written boldly across both the knuckles on his hands and Ali had just (appropriately) picked it up and amplified it …

In addition to joint work, we often work individually with siblings. This can bring up projections on the clients' part that we, the therapists, are siblings and we recognise that we can appear to have a sister-like relationship. An example of this was with two adolescent sisters, referred owing to a third sibling's death, whom we worked with individually for several months and who endeavoured to repeat unhealthy family patterns. This proved hard going in the sense that the girls frequently, both consciously and unconsciously, tried to cause difficulties between us. On one occasion they both said in their individual sessions that the other sister was unhappy with their therapist and they both wanted to see the same one. Another time, a session happened to fall on the birthday of one of the sisters and an elaborate party emerged within the drama. In the other sister's next session, she 'confided' a dilemma: should she report to social services that the therapist had taken her sister to McDonald's and given her a present? Alyson asked Ali whether she had in fact been to McDonald's, which caused tension until the birthday drama session could be unravelled in peer supervision. Thus the shame, humiliation and envy that we sensed was present between the girls had briefly been transferred into our dynamic. Careful consideration in individual and joint supervision, as well as meticulous record-keeping, enabled robust containment and minimised splitting (Winnicott, 1971). However, strong parallel processes occurred within the girls' school; safeguarding issues became complex as professionals mirrored family dynamics. There was no neat ending to this case. A period of co-facilitation with both girls together was helpful in some ways, with progress made in terms of their communication with each other and empowerment to get their needs met in a healthy way, but the family then moved to a different borough. We endeavoured to create some form of handover but this was not easy, as the family appeared to be making a 'fresh start' with new professionals and to put barriers up to our communication.

Sharing safeguarding within a professional team is essential to good practice. For arts therapists, safeguarding issues are often embedded within the symbolic material, making decisions around when, how and whether to take these outside of the session a complex responsibility. Co-facilitation allows one therapist to be fully within the action while the other can work wearing more of a safeguarding hat. One particular client's repeated direction for violence between roles he created led us to make a safeguarding referral. Through co-facilitation we were able to explore this more fully, one of us alongside him within the metaphor, the other observing more objectively. Two perspectives offer greater rigour when understanding and presenting the material in the necessary, wider safeguarding process. Due to the robust nature of our joint safeguarding practice the referral was taken up by social services and the child found to be at significant risk.

Co-working with Different Modalities

The term 'co-working' can be used to refer to a therapist working with the child and another professional, perhaps a teacher or mentor. A social worker working with the parent or carer can parallel separate therapeutic work. In such situations all parties might at specific times work together therapeutically and psychodynamically, offering another pair of ears and eyes (McFarlane and Harvey, 2012). In group therapy it is common practice to have two or several co-therapists whereas this mode of working is far less common with an individual client.

In art therapy it is rare to work as co-therapists with one client. There is limited evidence of art therapists co-working effectively within a child protection system with different disciplines; most examples of good practice with co-therapists are derived from combinations of different agencies co-working to support the clients, and usually with groups rather than individuals (and not directly with the client). However, Manicom and Baronska's research (2003) proposed that the bringing together of different disciplines enables personal and professional narratives to combine, creating multiple ideas and ways of seeing differences in the life experiences of individuals and their families.

Practice

The following client work is an amalgamated case, brought together from many clients we have worked with where themes and patterns have emerged. Within this vignette we will focus on the use of role within co-facilitated sessions.

Sarah

Sarah is a 13-year-old girl with a life-threatening condition who attends a special educational needs school. Our work with her took place weekly in an activity room at the school. The intervention was long term and took place over several years. During this time Sarah learned to utilise many dramatherapy tools and became very familiar with enactment of story, improvisation, ritual beginnings and endings, and voice work. She also developed ways of guiding the therapists to create the landscapes, people and situations necessary to the processing of her specific emotional issues. Over time she learned to 'be' within pauses and silence, to allow action to unfold and inner shifts to take place.

The Room and Support Worker

The presence of a support worker in our practice is not unusual. Often the client is dependent on them for medical support, mobility and communication needs. Risk assessment results in their being with the child or young person at all times. In dramatherapy they will take on roles within enactment and are actively involved in the creative material that emerges. With experience of sessions and regular opportunities to meet and discuss how the dramatherapy might be working, many of these support workers become invaluable resources for the client within sessions – an extension of the client themselves. Although we are not focusing on the role of support worker within this chapter it is an important part of the work.

As sessions need to take place in a variety of community settings, there is no single dedicated clinic room. The therapeutic space is created in each session through ritual and dramatherapeutic techniques. We may see a particular child at school, at home, in hospital or at a hospice. It was evident early in the evolution of the service that we needed to be creative and flexible in order to accommodate the often chaotic day-to-day family patterns of our clients. If we couldn't offer this, then the children and young people could not benefit from continuity. It has become a strength of the service that the working alliance adapts to meet this challenge.

Clinical Material

This is an extract from a session that took place two years into the overall process of the work. It was the first session after Sarah had come back to school following a lengthy hospital admission.

Ali: What was it like being in hospital?

Sarah: It was boring. Nothing to do. I hated it.

Alyson: So it was boring? When was it most boring?

Sarah: It wasn't boring all the time. Some of the nurses were really nice. Funny. Claire brought me in a DVD and we watched it on a big screen. I really liked that. And there was always someone to talk to, even in the night.

Support worker: Do you still wake up in the night a lot?

Sarah: Yes. Then it's really boring because I don't want to wake anyone up. So I just lay there getting really bored.

Alyson moves her chair out of the main informal talking circle and sits further out, nearer the wall. She starts to yawn quietly, slowly becoming more visibly bored. Neither Sarah, nor Ali nor the support worker stop their conversation or look over at Alyson in the role of Bored, but they are aware she is there.

Ali stands up, shifting the energy. She asks Sarah who she would like her to be. Sarah tells her to be the nice nurse who brought her the DVD.

Ali (in role of Nice Nurse – lively, fun, light energy): Have you seen this one? I thought I'd bring it in.

Sarah (in role of Sarah as patient): No I haven't. Put it on!

Sarah calls over to Alyson and directs her to be 'more bored'.

The action continues with Sarah directing the support worker to move to a different part of the room and take the role of The Film, making Sarah (in role of Sarah the Patient) laugh. Alyson continues in the role of Bored, yawning, sighing, becoming more exaggerated as Sarah instructs …

The role of therapist is made up of several merging roles within the co-facilitation role, with the therapists moving fluidly between them

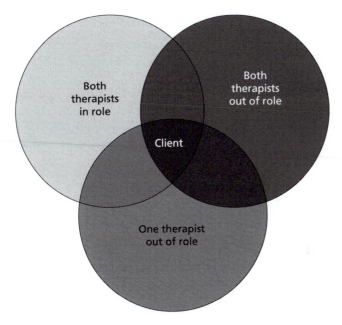

Figure 8.1 Internal positions adopted by therapists in co-working

all. The diagram in Figure 8.1 illustrates the way in which either one of us may take on different aspects within the therapeutic relationship at varying times within the session. These aspects can be loosely defined as, firstly, both therapists in role within the enactment/drama action; secondly, one therapist in role within the action while the other therapist is witness; and finally, both therapists out of role. Within these inner positions, more detailed elements may be utilised. Whereas one therapist may assume a particular internal position, both therapists may take on any/all of the positions, thus intensifying the client's experience. This serves the purpose of offering a more rigorous process and/or of containing the most complex psychological and emotional processes of the client. Landy (1994a, p. 7) describes role as 'a container of the thoughts and feelings we have about ourselves and each other, as a basic "unit" of personality'. Dramatherapy is action-based and therefore can benefit from the availability of a range of possibilities offered by more than one therapist. The potential in the 'potential space' (Winnicott, 1971) can be maximised.

Common to all three of these inner states is communication between us in sessions. Frequently this takes the form of 'thinking aloud' (Beddoe and Davys, 2016, p. 218) which allows transparency and includes the client. For example: Ali says, 'I'm wondering whether we might come out of this scene now?' In this Ali communicates to Alyson that she has picked up that the client would benefit from a breather from the drama-based action. Sometimes when both therapists are in role they may address each other directly from these roles – a layer of communication spoken through the voice of the character.

Both Therapists Out of Role

We find that the beginning and ending of the sessions tend to be times when neither of us is in role, the focus being on the person-to-person or real relationship (Clarkson, 2003), reiterating the working alliance, holding a time boundary or attending to practical elements of the session. The 'normality' of being together out of the drama can focus the session, reconnecting with each other and helping the client to arrive in the space. Likewise, as part of an ending preparation, client and therapists all being out of role together enables a coming back to the here and now and allows readiness for engaging once again with the world outside the space. On occasion, whole sessions may occur outside of the drama – perhaps when the client spends time reflecting or processing more consciously. Sometimes being out of role acts as a mechanism introduced by the client or the therapist to impact the pace of overall psychological unfolding. It may be that as therapists we sense the client needs 'anchoring' outside of creative work, and with both therapists making themselves available for a more conscious encounter the client can spend time in less symbolic, more concrete territory.

We had been working for over a year with a teenage boy, Bekhir, who had a life-limiting, degenerative condition. His condition had begun to progress during the last six months of our work together and he had been unable to attend school during this period. Our work with him at this time focused on the deterioration of his condition and health; his anger and sense of injustice were themes he brought each week when we worked with him in his home. He had initially been very resistant to working therapeutically. However, one of his great joys in life were his pets – cats, a dog, guinea pigs – and a shift occurred in our work with him when on one occasion we brought our two large puppy-sized (and realistic) dog puppets with us. There was an immediate engagement with them, and this developed and continued for the remaining time of our work with him. Where he had struggled to make eye contact with us and his language had been generally monosyllabic, with the two dogs a new intimacy emerged in our relationship; it was as if there were now five of us in his room. We were present but the interaction and conversations were between Bekhir and the dogs. Intellectually, Bekhir was aware of the 'role play' nature of using the dog puppets, the dramatic device allowing him to talk with them almost as if we were not present. He endowed each of the dogs with different personalities: one of the dogs (Ali) was an angry, rude dog that often got into trouble, while the other dog (Alyson) was the more fearful and vulnerable. When he was admitted to hospital, Bekhir's parents contacted us to let us know that he had asked to see us there. With the support of our consultant we discussed how we might make the most appropriate, therapeutic use of the visit, which would be governed by certain constraints (for fear of infection we couldn't take the dog puppets with us, and privacy and confidentiality were certain to be problematic). We discussed what we might be able to offer Bekhir, and how we might go about it. Our consultant offered to record some brief video footage of us both with the dogs, having a conversation about and for Bekhir – what they had enjoyed about the work with him, that they would miss him, what they would remember, and a recap of some of the work 'they' had done with him. In this sense the containment of the therapeutic work was preserved safely within a DVD. We took the DVD with us when we went to the hospital to see Bekhir. He was very sleepy but aware of our presence. One of his pleasures in the hospital was his laptop and earphones, with which he could listen to his music and watch DVDs either directly on his laptop or via the flat screen at the end of his bed. We sat with him and watched the DVD. While video is sometimes used as a tool by dramatherapists within sessions (Emunah, 1994; Landy, 1994b), our use of it in this instance was with a very specific and different intention: that of containment, immediacy and privacy. On a practical note, using film also offered a creative response to the work-limiting conditions of his situation involving risk of infection and lack of space.

One Therapist in Role, One Out of Role

Three or four people in the room, far from being too intense, can actually lessen intensity and provide more space. Whereas one therapist and one client can replicate the mother–child relationship, which can usefully be explored, two therapists and one client offers an opportunity for the parents-and-child relationship to be explored. Co-facilitation also allows a client to step in and out of that intensity, playing with the notion of distancing and under-distancing (Jones, 1996). The second therapist in the role of witness provides a third element which, where useful, may also lessen intensity. The model offers the possibility for the relief of deflection as the client can choose which of the two therapists to speak or interact with. It presents the opportunity for the client to move away from one particular therapist or issue if they need to. The overwhelming element of bereavement means that the therapist out of role steps into a more supervisory role, enabling a wide range of responses and feelings to be contained safely within the space. This is supervision in action and can evolve into taking on roles of challenge and authority when appropriate. This is similar to a family therapy model (Jones, 1993; Burnham, 1986) where a tutor or senior colleague may work, model and support a primary therapist as a meta-consultant. Our co-working provides a 'live supervision' (Burnham, 1986) and peer 'consultation exchange'. The definition of 'consultation' is to consider jointly: Bateson (1978) postulated that obtaining more than one view of an event enables the achievement of the cognitive or emotional equivalent of binocular vision, gaining (in a metaphorical sense) perspective on observations and experiences. We use a 'therapeutic consultation' framework as an integral part of the work within the therapeutic session, modelling transparency with the client. There is a culture of 'live supervision' (Burnham, 1986) in family therapy, where co-working can involve one of the therapists being behind a two-way screen; our framework involves both therapists physically present in the space, in consultation with the client. At times a theatrical device creates the equivalent of the family therapist's screen, offering further transparency. It demands that the client enters into the theatrical illusion of the invisibility of the second therapist, who is physically present but then dissolves their presence in order to 'disappear' and then 'reappear' where they can contribute information from their internal supervision. For example, in the earlier vignette involving Sarah, Alyson was able to 'appear' and 'disappear' in the role of Boring when she intuitively assessed it to be beneficial for the client's exploration.

This 'appearing' and 'disappearing' or, as Pitruzzella (2016) describes, 'disassembling' and 're-assembling', is a strong and unique characteristic of the model we have developed. It enables one of the therapists to focus on their 'internal supervisor' (Casement, 1985) and its contribution to the direction of the session through responding within the creative form to the transference is only possible where two therapists are working closely together.

'Drama can be the place where body, relationships, knowledge, roles and narratives gradually and delicately, can be put again into play; we can play with them, disassembling and then re-assembling them and creatively redefining and recombining them.' Pitruzzella, (2016, p. 107)

Dramatherapy during a period of pre-bereavement can rely heavily on transferential processes to inform the therapist–client relationship and the therapeutic work that comes out of that relationship. The transferences experienced by the therapists in these sessions can be powerful and, at times within the context of the session, overwhelming. When two therapists are actively engaged in the psychodynamic element of the practice, the informative nature of these possible transferences can be fully utilised for the benefit of the work.

A Triadic Therapy model (Donigian, 2005) shares some core principles with our model – for example in the sense that several people are involved in the action – although it differs in that we still consider two therapists working with one client as individual work. Triadic Therapy is based on philosopher Bert Hellinger's insights (1999) that therapists are changed not only by the experience with the client but through the encounter with each other, the clear aim remaining for the benefit of the client.

In playback theatre, the facilitator is also re-creating the client's narrative but within co-facilitated dramatherapy sessions the client may well also be in role – which is not the case in playback. Co-facilitated drama-therapy encourages the client to guide where they want the action to go. The client can direct the action from in or out of role where the therapists attune to the client accordingly. Co-facilitation allows the level of detailed support that a very unwell child may need in order to direct, freeing the 'other' therapist to be active in the drama.

There are inevitably times when one therapist is absent. On occasions when one of us has been unable to be physically present in a co-working therapy session, we have been able to draw on the 'other' from both in- and out-of-role positions. For example, during one session where Alyson was absent, Ali was able to lean on the triadic dynamic and knowledge of the client and their knowledge of us. The client was able to respond with ease when asked, 'What do you think Alyson might have said about that?' A client might respond very directly and literally to a question like this, or they might remember a role that one of us had taken within their drama and respond according to that. This could be usefully seen as one therapist in role and the other therapist out of role.

Both Therapists in Role

At times, both therapists may take part in a myth or story enactment, enabling the individual client to experience their own chosen role from within a fuller 'supported' enactment – where the other participants (the therapists) are taking on roles focused specifically towards supporting the individual client's process. This stands in contrast to the more general-ised nature of a typical group process. The therapists draw on a number of elements when making an intervention in these client-led improvisa-tions: informed intuition, knowledge of the client's overall therapeutic process, external circumstances which are fed into sessions by family and professionals, previous roles the client has brought to sessions which the therapist considers useful to the client's psychological process in that moment, and further development of previous plots. Pitruzzella says that dramatherapy:

> provides people with a special and safe stage upon which their representa-tions of themselves and of the world can play together, transformed by

imagination and re-signified by metaphorical shifts; in it the person's nucleuses can find the space and the languages for encountering and renovating each other. (Pitruzzella, 2016, p. 107)

In Sarah's vignette the client put Ali in the role of Nice Nurse and the support worker in the role of The Film. Her decision to play Sarah the Patient may have taken into account her knowledge that the session offered the capacity to compensate for danger and unpleasant feelings by ensuring that Sarah the Patient was cared for by the Nice Nurse, while employing the support worker to provide a reliable and comforting presence when needed. This enabled Sarah (the client) to implement the safety elements she required in order to take creative risks. The strength of this model is that the client themself can identify the exact mechanisms needed in order to create the conditions necessary for the work to take place, guiding the therapists directly. This is aided by the therapists' sensitivity to the transferences present; each therapist is able to intensify or lessen the focus on each of their roles as they closely follow the improvisation and story building.

Themes from previous sessions may be reintroduced by a therapist through role. For example, the confident, older and knowledgeable Head Teacher, which Sarah had developed within an earlier improvisation, was reintroduced by Ali in a later session to offer the opportunity for integration of Sarah's own confident, mature and knowledgeable qualities. Sarah (the client) directed the Head Teacher (the therapist in role) to get her out of difficulty. In this way Sarah was able to identify, explore and develop the resilient, problem-solving element within herself.

Similarly a different client, a young man named Luke, whom we had been working with for many years at school and then college, invited us to be advocates at a mental health capacity assessment set up by a hospital psychologist, at which important decisions needed to be made about medical issues affecting his quality of life. Owing to his degenerative condition, Luke's use of words had become extremely limited. He presented as profoundly physically disabled and he was concerned that college staff didn't know him sufficiently. Not only had we developed specific methods of supporting Luke to communicate, but he had also guided us to a specific way of listening. Alongside the individual's role in self-expression, agency – the capacity for human beings to make choices.

Agency requires an active or effective listener (or listeners) (Lundy, 2007)

Co-facilitation allows one therapist to support the 'speaking' and the other to provide bespoke 'listening'. With some clients it is not enough to be a 'good' listener. Attention needs to be given to the understanding between the 'speaker' and the 'listener'. Where illness and disability so severely impact a client's ability take part in life, co-facilitated dramatherapy sessions can create a form of immersive theatre experience (Machon, 2013), allowing life to come to the client. It can allow the clients to be *'producers of experiences and shapers of events'* (Bandura, 2000, p. 75; Ramsden, 2014).

The psychologist had brought visual prompts and pictures but it was clear that Luke was struggling to make himself understood and have adequate time to consider such complex and emotional choices. As the meeting progressed Luke suggested that he wanted to use some of the familiar drama techniques from therapy. We spoke with him confidentially and he asked for our help to explore these choices. This involved improvising several scenarios around the specific ethical decision, with him being able to direct the action. He chose who he wanted each of us to play, based on his knowledge of us and the longevity of our relationship. He chose Alyson to be him in life and then death, and Ali to play the role of both doctor and father.

Through the layering of roles (for example: the doctor is also the father who is also authority figure) we were able to encapsulate and represent our knowledge of Luke over many years, incorporating his spiritual, emotional and psychological life journey. The three scenes he set up involved, firstly, the medical intervention improving the quality of his life, next the operation being unsuccessful, lastly, one where he would die as a result. Each scenario was a realistic possibility. We were able to enact these fluently, one after another. He then asked to go back and repeat certain elements. We needed to think quickly and with the utmost discipline in order to ensure this entirely reflected his ideas. As we worked together with him we were able to acknowledge our own feelings and responses to the questions put to him without allowing them to overwhelm or overly influence his voice.

> Client voice in dramatherapy therefore, can be described as the client's awareness of their agency and capacity to make choices of self-expression, and to have their communication actively and effectively heard by the therapist, who supports the development of a self-initiated process of change. (Ramsden, 2016, p.34).

Conclusion

Each client we have worked with over the last 16 years has contributed to the development of our co-facilitation model. They have advanced our practice through their unique set of circumstances, compelling us to discover new elements of the potential of dramatherapy co-facilitation.

The key elements that lead to successful co-facilitation work are: robust preparation and research of the issues surrounding the client; nurturing the whole relationship between co-facilitators and not simply the therapy element; external specialist consultation; joint and individual supervision; valuing of similarities and differences; a relationship that is sufficiently robust to ensure challenge to each other; flexibility; training; sense of humour; balance; allowing each other to do what the other does best; non-agenda-based generosity; different types of creative risk taking; and allowing the time and space for all of the above to take place.

References

Bandura, A. (2000) Exercise of human agency through collective efficacy. *Current Directions in Psychological Science, 9*, 75–78.

Bateson, G. (1978). *Steps to an Ecology of Mind: Collected Essays in Anthropology, Psychiatry, Evolution and Epistemology*. London: Paladin.

Beddoe, L. & Davys, A. (2016). *Challenges in Professional Supervision – Current Themes and Models of Practice*. London: Jessica Kingsley Publishers.

Burnham, B. J. (1986). *Family Therapy*. London: Routledge.

Casement, P. (1985). *On Learning from the Patient*. London: Routledge.

Cattanach, A. (2005). Co-working with adoptive parents to support family attachments. In A. M. Webber & C. Haen (Eds.), *Clinical Applications of Drama Therapy in Child and Adolescent Treatment*. New York, NY and London: Brunner-Routledge.

Clarkson, P. (2003). *The Therapeutic Relationship*. London and Philadelphia, PA: Whurr Publishers.

Donigian, J. (2005). *Systemic Group Therapy: A triadic Approach*. Boston, MA: Cengage Learning.

Emunah, R. (1994). *Acting for Real – Dramatherapy, Process, Technique and Performance* (p. 227). New York, NY: Routledge.

Gersie, A. (2012). Consultation session, London.

Haythorne, D. & Cedar, L. (1996). *The Story of Roundabout; Creation of a Group Practice* in *Discovering the Self through Drama and Movement*. London: Jessica Kingsley.

Heidegger, M. in Ladkin, D. (2010). *Rethinking Leadership: A New Look at Old Leadership Quotes*. Cheltenham: Edward Elgar Publishing Inc.

Hellinger, B. (1999). *Acknowledging What is: Conversations with Bert Hellinger Zeig*. Phoenix, AZ: Tucker & Theisen Inc.

Jones, E. (1993). *Family Systems Therapy, Developments in the Milan-Systemic Therapies*. Chichester: John Wiley & Sons Ltd.

Jones, P. (1996). *Drama as Therapy – Theatre as Living*. London: Routledge.

Landy, R. (1994a). In Jones, P. (Ed.), *Drama as Therapy – Theatre as Living*. London: Routledge.

Landy, R. (1994b). *Dramatherapy: Concepts, Theories and Practices* (2nd ed., p. 151). Springfield, IL: Charles C. Thomas.

Lundy, L. (2007) 'Voice' is not enough: Conceptualising Article 12 of the United Nations Convention on the Rights of the Child. *British Educational Research Journal*, 33(6), 927–942.

Machon, J. (2013). *Immersive Theatre, Intimacy and Immediacy in Contemporary Performance*. London: Palgrave Macmillan

Manicom, H. & Baronska, T. (2003). Article in *The Association for Family Therapy and Systemic Practice*. New Jersey, NJ: Blackwell Publishing.

McFarlane, P. & Harvey, J. (2012). *Dramatherapy and Family Therapy in Education, Essential Pieces of the Multi-Agency Jigsaw*. London: Jessica Kingsley.

Pitruzzella, S. (2016). *Drama, Creativity and Intersubjectivity – The Roots of Change in Dramatherapy*. London: Routledge.

Ramsden, E. (2014). *A practitioner-researcher inquiry into choice, voice and agency in individual dramatherapy sessions: co-researching with children in a primary school setting*. [PhD thesis]. Leeds Beckett University.

Ramsden, E. (2016). Supporting agency, choice-making and the expression of voice with Kate: Dramatherapy in a mainstream primary school setting with a nine-year-old girl diagnosed with ASD and ADHD. In D. Haythorne & A. Seymour (Eds.), *Dramatherapy and Autism*. London: Routledge.

Rothschild, B. (2000). *The Body Remembers – The Psychophysiology of Trauma and Trauma Treatment*. New York, NY: W.W. Norton.

Yalom, I. D. (2005). *Theory and Practice of Group Psychotherapy*. New York, Basic Books.

Winnicott, D. (1971). *Playing and Reality*. London: Routledge.

9

Body, Movement and Trauma

Aleka Loutsis

Introduction

New paradigms in body psychotherapy informed by research in trauma, neuroscience and attachment theory have inspired and influenced my practice as a dramatherapist and dance movement psychotherapist. I will focus on developmental trauma and the impact of this on the body and movement with a particular emphasis on five key developmental gestures.

In response to these new paradigms I offer another dimension to the existing Sesame Approach to Drama and Movement Therapy. This symbolic and Jungian-based approach encompasses both individual and collective levels of being which lends itself to further exploration, particularly in relation to developmental themes.

Essentially, I am proposing the inclusion of another form of processing which is to bring attention and awareness to the body moving in the present moment. The potential of moving to and fro between implicit knowledge and explicit articulation enables a different experience to the current approach of remaining purely in the art form. I will also suggest how we can adapt existing reflective practice following immersive movement work to cognitively integrate the embodied experiences.

The world of talking therapies has become increasingly interested in the non-verbal dimension within therapy. I have witnessed this interest grow both within my workplace in the NHS Mental Health Services and through my engagement in continuing professional development (CPD) particularly in relation to the impact of trauma on the body *and psyche* of an individual. So what is it about the non-verbal dimension that has drawn this interest?

Top-down approaches (primarily verbal, cognitively driven and left-hemisphere-of-brain dominant) have been identified as limited in their effectiveness when treating people suffering from severe and enduring mental health problems. These chronic and disabling illnesses or disorders of the self invariably carry complex histories and disturbing personal narratives that are often rooted in early experience. Research in trauma informed by neuroscience tells us that adverse developmental experiences are held in the body and that emotional and cognitive processing can also be severely affected (Schore, 2012, pp. 71–117; van der Kolk, 2014, pp. 105–122). If we are to take the above mentioned as a premise for considering effective mental health treatment then the pathways to recovery must also include bottom-up approaches (primarily non-verbal therapies and right-hemisphere-of-brain dominant) such as the arts therapies and body-oriented psychotherapies (Rohricht, 2009).

Peter Levine refers to the therapeutic limitations of top-down processing where body language is neglected and strongly suggests that bottom-up processing in the early stages of psychotherapy is essential. He says that 'addressing a client's "bodyspeak" first and then, *gradually,* enlisting his or her emotion, perception and cognition is not merely valuable, it's essential' (2010, p. 45). Allan Schore corroborates this, noting that approaches that focus on 'conscious cognitions alone, without changes in emotion processing, are limited' (2012, p. 5).

Bottom-up begins with the body; observing 'how arousal, postures, movements, expressions, gestures and sensations of the body affects emotional and cognitive processing' (Ogden and Fisher, 2015, p. 773). In addition to paying attention to these processes in the present moment, this approach of embodied self-awareness also lends itself to spontaneity, creativity and change. Top-down begins with cognition as the place from which to enquire about that embodied experience and studies 'how thought processes (insight, beliefs, reasoning, reflection, and so forth) affect the body and emotional processing' (Ogden and Fisher, 2015, p. 773). The balance between non-verbal and verbal interventions in arts therapies practice prompts questions such as the integration of top-down elements with embodied and creative-based approaches. Dramatherapists are working with the body and the imagination as well as the intersubjective field of relationship but could benefit from enhanced understanding of body-based techniques which draw upon recent research. This chapter will offer an innovative approach to working with the body, emotions and cognitions, utilising both bottom-up and top-down approaches in the context of working with developmental trauma in dramatherapy. This approach involves experiential, reflective and integrating components when working through the body with five key developmental gestures.

The five gestures – 'yield, push, reach, grasp, pull' – can be seen as a framework within which we can study the body in relationship to another person, object or idea. This framework can either be utilised as a sequential process or each gesture can be used individually. In any case this approach encompasses both bottom-up and top-down processing and progresses through a series of three stages. In the first instance, the dramatherapist is consciously paying attention, being curious and noticing the way in which the gesture is performed. Secondly, the gesture is supported to become a gateway to a less conscious realm of spontaneous movement. The third part relates to integration, i.e. finding ways to bring the wisdom of body, emotions and thoughts together. This framework encapsulates both form and spontaneity, leading to new experience directly relating to the idea of praxis.

A gesture such as 'reaching' is one that we can easily recognise. We see it in early development in relation to a significant other and, if fostered, it becomes part of the non-verbal movement vocabulary which communicates a desire to connect to others. The way this action is performed will be dependent upon early developmental experiences (Ogden et al., 2006, p. 19). In other words, how 'reaching' was responded to during infancy and what was understood from these responses will shape the mind/brain/body, informing relationships and styles of functioning in the world (Schore in Green, 2003, pp. 24–27). Consequently, forming relationships in the present moment will also be shaped by the meaning we made from these early experiences in the past. This concept will underpin my exploration of five key developmental gestures that are universal to humanity.

Body Holds the Key

The body as symbol of Self, when viewed from a Jungian perspective, contains all experience both at a cellular and archetypal level and this therefore includes developmental themes, both personal and collective (Chodorow, 1991, p. 118; Adler in Pallaro, 1999, p. 195). The idea of body containing all experience also points to traumatic experience being held in the body and this concept is now well established in the field of trauma (Ogden et al., 2006; Levine, 2010; van der Kolk, 2014). According to research it is evident that the impact of attachment-related trauma on the infant's development can have devastating and lasting effects (Gerhardt, 2004; Schore, 2012). Psychological wounds are not uncommon experiences in human development and individuals' responses to these wounds range from mild distress to severe psychiatric disorders. The primary caregiver provides the template for the future development of the whole organism of the infant through the non-verbal, emotional, social and embodied relationship (Schore, 2012, p. 27). Through the 'social engagement' system of facial expressions, eye contact, prosody (emotional tone of voice), touch, gesture and proximity awareness the infant/client learns communication cues for assessing safety (Porges, 2011). This interactive and affect-regulating system helps establish a secure attachment and maintain homeostasis. But when this is not the case, insecure or disorganised attachment patterns are borne out along with dysregulated states (Bowlby, 1969; Schore, 2012, p. 19). Van der Kolk stresses the importance of integrating work with the body without which recovery in trauma is not possible. Overwhelming trauma strikes to the very core of our being and 'for real change to take place, the body needs to learn that the danger has passed and to live in the reality of the present' (van der Kolk, 2014, p. 21). It is clear that re-establishing a sense of embodied safety is of prime importance in stabilising the organism so that psychological wounds and trauma can be processed. Papadopoulos, in her paper 'The Body as Home', also reinforces the notion that the body is central in both establishing a sense of safety and enabling transformation (Papadopoulos, 2015). We also know that attachment plays a vital role in the developing brain, mind and body of the infant who is dependent on the caregiver to facilitate the best possible environment and provide interactive regulation for the whole system (Schore, 2012, p. 228). In a recent masterclass Schore confirms that: 'The in utero and immediate postnatal environments and the dyadic relations between the child and caregivers within the first years of life can have direct and enduring effects on the child's brain development and behaviour.' (Schore, 2014)

These 'embedded' habitual and procedurally learnt ways of being and communicating through gesture and movement are interesting features to further consider. They are also 'implicit communications within the therapeutic relationship' (Schore, 2012, p. 38). From the perspective of developmental trauma, they will be 'coloured' by our attachment history and held in the body. They are embodied relational 'stories' that are expressed through the way we carry ourselves, and by getting to know them we can rehearse new possibilities. If we accept the premise of the body as container of all experience, and that movement is a means of communication and self-expression (body and movement bridging the conscious and unconscious realms), then the therapist is potentially in relationship with the client's developmental patterns, collective or archetypal themes and the narrative of the traumatic experience. By engaging with these through the conscious study of the gestures initially in the first stage, and then when appropriate through the unconscious realm of spontaneous movement in the second stage, there is potential for the reparation of early deficits and for rediscovery of lost parts of Self. Consolidating the body-based, bottom-up work with top-down reflective processing supports the re-integration of both aspects and refers to the third stage. The next part of the chapter focuses on the conscious study of the gestures.

Five Key Developmental Gestures

The five gestures of yield, push, reach, grasp and pull originate from the work of Bonnie Bainbridge Cohen's research on *infant movement development* which forms the basis of her practice known as Body-Mind Centering (BMC), the principles of which are featured in her book, *Sensing, Feeling and Action* (1993).

> The first is yielding to gravity and a primal contact with the object world. The ability to yield and be in touch underlies the ability to take appropriate and effective action. Separating from the contact requires pushing. This action gives the ability to sense one's body and mobilize one's own weight, thus empowering one to explore the world'. Pushing provides the ground and gives support for reaching, which expresses an infant's curiosity, desire, or compassion in extending into space. Grasping and pulling are the logical extensions of reaching, and are the culmination of successful yielding, pushing, and reaching. (Aposhyan, 1999 in Bloom, 2006, p. 12).

These five developmental gestures are universal actions or movements associated with forming and maintaining relationships. They are embodied communications that will have been shaped by the quality of responses we have received during our early development. The process of self-discovery by paying attention to what happens when the action of the gesture is slowed down heightens awareness and can be an intense physiological and psychological experience. Practising this in relationship with another provides an opportunity to notice impulses or restrictions, tensions and sensations in the body. Feelings and thoughts may arise as well as moments from our early developmental life when certain implicit beliefs were formed about ourselves, others and the world around us. This type of study can help to reveal the quality of the gestures that have been either inhibited, blocked, exaggerated or adjusted and provide an opportunity for reparative experimentation when there are obvious psychological wounds or trauma. This way of studying the gestures is useful for training therapy students as well as for clinical application.

As a child or adult going back to embody these early movements, memories and feelings related to the original experience may be evoked, and insights can emerge from consciously re inhabiting the moving body and the memories held within it. (Hartley in Totton, 2005, p. 131)

As I present each of the five gestures I will outline four categories to cover: definition, deficits as a result of early developmental experiences, observations from practice and possible interventions. All the definitions will be taken from the Merriam-Webster online dictionary.

The focus on the five gestures will be within the context of relationship, studying how the action is performed and if there are any associated feelings or thoughts, images or memories that emerge. The focus is on present-moment experience, paying attention to what is happening 'inside', observing the process of the action or gesture in relation to other and simply noticing what emerges. Here the study also involves verbal interaction and curiosity. The following examples are presented to support an experiential exploration of each gesture and to stimulate progressive understanding of how they might inform dramatherapy training and practice. Within this, I use a convention whereby I offer examples of facilitation and exercises which demonstrate how these gestures are worked with in practice.

These examples have come together from different sources that include my teaching, clinical practice and professional development. This approach requires working in relationship with another person and incorporates touch so a working alliance needs to be negotiated and agreed as in any therapeutic encounter or teaching environment.

Five Developmental Gestures: Yield, Push, Reach, Grasp, Pull

Yield

The ability to yield and be in touch underlies the ability to take appropriate and effective action. (Aposhyan, 1999 in Bloom, 2006, p. 12)

Definition

Yield: to surrender or relinquish to the physical control or cease resistance.

Yield relates to the capacity to give one's weight to the ground, to be supported by the ground beneath our feet as we walk, to allow Mother Earth to hold us, to trust being held and to let go without fear of being dropped or falling apart. Releasing the breath and relaxing musculature helps to surrender to gravity and to earth energy. Yielding enables receptivity and the taking in of nourishment. It is an active and relational state, in which we let go and let ourselves be supported by the ground, by a chair, by another human being. Through this experience of being held it is possible to leave the secure base for new experiences knowing there is always a place of safety to return to. With good enough early experiences, the infant feels supported through body and skin to take in the goodness. They can breathe easy and deeply, they can rest in the safety of the holding and loving care.

Deficits

When this state is missing in early experiences, through lack of love, empathy or good enough care and safety, then the holding has to be self-generated. Muscles become tense and the breath may be held or shortened. The sense of ground feels far away, is unfamiliar, feels shaky or absent and this less grounded feeling can provoke a sense of insecurity, fear or anxiety. This lack of external support and the feeling that nobody is there prompts a withdrawal, a pulling in, disappearing or giving up and collapsing into a more passive state. Generally, there is an absence of connection to the instinctual body with consequences later in terms of being attuned to individual needs.

Observations

A client may struggle to yield to the support of a chair, remaining mobilised, body poised, perhaps leaning forward, muscles tense and breath held, ready for action at any moment. Or, the client might be in constant motion, unable to pause or take a deep breath. Resting is not part of the learnt embodied repertoire. In contrast, a person sits heavily on the chair, body language collapsed and passive, struggling to initiate any movement. They are in a shell of a body but not present. Some people struggle to take in information or to receive an object, such as catching a ball and bringing it in towards their body. The natural movement of taking something in is inhibited. Many will have difficulty with the flow of movement as a consequence of trauma. An example may be the lack of flexibility in joints or movements that appear 'jerky', over-controlled or 'stuck'.

Interventions

Explore how much or how little weight is given or allowed for the partner to hold. This could be with a hand or a foot, leaning into or back to back with another. Notice what happens to the breath, the muscle tone, quality of contact with skin, body sensations and allow feelings to surface or thoughts to arise. The person supporting can help their partner to remain focused on the task by encouraging them to observe with curiosity and an open mind. Images or memories may also surface.

Experimenting with eye contact by opening and closing eyes at intervals while a partner maintains attention is a useful way of exploring contact and being held by another through the gaze. Notice any body tension or changes in breathing as this is done. Other ways to study this when touch is not an option is to yield weight to gravity by lying on the ground and notice any tendency to hold or collapse the body. Or, lying inside a cloth and being held in it, being rocked, by another. Leaning against a wall or an imagined tree, holding an object that represents something precious and practise letting it go or self-touch, such as squeezing and releasing a hand or an arm. All of these can be studied with the same quality of attention and with the support of a partner. Notice if any beliefs come up, such as 'it is not safe to let go' or 'I have to hold on'.

Push

> Separating from the contact requires pushing. This action gives the ability
> to sense one's body and mobilize one's own weight, thus empowering one
> to explore the world. (Aposhyan, 1999 in Bloom, 2006, p. 12)

Definition

Push: to use force to move someone or something forward or away from you.

If the experience of yielding into contact with a significant other has
been good enough, the infant has the resources to push away and separate
from the caregiver. They can push with their arms away from the ground
to see from a different vantage point and raise their upper torso and
eventually crawl which will help develop body awareness. They develop
strength, balance and timing and will have a good sense of self from their
centre, their core within. These types of early experiences help to establish a sense of mastery and control and develop self-confidence. Pushing
away and separating from the caregiver is also the playground for learning
about nearness and distance, the space between and boundaries.

Deficits

When the attachment has been strained, leading to either insecure avoidant or ambivalent patterns of relating, the infant learns to adapt to that
environment in order to maximise the best possible outcome. This could
mean a need to push onward and grow up very fast or to be a high achiever
in order to please or feel accepted. Or the infant may be left feeling
that whatever they do makes no impact. Gaining the attention needed
or pushing away the unwanted attention is diminished or unsuccessful.
Here we can also see the beginnings of how boundaries are being experienced and the potential beliefs formed, such as needing to keep busy all
the time in order to minimise contact, keeping a distance between you
and others, curbing spontaneity and play, to name but a few examples.

Observations

With these insecurities, we may observe a tendency to push too much, too little or not at all. A client may struggle with knowing how much or how little effort to put into their actions or movements when being with others. This could be experienced by others as an aggressive action, disinterest or as a withdrawn state where the client is barely noticed. The quality of intensity or weakness is observed at both a physical and psychological level. There could be a struggle with how close or far away to position themselves in relation to others. Either way, gauging the sufficient amount of energy, effort or distance towards the desired contact or connection with others will not have been learnt and embodied. This will put pressure on future relationships and on styles of functioning in the world of work and recreation. Spatial awareness and negotiating boundaries will be affected.

Interventions

> Children need to feel at home in their own bodies and so to gain body mastery (Sherborne, 2001, p. xiii)

Experiment with a partner pushing against feet or other parts of the body. Try sitting back to back and take turns to push them along the floor, which will encourage use of the core muscles in the centre of the body, pushing with your head or facing each other and pushing away with eyes. Push with hands and notice how this action is performed. Do you push with the edges of your hands or with fingertips? Where in the body does the push begin? Explore pushing from the back and shoulders, through the arms into the hands. Is the push executed with sufficient mastery to control or contain your strength? Notice how your muscles are activated when you push. When pushing, are you using too much or not enough energy or effort? Notice any beliefs that come up as you try these exercises, such as 'I am too strong' or 'I am not strong enough'.

Practise pushing against a wall with your partner witnessing and supporting you to notice how the body performs this action. Notice if the core and hips are engaged, how the legs are positioned, whether knees are bent or straight during this action and how firmly the feet are planted on the ground. Props can be used, such as a cushion or a large gym ball. Sometimes using props to explore and create visual and concrete boundary shapes can also be helpful. Perhaps the pushing action has an aggressive quality, is sudden, hesitant or perhaps fearful.

Pushing can trigger painful memories and emotions or it may also trigger beliefs associated with trauma. If you have been unable to successfully push away repeatedly harmful and intrusive experiences, then there will be associated negative beliefs and a need to discover and develop new experiences that are effective.

Reach

Pushing provides the ground and gives support for reaching. (Aposhyan, 1999 in Bloom, 2006, p. 12)

Definition

Reach: to touch or grasp by extending a part of body.

Reaching, whether by a hand, with eyes or facial expression, from the heart or through sound is an outwardly directed action or movement that has the aim of making contact with another being. A young infant will initially seek out proximity by drawing their caregiver towards them until such time as they are able to perform gestures or move themselves towards the caregiver or desired object themselves. The young infant's gesture of reaching out with arms to be picked up and carried or consoled is a familiar image. Their fear or uncertainty is reassured by the caregiver's prompt response. If this dance of reaching for contact and receiving loving responses is established then the learnt embodied knowledge and implicit memory is of trust that the reach will be met in a healthy way. The gesture of reaching will have a feeling of congruence, of wholeness and safety. Reaching outwardly also indicates a readiness to begin exploring the surrounding world and to be spontaneous, curious and interested to play.

Deficits

Proximity-seeking actions attempted within an insecure attachment profile of either avoidant or ambivalent patterns are likely to lead to the infant either inhibiting their reach, having to be self-reliant or overly adapting in some way to the caregiver's needs or limitations. Reaching gestures may therefore become distorted as a consequence of repeatedly inadequate or negative responses. In some cases, such as with a disorganised/disoriented attachment, the belief will be that it is simply not safe to reach out.

Observations

Reaching implies an action or movement away from one's current position towards another or something other and so requires an extension of the upper limbs or mobilisation of lower limbs to move towards, or a shift in alignment and balance, such as leaning towards the desired object. In clinical settings, clients may struggle to extend within or to the limits of their personal space (as far as one can reach) and these difficulties will unconsciously precede the impetus to move one's body or impede the movement in the direction of the desired object. When the physical and psychological ground has not been adequately prepared, then the initiation and follow through of the gesture is compromised.

The feeling or belief is that there's no point in even trying to reach, that any effort will be misunderstood, not recognised or that their need is not important.

Interventions

As this is essentially a gesture of seeking to be met and to make a connection with another, experiment initially reaching with eyes and facial expression, then with your body leaning towards the other. Perhaps as you explore this theme there are sounds that want to emerge? Try reaching with your arms or from your hands. Do you use one or both? Notice how this movement and gesture is performed. Is the action sudden, uncontained or lacking in focus? In contrast is the quality uncertain, tentative or held back? Perhaps the intention to reach is there but you find your hands clenching or resisting the action. Does the movement begin with a finger? Notice the position of your hand; are your elbows straight or bent? Does the movement come from your back or from your shoulder? Notice your breathing or any other information emerging in this process. Another way to explore this is to try moving towards your partner, taking time to notice any sensations or other internal activity as you do so. Try experimenting with either increasing or decreasing speed, approaching from different angles, or explore your own variations on the theme of this approach. Proximity-seeking actions require attention and response from another so there could be some playful explorations around how to gain that attention.

The use of props can be supportive, especially when direct relationship feels too challenging. Find an object and imagine that it represents something you really want or need. With the same attitude of interest and curiosity, study what arises in the body as you prepare to reach towards, approach and take hold of this object. Are there any sensations, feelings, thoughts or memories that surface?

Grasp

> Grasping and pulling are the logical extensions of reaching, and are the culmination of successful yielding, pushing, and reaching. (Aposhyan, 1999 in Bloom, 2006, p. 12)

Definition

Grasp: to take and hold (something) with your fingers, hands etc., to understand or comprehend, to make a motion of seizing.

To grasp is to seize the moment or an idea with confidence and energy. Grasping can also suggest a desire to hold onto someone or something and to cling on to someone for dear life. A baby will latch on to the breast. An infant might hold on to extend a hug or a cuddle. Grasping also enables exploration of the object being held in the hand/s to be gathered in towards the body and incorporated. Reaching out successfully towards the subject/object of desire, it can now be held with confidence and with delight.

Deficits

When the reaching out has been thwarted and the child is insecure, these experiences will inhibit their confidence in taking hold of an object or there might be a desperation to seize and hold onto that object. The grasping gesture will be incomplete in some way either because too little has been caught or too much has been grabbed and because the limiting beliefs associated might feel disappointing or overwhelming. Due to the relational nature of making contact, this will involve touch and gaze both of which can be experienced as negative when the attachment relationship is insecure or unsafe. Repeated experiences of disapproval, denial, rough handling or a harsh look with the eyes could lead to a complicated dynamic with regard to contact, both physically and psychologically.

Observations

A client may give the impression that however you respond, it will never be enough and they will latch on to you, following your every move, or do everything possible to catch your attention, while at the other end of the scale, a client may struggle to catch hold of a task or intervention, and may take hold of it only for a very brief moment before dropping it or skirt around the edges. You may notice held breath or muscles that are tense. Perhaps you see a hand that is clasped or toes that are drawn in. Eye contact may lead to increased paranoid states and contact is avoided at all costs. The action of taking and keeping hold of an object such as a cloth or a ball may be incomplete.

Interventions

With your partner, study the experience of holding on to an object with the idea that you will not let go. Imagine that object is some prize possession of yours. Notice the amount of effort and energy involved in this response. Notice any body sensations after having performed this exercise. You could also experiment with holding onto an object with your toes or fingers or study the action of latching on with your mouth. Practise grabbing a cushion and holding it tight against your body as if hugging someone. In agreement with your partner, practise grasping and holding on to their arm, hand or leg. Your partner could also hold you, either at standing or floor level. Take the lead as to how much or little enclosure or holding feels right and the time to notice body responses.

Try using eye contact and facial expressions to keep hold of your partner's attention. This exercise could extend into moving around the room with your partner and working very hard to keep their attention even when they are not looking directly at you. You can use sounds and movement to get their attention. Although some of this is very active, take a moment to notice what comes up when engaged in this activity. Is it familiar or alien territory for you?

Pull

Grasping and pulling are the logical extensions of reaching, and are the culmination of successful yielding, pushing, and reaching.' (Aposhyan, 1999 in Bloom, 2006, p. 12)

Definition

Pull: to hold onto and move (someone or something) in a particular direction and especially toward yourself.

Having successfully reached out and taken hold of the desired object, the infant can now draw it in towards themselves and explore through the senses. With the acquired stability and strength from the yielding and pushing through to the good enough experiences of reaching out, exploring personal space and travelling in the shared space the infant has the confidence to seek out and pull the caregiver towards them or bring themselves closer to the caregiver in the knowledge that they will receive the love and nurture they need. The action of pulling brings the object closer and therefore changes the distance between them.

Deficits

When the attachment relationship is insecure, the action of pulling in towards oneself can be confusing or precarious. The pull may not acquire the desired outcome and the action could turn into pulling away from the caregiver rather than pulling them in. Or there might be a pulling in through the body in an attempt to protect oneself from external forces that are potentially threatening.

Observations

In clinical settings the action of pulling may be hard to regulate and can be experienced as either too strong or ineffectual. Increasing proximity as a result of pulling may feel threatening or intrusive. A client may get pulled into something without having the resources to extricate themselves safely from the situation (such as some form of exploitation). Therapists and other professionals may also get pulled into a complex dynamic.

Interventions

With your partner, experiment pulling with eyes or with facial expressions, or gesture with hands to pull them in. Try gathering actions towards your body, with arms and hands and gradually slow this down to study the body and breath. Experiment pulling yourself up from a sitting position and study the way you execute this. Explore what happens while increasing proximity with each other, as you pull them in or they pull you in with gesture, facial expressions or sounds. You can also explore different ways of pulling by using props such as a cloth, pulling in towards one another, pulling someone or something along, or pulling away. Being pulled along in a cloth can promote relaxation and yielding patterns providing an experience of being contained and held.

Gesture as a Gateway to Spontaneous Movement

From this intervention of yielding being invoked we can see the cycle of these developmental patterns as part of a natural flow of movement. Each of these five gestures of yield, push, reach, grasp and pull can be worked with individually or in whichever order feels appropriate at the time. The advantage of studying the gestures in this first stage is that the client remains focused on their experience in the here and now initially and although memories may emerge, processing at a deeper level will depend on the client's readiness to use this structure to cultivate spontaneity. The studying of these developmental patterns provides material to reflect upon and can be considered to be an appropriate approach for helping 'to cultivate the sense of an embodied self, and can provide safety, structure and an opportunity to strengthen ego boundaries' (Hartley, 2004, p. 58). It is a bottom-up approach that also incorporates top-down processing and in this way it remains in a more conscious domain.

Equally, either as a cycle or individually, the study of the gestures can lead to an exploration through spontaneous movement. I am adopting this phrase 'spontaneous movement' to capture the notion of working from inner impulses and to follow the flow of sensations, feelings etc. as they arise. In terms of Laban movement analysis, the 'felt sense' of this experience relates to the 'element of flow linked to feeling, to breath, energy & life force, the experience of emotion in the body' (Bloom in Totton, 2005, p. 65) or to the 'body moving of its own volition' (Levine in Totton, 2005, p. 39). As in the previous section, the work begins with the body and while there remains a reflective component, this time the cognitive processing will be incorporated after the movement experience.

This spontaneous movement approach is strongly influenced by Jungian ideas, especially those relating to active imagination and authentic movement. Both also convey the value of the mover being witnessed and of movement arising from within as well as having a personal and transpersonal dimension (Chodorow, 1991, p. 117; Whitehouse, 1999, p. 78; Adler, 1999, p. 194 in Pallaro, 1999). However, there must be a note of caution as this less conscious approach may not be suitable for those who have a fragile ego. The choice of approach will depend on the clinical need being presented but for training students, engaging with the progression between the two would be beneficial. This second stage involves a deepening exploration into the embodied self through the art form of creative movement. Through eliciting and playing with spontaneity, listening and following the wisdom of the body and allowing the unconscious to do its work through movement it might also be possible to experience ourselves reaching towards another person or idea of 'other' and discover something new or rediscover a lost part of Self.

Having studied the five gestures as described in the first stage, identify a moment that has particularly resonated such as a memory, image, feeling, sensation, belief or thought and use this as a gateway to deepen the experience, knowledge and understanding. Below is an example of how the process of the second stage can be facilitated through the gesture and pattern of yielding. Follow the ebb and flow of breath, the opposites of open and close, holding on and letting go, contraction and expansion and allow movement to emerge from there. Notice the body's rhythmic impulses and inner sensations and allow these to be expressed through moving forms or shapes. Close eyes when attending to internal landscapes or open eyes when needing to orient to the external space. Perhaps movement begins at floor level, exploring the body's relationship to gravity, rocking and rolling, moments of resting or waiting for the next impulse to be moved. Maybe the exploration begins at standing level, leaning against a wall, swaying gently. Perhaps an image or memory or a viscerally felt emotion related to the gestures is the starting point. How is this given expression? The body and movement find their own unique flow between inner and outer worlds. All these themes can be amplified through spontaneous movement. The witness pays attention to the mover and may also use movement, sound and mirroring themselves to support this process. The witness holds 'real' time and accompanies the mover until it is time to return from the unconscious realm back to the present moment. Later, verbal reflections can be shared. This transition between inner and outer worlds as we emerge from immersive work is important and deserves consideration as it forms part of the process of integration.

> It is within the relationship that the mover may begin to internalize the reflective function of the witness, i.e. to yield to the unconscious stream of bodily felt sensations and images, while at the same time bringing the experience into conscious awareness. (Chodorow, 1991, p. 113)

Integration – The Wisdom of the Body, Emotions and Cognitions

The body offers a bridge between unconscious and conscious processes: the immersive movement experience, both in the study of the five gestures and in the deeper exploration through creative and spontaneous movement, is a bottom-up experience and requires top-down processing at the appropriate time. It is in this transition period that the body becomes central in the holding of the experience. Verbal reflections help to integrate the sensory and emotional experiences as between them they engage both the right and left hemispheres of the brain. However, finding the words or language to reflect upon an experience is a delicate subject, especially when one has been working in the non-verbal field of movement. Gendlin (2000) suggests finding the right words to describe the 'felt sense' of an experience is a creative process that emerges from below the surface, it has to rise up and find its form, a kind of poetic language. Fogel describes this as 'evocative language' (2013, p. 32). This notion of finding a way to articulate an experience links the bottom-up with the top-down approach.

I propose an adaptation to our existing approach with regard to reflective practice following immersive work, with a focus on integration of the bottom-up embodied study and creative exploration with a top-down consciously oriented approach to processing the experience. The 'bridge out' is the fifth of the six-part Sesame session structure that is a transition from the main theme to the closure and where the participant/s emerge from the depths of the unconscious world. The quality of elongating time is important here and creating space for the beginnings of conscious reflection through paying attention to the 'felt sense' of the body from the movement experience, perhaps pausing in moments of stillness, breathing into shapes or sculpts and searching to find an 'evocative language' for what may be surfacing. This allows time and space for the meaning-making to be constellated even if in embryonic form. This is not a linear process but rather these different forms will flow in a dialectical manner between inner and outer worlds and draw closer until integration becomes possible. Dream world and real world are partners in this dance, complementing each other and potentially bringing meaning and wholeness to the experience supported by the witness.

Conclusion

The flow of processing between bottom-up and top-down approaches has been explored through the framework and study of the five developmental gestures, spontaneous movement and the process of integration. With the support of working with another person on the gestures it is possible to bring implicitly learnt embodied patterns and beliefs to consciousness, notice and articulate them verbally as the study takes place. In contrast, the less conscious work of developing a specific moment of resonance using spontaneous movement enables another form of implicit knowing. The poetic or evocative language brings this experience closer to consciousness and eventually can be articulated more explicitly through words. In this way the balance between non-verbal and verbal dimensions in dramatherapy has also been considered.

In terms of therapeutic interventions, the usefulness with regard to the differentiation of bottom-up and top-down approaches in trauma treatment is necessary as very little can be achieved until this bodily based feeling of safety is established. The first stage in studying the five gestures can be successfully and safely applied when working with developmental trauma as essentially the work is being held in a more ego-directed way.

The second stage, working with spontaneous movement, would only be suitable for those with a strong enough ego structure.

This framework of the five developmental gestures could enrich the Jungian-based drama and movement therapy training at the Royal Central School of Speech and Drama: for example, applying these to character formation and role play in drama and myth enactments or reflecting upon the subtleties in the quality of the reach towards a symbolic image, the pull towards shadow aspects or grasping an archetypal theme from within a story. The gestures are useful for training students and can also be applied as an assessment tool. They are versatile and offer an additional approach to clinical work, especially when facing clients who have highly dysregulated affective states including those suffering from trauma and severe mental health conditions.

There is potential here to create a bridge between developmental and archetypal paradigms, holding the personal and collective dimensions. 'When we use our bodies to express the imagination, the vividness of the sensory-motor experience tends to take us to complexes that were constellated in infancy or early childhood.' (Chodorow, 1991, p. 6) It is interesting to note that Levine also points to some interesting parallels between this and Jung's process of psychological individuation (2010, p. 257).

I leave you with a final thought.

We are now faced with the problem of how this rapidly expanding body of discoveries in development and neuroscience will be used in the mental health professions, not only in the delivery of service but also in the training of the next generation of psychotherapists. (Schore, 2012, p. 9)

References

Bloom, K. (2006). *The Embodied Self.* London: Karnac Books.

Bowlby, J. (1969). *Attachment and Loss. Vol 1 Attachment.* New York, NY: Basic Books.

Carroll, R. Interview with Allan Schore. Available at: www.ThinkBody.co.uk.

Chodorow, J. (1991). *Dance Therapy and Depth Psychology. The Moving Imagination.* London: Routledge.

Cohen, B. B. (1993). *Sensing, Feeling and Action*. Northampton, MA: Contact Editions.

Damasio, A. (2000). *The Feeling of What Happens. Body, Emotion and the Making of Consciousness*. London: Vintage.

Fogel, A. (2013). *Body Sense. The Science and Practice of Embodied Self-Awareness*. New York, NY: W.W. Norton.

Gendlin, E. T. (2000). *Introduction to Focusing and Felt Sense. Part 1, Presentation at International Conference in Toronto*. Available at: youtube.com/watch?v=j7PEC5Mh5FY. Accessed online from the Focus Oriented Psychotherapy Institute

Gerhardt, S. (2004). *Why Love Matters. How Affection Shapes a Baby's Brain*. East Sussex: Brunner-Routledge.

Green, V. (Ed.). (2003). *Emotional Development in Psychoanalysis, Attachment Theory and Neuroscience. Creating Connections*. East Sussex: Brunner-Routledge.

Hartley, L. (1995). *Wisdom of the Body Moving. An Introduction to Body-Mind Centering*. Berkeley, CA: North Atlantic Books.

Hartley, L. (2004). *Somatic Psychology. Body, Mind and Meaning*. London: Whurr Publishers Ltd.

Levine, P. A. (2010) *In an Unspoken Voice. How the Body Releases Trauma and Restores Goodness*. Berkeley, CA: North Atlantic Books.

Merriam-Webster online dictionary

Ogden, P., Minton, K. & Pain, C. (2006). *Trauma and the Body. A Sensorimotor Approach to Psychotherapy*. New York, NY: W.W. Norton.

Ogden, P. & Fisher, J. (2015). *Sensorimotor Psychotherapy. Interventions for Trauma and Attachment*. New York, NY: W.W. Norton.

Pallaro, P. (Ed.). (1999). *Authentic Movement*. London: Jessica Kingsley.

Papadopoulos, N. (2015). The body as home. In *ADMP e-motion, 25*(3).

Porges, S. W. (2011). *The Polyvagal Theory. Neurophysiological Foundations of emotions, Attachment, Communication, Self Regulation*. New York, NY: W.W. Norton.

Rohricht, F. (2009). Body oriented psychotherapy. The state of the art in empirical research and evidence-based practice: A clinical perspective, body, movement and dance in psychotherapy. *An International Journal for Theory, Research and Practice, 4*(2), 135–156, DOI:10.1080/17432970902857263.

Schore, A. N. (2003). The human unconscious: The development of the right brain and its role in early emotional life. In V. Green (Ed.), *Emotional Development in Psychoanalysis, Attachment Theory and Neuroscience. Creating Connections* (pp. 23–54). East Sussex and New York, NY: Brunner-Routledge.

Schore, A. N. (2012). *The Science of the Art of Psychotherapy*. New York, NY: W.W. Norton.

Schore, A. N. (2014). *The Science of the Art of Psychotherapy*. Masterclass. London, UK.

Sherborne, V. (2001). *Developmental Movement for Children*. London: Worth Publishing Ltd.

Totton, N. (Ed.). (2005). *New Dimensions in Body Psychotherapy*. Berkshire: Open University Press.

van der Kolk, B. (2014). *The Body Keeps the Score. Mind, Brain and Body in the Transformation of Trauma*. London: Allen Lane/Penguin Books.

10

Multimodality

Rachel Porter

Over the last 10 years I have had the opportunity to study a unique and key element of the Sesame Approach to Drama and Movement Therapy: Movement with Touch and Sound (MTS). I have investigated this discipline in great detail both through my clinical practice and my role in teaching the MTS strand at the Royal Central School of Speech and Drama. In this time many of my own ideas about the function, purpose and nature of MTS have evolved.

Movement with Touch and Sound was developed by the founder of the Sesame approach, Marian Lindkvist, as a means of reaching clients who inhabited non-verbal and pre-verbal states e.g. profound autism, profound and multiple learning difficulties. These are growing communities. The reasons for the increase in the diagnosis of autism is not conclusive; it may be partially due to increased awareness and improved methods of diagnosis.

There are studies that show how improvements in neonatal care and the lessening of child mortality have led to considerable increases in the number of brain-damaged babies reaching birth. A percentage of these children will be identified as having profound and multiple learning difficulties (PMLDs), thus resulting in rising recorded cases of people with PMLDs (Costeloe et al., 2012).

Another expanding community is the elderly (Prince and Jackson, 2009), of which a significant number re-enter pre-verbal states due to dementia and age-related cognitive decline.

Since these are groups that MTS was created for, this element of the Sesame approach has become more relevant now than ever before. It therefore seems curious and unfortunate that the discipline continues to remain relatively unknown outside of the Sesame community.

This chapter aims to raise and develop awareness of this unique aspect of dramatherapy practice. I will seek to dynamise the subject by challenging its current theory base. I will critique the continuing relevance of Erikson's developmental model (Erikson, 1950) in relation to the Sesame approach, while reaching for new ideas about the subject and positioning MTS as an effective form of therapeutic non-verbal communication/interaction. I will also look to identify and clarify techniques that MTS practitioners instinctively reproduce in their practice but struggle to name (Porter, 2014).

Through my own practice and research I have come to the conclusion that at the heart of the successful application of MTS is the ability to work with multimodal attunement. The discussion here will pivot around this point as a central theme. I aim to demonstrate that although this approach has not attracted much academic examination, such studies would illuminate and clarify more subtle elements alive within the dramatherapeutic encounter.

In examining MTS we reveal a particular type of intelligence, which can be found at the root of all pre-verbal engagement with the other. This essentially involves a creative process in the form of episodic improvisations; scenes of both a dramatic and somatic nature. I will explore the qualities required for practitioners to work effectively with MTS and show that these fundamental competencies benefit not only the practice of a therapist but also the craft of a performer.

So this chapter seeks to examine the concept of multimodality as a specific element within the Sesame Approach to Drama and Movement Therapy. Multimodality is a term that describes ways of communicating that combine different forms and mediums of correspondence, e.g. linguistic, visual and aural.

'Multimodal literacy' (Bateman, 2008) is a key competency for students training in this approach. The training combines intensive studies in the application of movement, story and drama, enabling students to synthesise these different strands into therapeutic interventions tailored to meet clients' needs. Within the study of movement is the subject of MTS. The essentially multimodal focus of this discipline is clearly evident in its title. It is designed to engage and support clients who present especially complex needs, requiring a more nuanced interpersonal propinquity. I believe that multimodal literacy is an essential element of the dramatherapeutic encounter. By describing different dynamic aspects of the pre-verbal relationship we can become conscious of facets that articulate a unique technique within dramatherapy.

To date in MTS training, Erikson's stages of human development have been used to indicate and assess where a client might be on a scale of psychic and somatic growth (Smail, 1999). Daniel N. Stern (1985), however, challenges the accurate scope of such systems. Essentially he identified a disjunction between his own observations of infant behaviour and those demarcated behaviours allocated to 'stages' as described by Erikson. While Stern acknowledged the 'domains' of change in the infant's life he attributed them more broadly and included the idea of phasic overlapping. He rejected the idea that the earliest stages remain as solely infantile zones that an adult only returns to in regressed states. Stern argued that these stages remain ever-present and active. He further suggested that verbalisation could all too quickly stunt the instinctive, sensorial parts of our being in communion with one another, and lead potentially to feelings of alienation: 'The piece that language takes hold of is transformed by the process of language-making and becomes an experience separate from the original global experience.' (Stern, 1985, p. 175)

In the creation of Stern's term 'vitality affect' (Stern, 1985) he avoided conceptualising his observations in a way that impeded the oblique aspects of human experience, 'Many qualities of feeling that occur do not fit into our existing lexicon or taxonomy of affects' (Stern, 1985, p. 54).

The oblique approach is an integral aspect of the Sesame philosophy (Pearson, 1996) and this is especially true for MTS because we are working with the most primitive elements of human relationship. It seems to me problematic for an approach that identifies itself as 'oblique' to rely on theories of human behaviour and development which appear at odds with the very obliqueness of human nature. Theories such as Erikson's require a particular mindset in application that I believe are discordant with that of the Sesame practitioner working with a pre-linguistic process. An overly prescriptive, cognitive-dominant process will be unhelpful as it is the antithesis of what is to be embodied by the practitioner working within the realms of the visceral. I am not suggesting that MTS is an approach without intelligence but that its particular form of intelligence is of a proprioceptive nature as well as being intuitive, interpersonal and empathic. Thought and words are not absent but they accompany and work *with* the main focus which is essentially sensory, feeling-based and ultimately of the body. When working with a client in pre-verbal states, one must inhabit that specific world of vitality affect, e.g. a grunt, a sigh, a slouch, a piercing stare, a sudden arm movement that leads to the flicker of a smile, all in one sequence of action. In a reciprocal interaction, we attune to rhythmic, tonal and other multimodal qualities. We are working through the aural, tactile and corporeal in a multimodal dance. One cannot work with a plan as such; though the session is shaped around the classic Sesame structure, the content is often a spontaneous interpersonal event that pivots around the client's idiosyncrasies.

Sesame therapists often reflect that MTS practice feels instinctive and difficult to put into words (Porter, 2014). This parallels the puzzlement of mothers in Stern's research who, after having engaged in attuned interactions with their children, found it extremely difficult to articulate what they had just done (Stern, 1985).

It appears to me that Stern's research and subsequent insight eclipses that of Erikson's, by capturing with such searing accuracy those essential elements which are key in MTS practice. His studies unveiled the intuitive genius of the primary caregiver in the attunement process. Here mothers were observed working within a multi-sensory vernacular mirroring the infant's innate 'cross-modal fluency'. Similarly analogous is the way in which Sesame therapists attempt to work within that pre-verbal domain, attuning to their clients through their use of movement, sound and touch.

We need not regard such processes as regressive but rather, and more accurately, as sophisticated forms of communion that might develop into rich and surprising communications. This type of work and its client groups can be so easily marginalised if the lack of verbalisation is associated with a sense of incompleteness. Stern was clear in attributing value and meaning to these forms of interaction through his own work: 'In spontaneous behaviour, the counterpart to artistic style is the domain of vitality affects.' (Stern, 1985, p. 159)

The Sesame Approach to Drama and Movement Therapy MA training requires that every student studies MTS both theoretically and experientially. This enables them to work with pre-verbal client groups. The rigour of the training ensures that students have both an understanding and a lived experience of this form of human encounter. It is required that students are able to work with an embodied understanding of attunement in a non-linguistic therapeutic relationship. Important to note here is how, in learning to work consciously in the domain of vitality affect, one's development as an artist may also progress. I believe this to be key: that every trainee dramatherapist should build a baseline understanding and literacy in the pre-verbal, non-linguistic forms of development and experience. And that in developing such competencies, the student's artistic sensibility will be enriched. Often the development of the artist is secondary to the development of the therapist in the art therapies. I suggest here that the unconscious drives that undervalue intuitive and somatic intelligence and prioritise instead those academic, cognitive-based structures and approaches are the same drives that attribute less importance to the arts therapist being also an artist. Within the particular theories of child development I am presenting here, the language of time-based forms is aligned with the pre-verbal language of mother and child. It is no coincidence that neither the language of pre-verbal communication nor that of the performance artist are considered essential parts of training for the arts therapist. While students are expected to understand theoretical ideas about both, they might not be trained in how to embody either. This I believe to be a fundamental flaw in our current arts therapy training systems.

New Perspectives in Developmental Psychology

In the 1970s, a group of researchers made a series of groundbreaking discoveries into the nature of pre-linguistic interaction. They were watching and examining film footage of interactions between mothers and their babies. They began to focus their attention on how babies, often only days old, where able to commune and communicate with adults in ways previously unimagined. Their findings at the time were considered controversial.

Two key figures in this movement where Colwyn Trevarthen and the late Daniel N. Stern. Stern's book *The Interpersonal World of the Infant* (1985) was considered groundbreaking and gathered considerable recognition and acclaim. However, it was Trevarthen who really prepared the ground through his research and writing from the late 1960s onwards. He and numerous other researchers at that time (Charlesworth and Kreutzer; Stern; Papousek and Papousek; Bateson) were discovering that young infants had an innate communal and communicative intelligence. For example, much was written about patterns of communicative intent in babies only days old, demonstrated through coordinated responses towards the primary carer. It was noted that blindness in newborns was difficult to detect because of the neonate's natural propensity for 'looking movements' as they searched out the carer's voice and reacted with agile physical responses, e.g. head rotation, reaching and grasping.

> And I talked about innate intersubjectivity even in conversation with a two month old. And I did it deliberately to be provocative, because I was using words that were not kosher; they were forbidden, innate. And I got the most amazing abuse, people mocking the idea that babies could sing along with their gestures and that they could communicate. But I realised I was onto something good.

> (Dialogue on intersubjectivity with Colwyn Trevarthen and Stein Braten (Stensaeth and Trondalen, 2012)).

Vasudevi Reddy (2008, p. 68) discusses in *How Infants Know Minds* 'the sceptical atmosphere of the late 1960s and early 1970s'. She contextualises that atmosphere, finding its roots in the beginning of the last century when psychologists from Freud to Piaget identified the young infant as unable to separate itself from its surroundings. They created a neonatal world of confusion.

This recreated infant is made up of memories, present re-enactments in the transference and theoretically guided interpretations. I call this the *clinical infant*, to be distinguished from the *observed infant*, whose behaviour is to be examined at the very time of its occurrence. (Stern, 1985, p. 15)

From this 'observed infant' a new wave of research burst forth which promoted radical new ways of thinking about the pre-verbal interpersonal relationship and challenged that existent paediatric hegemony. This particular group of researchers' commitment to those preliminary discoveries was resolute and they went on to pioneer new areas of research and practice within developmental psychology. The communing and communicative body of the mother/child dyad with its innate and self effacing wisdom was the great discovery.

Trevarthen originally trained as a biologist. A fascination with the world of infant communication emerged at Harvard in 1967 and his research was the first of its kind. Stern and Trevarthen, along with others in this new wave, became friends and colleagues. Their mutually exclusive discoveries developed in parallel before combining to form a whole new field of infant research.

Stern trained as a psychiatrist in 1964 and a psychoanalyst in 1972. One aspect of his work was to bridge a gap between the psychoanalytic world and that of developmental theory. His thinking and research brought profound and far-reaching challenges. His ideas and insights were grounded in the actual recorded experiences of the mother/child dyad. His study focused on the early developmental years of the infant. He took a thoroughly modern approach, employing cutting-edge technology to examine and measure the reactions and responses of his subjects in micro detail. Previously established theories of infant life were re-examined and re-evaluated in the bright new light of his methods and subsequent findings.

The scope of challenge brought about by Stern's research leant against the work of several recognised and high-profile theorists such as Freud, Mahler and Erikson. It questioned their pathomorphic assumptions about infancy and their tendencies to create phasic structures around childhood development. Stern identified and brought attention to discrepancies between their ideas related to the timing of specific developmental events.

> The early life narratives as created by Freud, Erikson, Mahler, and Kohut would all be somewhat different for the same case material. Each theorist selected different features of experience as the most central, so each would produce a different felt-life-history for the patient. (Stern, 1985, p. 15).

Stern was not, however, in total disagreement with the prevailing clinical view of infancy but he felt it should not dominate. His idea was that both views had something to offer each other. In his own work he attempted to merge the objectivity of the observed infant with the subjectivity of the clinical infant.

Stern argued that the concretising of developmental changes into hierarchical frameworks was not collectively accurate. He worked to demonstrate how the reductive tendencies of certain psychoanalytic approaches were too far removed from the interpersonal encounter itself. It seems here a drive developed in him to take a normative approach to the research while utilising the subjective reflexivity of psychoanalysis.

Stern appeared fascinated in the new detail that could be extracted from video technology. Mother/child interactions could be carefully analysed and broken down into the tiniest splinters of behaviour. The resultant findings went beyond anything that had been previously identified. This group of developmental researchers now had a new-found confidence to challenge the long-standing bedrock of developmental theory. They were each individually arriving at the same conclusion: that within the infant experience was a vast and mysterious intelligence beyond anything previously imagined or discussed within scientific realms.

It was during this same era that Marian Lindkvist began her groundbreaking work with autistic children. In 1973 she encountered profoundly autistic children who were 'all over the place physically' and 'in their own world' (Lindkvist, 1998, p. 75). With all of her previous client groups, story had been at the centre of her approach. However, at a particular point, Lindkvist discovered that certain clients could not respond to what she referred to as 'action plots'.

Driven to reach these remote children she adapted her approach. She began working directly though the body and voice and in ways unmediated by story. This work was one to one and involved mirroring and attuning to the child until she connected with them directly, in and through their unique and idiosyncratic world of experience. Eventually, once a kind of complicit unification had developed between the therapist and autistic child, variations could be introduced that met the child's own capabilities, capabilities that had previously been swallowed up by the consuming tsunami of their isolation.

In her own work, Lindkvist was echoing and embodying the very same qualities of the infant's interpersonal world that Stern and Trevarthen were simultaneously discovering in America. At this time their work was unknown beyond their particular scientific community. When it came to Lindkvist describing her technique theoretically, she naturally relied upon the prevalent and widely recognised ideas of Erik Erikson. His 'life stages' model was the prima facie model: a popular and accessible developmental approach that codified developmental levels relating to pre-verbal work and indicated developmental progressions within and beyond it.

As discussed above, Stern was quickly discovering that Erikson's staged theory was limited when compared to the expansive domain of pre-verbal awareness and multimodal communication that was being revealed to him through his research and clinical observations. The tectonic plates underlying developmental theory were beginning to shift.

In writing on the meaning and efficacy of the creative arts therapy encounter, Marian Lindkvist and the movement therapist Audrey Wethered (Wethered, 1993) discuss the notion of 'informed instinct' (Lindkvist, 1998). In describing this they explain how a theoretical underpinning can complement an intuitive 'oblique' approach. Despite their efforts, it is this aspect of our practice, involving instinctive processes (the vital components of maternal and therapeutic attunement) that appear to arouse continuing suspicion and scepticism. It is often regarded as mysterious and irrational, and therefore denied recognition as a valid, emergent ideology capable of shaping and defining future art therapy practice.

The philosophers of science and mathematics have drawn a great black line between propositional language used to state facts as unequivocally and literally as possible, and all other kinds of expression and their various purposes which are lumped together under one caption, 'emotive'.
(Langer, 1967, p. 80)

A thorough re-appraisal of this discrepancy feels timely. I believe the example of Stern and Trevarthen can inspire and support an evidence base to underpin the efficacy and recognition of MTS. In citing and bringing attention to their scientific examination of these most instinctive of human processes, we are able to articulate an integrated argument for the phenomenon of pre-verbal acumen. Their work creates a dynamic space around the primary relationship and reflects upon it as an endless source of wisdom. Both Trevarthen and Stern continued to explore their ideas in an experimental way, both moved into the fields of various art forms and worked alongside artists and arts therapists. Fascinating is their journey from mother/child interactions to art forms. The fact that both travelled this route, each uniquely, proves something of this connection between pre-verbal communion and Stern's 'dynamic experience in the arts' as well as Trevarthen's 'musicality' (Trevarthen and Malloch, 2009).

Their work has brought such vitality and passion to this *world before words* and yet a puzzling question remains: why do people and professions whose work involves engagement with pre- and post-verbal individuals still suffer such poverty and disregard? 'These pre-verbal origins of language and communication are generally disregarded (if not dismissed [e.g. Pinker, 1994, 40])' (Dissanayake, 2000, p. 46).

A recent article in *The Guardian* (Hammond, 2016) exposed the closing down of most 'continuing care' stand-alone units in the UK for people with extreme dementia and challenging behaviour. Some years ago a specialist unit for people with PMLDs had an innovative department for Movement with Touch and Sound at Orchard Hill, Wallington. That unit was closed and the dramatherapy service wound up. I have worked in Belgium on a unit where young non-verbal adults with severe learning difficulties and challenging behaviour are left strapped to their beds and crying out for attention because there were not enough staff on duty. Challenging behaviour is often not examined in depth or treated therapeutically but instead is simply medicated. I have sat by the bed of a child with contorted, twisted limbs, born healthy but brain damaged later in infancy and placed in permanent institutional care where he didn't receive enough physical stimulation. His physical disability was preventable. I have worked in day units where PMLD clients have minimal facilities, small rooms, no outdoor space. No space for private therapeutic work. Care workers in some of these settings often have little or no training in pre-verbal communication although they are working extensively with pre-verbal clients.

It remains extremely difficult to secure funding for individual therapeutic work with the post-verbal elderly or pre-verbal profoundly disabled. In a time of cuts and austerity, this challenge will only increase and all against a backdrop of the steady, silent growth of these communities due to our ability now to prolong life as never before. It could be that arts therapists can play an urgent and important role here, as the creative elasticity of our work enables us to reach, meet and meaningfully engage such individuals. While embodying the pre-verbal we can also access research material that invigorates and energises arguments around human rights for people who inhabit the non-verbal domains. By drawing upon studies of mother/child interaction, we can learn so much about fundamental communicative and creative forms. We have the opportunity to innovate a new skill set inspired by a wealth of developmental research and in so doing raise awareness and build recognition and respect for what remains an essentially under- and/or devalued way of being in the world. We have well-founded research here which establishes the wonder, value and skill that is hidden in the world of the wordless and yet it is still commonly regarded as the most basic way of being and working. I would like to challenge that idea. It is my contention that by developing multimodal literacy within the pre-linguistic realms, drama and movement therapists can evolve a stronger and more profound grounding in the fundamental processes of the creative encounter. These fundamentals are often taken for granted, assumed or overlooked.

With this in mind I will explore several key elements of this non-linguistic interpersonal world, my aim being to introduce and articulate those ideas which support and develop multimodal articulacy within the context of attunement.

Amodal Perception

During the 1970s the researchers I have mentioned above (e.g. Stern, Trevarthen) examined the infant's capacity to operate multi-sensorially through interactions with their external world. The discoveries made were surprising at the time. In 1979 Meltzoff and Borton discovered that babies as young as 3 weeks were able to recognise objects via the unseparated modes of sight and touch. Other researchers experimented with levels of light and sound and found there was an audio visual fluency in the young infant's sensing of the environment. This debunked earlier theories of staged learning; the infant's knowledge was tacit, channelled via a pre-existing amodal acuity.

This amodal state generates a global experience of sensorial and experiential unity that Stern believed verbalisation separated us from. Though separation may be a vital human developmental process that assists individuation, the extent of such separations could also be a cultural side effect of a logos-dominated system where thought and reason rule over instinct and soma.

Kathryn Linn Geurts's anthropological study *Culture and the Senses*, 'Bodily ways of knowing in an African community', investigated the sensorial meaning system of the Anlo-Ewe speaking people in south eastern Ghana. The work challenged the idea of a five sense model (she presents this as an already proven argument) and explores this through the description of a Ghanan tribe's cross-modal experience of their senses. This creates a more expanded way of being in the body and relating inner and outer experience: 'a gestalt of all bodily experiences and inner states' (Geurts, 2002, p. 45).

As I relate to any client in a non/pre-verbal domain, there are moments where I might need to resurrect this state of sensory unity in order to connect to the client's mood, or inhabit their universe. This can be experienced as sinking into a more visceral realm which connects environment and other. If reached, one can tap into an instinctive wisdom that transcends logical thought, defies the rational, and reaps vital information via a rich non-linguistic communication system, essential if someone cannot tell you what they want or don't want verbally. The body becomes a sensitised receptor through what I experience as a process of refinement. I believe this not to be a regressive state in the sense of returning to base functionality, but the retrieval of an innate mastery of sensory multimodality that was once an amodal state. A stripping back of self-hood is required, quite a challenge in a culture where health and identity often appear as synonymous. On the Sesame MA Drama and Movement Therapy training, I have witnessed some students struggle immensely with the amount of 'letting go' this type of work requires. Stern's domains of relatedness (as opposed to developmental stages) were believed by him to be co-existent and present throughout life (as opposed to abandoned to infancy). Therefore, in theory we can access them at any time, if we are not defended against them. Maybe this is not something we can teach but rather facilitate as a kind of unlearning. Isn't this what Jerzy Grotowski attempted with his 'via negativa' and Jacques Lecoq explored with his use of the neutral mask? 'Ours is then a via negativa – not a collection of skills but an eradication of blocks.' (Grotowski, 1968, p. 16)

Vitality Affect

Stern was responsible for the conception of the term 'vitality affect' (Stern, 1985). He was searching for a new lexicon that helped him capture a realm of affect that functioned beyond taxonomological confinement. He observed infants expressing a dynamic range of emotion, kinetic in nature, out of range of Darwinian categorisation. Rather than attempting to limit a definition of this polymorphous process, it is described through a myriad of adjectives and adverbs, e.g. languorous, rushing, pulsing, halting and tightly:

> They are not acts as they have no goal state and no specific means. They fall in between all the cracks. They are the felt experience of force — in movement — with a temporal contour, and a sense of aliveness, of going somewhere. They do not belong to any particular content. They are more form than content. They concern the 'How', the manner, and the style, not the 'What' or the 'Why'. (Stern, 2010, p. 8)

This description of vitality affect fits also the contoured expressive experience of non-verbal people with profound disabilities, possibly even people on the extreme end of the autistic spectrum. I am suggesting this could be the expressive mode of anyone who doesn't have access to the verbal function.

Stern goes on to describe how vitality affect is also the language of time-based art forms, namely dance, music and drama. Vitality affect as a concept is particularly useful to me when teaching because it helps the students to conceive of states that exist beyond categorical affect. This is important; as already stated, most clients who are disabled to the point of being pre- or post-verbal inhabit such a space. A therapist who works in this field must be able to enter that world beyond the boundaries of reason that living through words builds around our experience. This is an existence where emotional states may change quickly or sometimes at an unfathomably slow pace, at rhythms that often evade logic and can seem abstract, even chaotic, to the inexperienced eye.

As an artist this can be a highly creative space one might even aspire to in order to create original works. In some particular performative styles, e.g. abstract and interdisciplinary forms, the final work is performed in this dynamic realm of vitality. As a performance artist I have found that study and practice within this area has reconnected me more deeply with my own practice. And I have witnessed countless students, who were also performers, discover a natural and deep connection with the subject of MTS which, at its heart, is a way of communing and communicating with the utmost sensitivity, spontaneity and intimacy (all qualities of skilled actors and dancers).

Affect Attunement

'Attune' in the online Oxford University Press English Dictionary is described in three ways: 'to make receptive or aware', 'to accustom or to acclimatise' and 'to make harmonious'. These accurately describe core aspects of Movement with Touch and Sound. One is attempting through attunement to enter into a pre-verbal communion/dialogue which stimulates receptivity to self and other, accustoms two people to one another through developing their capacity for interpersonal relations, and works with ideas of opposites and balance in order to harmonise disparate energy.

In Stern's final book, *Forms of Vitality*, he defined affect attunement as 'vitality form matching'; here a direct correlation is made between maternal attunement and vitality affect. Affect attunement is a specific form of attunement that primary carers instinctively carry out with their infants: 'she imitates faithfully the dynamic features but with a different content in a different modality' (Stern, 2010, p. 113). So attunement is, by nature, a multimodal process within which the mother takes an expression of the child that could be embedded in any non-linguistic vitality form and she translates it into another mode of expression while holding on to the underlying affect.

Stern also identified a spectrum of nonattunements, misattunements, selective attunements and communing attunements (Stern, 1985). One can utilise this spectrum as an aid to the drama and movement therapist's understanding of the choices they make in the process of attuning to the client. It can enable the therapist to recognise their own attunement patterns and to see the process as a varied and dynamic system; though instinctively triggered, such awareness can fine-tune the therapist's approach.

It feels important to mention some other terms that fall into the same classification group as attunement but differ in nature. It could be assumed that an empathic demeanour would enable a person to work successfully with MTS. While empathy requires a resonance with another person, it also involves a cognitive process: 'the integration of abstracted empathic knowledge into an empathic response' (Stern, 1985, p. 145). Stern believed that empathy was 'enormously complex' and warned against simplifying it; he believed attunements were more instinctive, in the sense they happened without awareness in a more reflexive manner:

> Attunement takes the experience of emotional resonance and automatically recasts that experience into another form of expression. Attunement thus need not proceed towards empathic knowledge or response. (Stern, 1985, p. 145)

Mirroring is another over-used term, holding different meanings for different therapeutic approaches and often involving several processes. It most typically refers to a process of synchronising with and reflecting back to the other, what Stern called 'true imitation'. This does not necessarily require an inner affect matching; it can be more superficial. It may involve a profound experience of oneness; it can also have a simplicity and a playfulness. Mirroring can be a useful tool, often a starting point in an MTS session, but for an experience of being with the other in a more complex exchange one must go beyond form or merging. Though attunement involves moments of inner and outer synchrony, it essentially operates without the need for such an echoic involvement. 'Attunement is a distinct form of affective transaction in its own right.' (Stern, 1985, p. 145)

This process of attuning to the other is, I believe, as key to working successfully with pre/post-verbal clients as it is to the healthy development of the infant. Some would argue attunement is the basis of any successful therapeutic encounter. Una McCluskey (2005) observed empathy and attunement working together as a goal-corrected process in professional care-giving relationships.

With non-linguistic clients one can be working with those same elements. Once a flow of successful attunements to vitality affect has occurred, a door often opens into the world of the client where an exploration takes place that is often followed by a 'pause' (Nind and Hewett, 2005), hence the idea of episodic explorations. These periodic non-linear narratives require an empathic facilitator who can also attune to a client's vitality affect through the expressive use of their body and voice. Being empathic alone is not enough. The ability to improvise freely with voice, movement and physical contact in order to match the client's vitality affect is an imperative. The communing presence of the therapist, the ability to 'be with' without doing, is vital. One must move in and out of communions and communications at varying levels of vitality, as a primary carer does, in order to regulate the client and support their self-regulation.

In these ways we can assist a client's exploration, an essential part of their therapeutic and developmental growth. The therapist supports this by providing momentary misattunements which create variation and can stimulate change.

I am placing the lexicon of attunement into the Sesame practice of MTS. I believe Sesame has been successfully pioneering clinical practice with non-verbal clients, yet we still lack a suitably evolved language to describe it. Sue Jennings's approach to drama therapy could be seen as academically driven and research based. Hers is a prolific body of written work. Marian Linkvist, Sesame's founder, was not an academic; her genius was the intuitive embodiment of the work, demonstrated through the practice, application and development of MTS, which seems radical even today. Jennings's most recent work includes an approach entitled 'Neuro-Dramatic-Play' (NDP) which is, in its own way, an approach that parallels MTS in its focus on pre-verbal communication and sensory interaction with the client. The Sesame approach has developed and been taught many years prior to that of both NDP (2011) and other similarly themed pre-verbal work such as the 'developmental drama' of Mary Booker (2011). These approaches tend not to explicitly reference Lindkvist in their research and writing, though she had been developing MTS in 1973. This is perhaps due to a lack of research and writing around the subject of MTS. It appears especially timely to now further articulate and define MTS as a distinct body of research and practice, to align it with a clear and well-established knowledge base and to reveal, examine and highlight its pre-eminent qualities in light of recent developments in the field. The language of the domains of vitality I have described might be a pathway for the non-linguistic skills of MTS to extend their reach into academic and clinical realms, so furthering discussion of the subject, raising awareness, extending the knowledge base and supporting accessibility by future clients.

Conclusion

We define musicality as expression of our human desire for cultural learning, our innate skill for moving, remembering and planning in sympathy for others that makes our appreciation and production of an endless variety of dramatic temporal narratives possible – whether those narratives consist of specific cultural forms of music, dance, poetry or ceremony; whether they are universal narratives of a mother and her baby quietly conversing with one another; whether it is the wordless emotional and motivational narrative that sits beneath a conversation between two or more adults or between a teacher and a class. (Trevarthen and Malloch, 2009, p. 4)

This concept of musicality is extremely helpful as it contains within it a multimodal approach to interaction which links it with other forms of experience. 'Communicative musicality' somehow gets to the heart of this work and assists me in understanding my practice of MTS as a kind of symphonic, sensorial, dance with the client.

When we work with a client in a pre-linguistic state we replace the layer of verbalisation with the language of vitality affect, through a multimodal medium. Instead of training in the use of a linguistic intervention base we must develop our technique in the spontaneous use of the art form in a more abstract sense. We have to be available to a range of modalities: tactile, audial, proprioceptive etc.

There are domains beyond a developmental stage or a particular mode of art where one communes with another beyond cognitive rule. Should we ignore that layer of our work simply because it doesn't fall into the category of form of our designated art therapy practice? Surely this is one of the vital places for examination, as it brings us closer to the ground from which the arts in therapy springs forth. Thus when one works through this source of human communication we transcend modality; the art form is at its purest expression: temporal, improvised, intuitive, musical and dramatic simultaneously.

Stern (1985) challenged modern psychoanalytic theories that perceived pre-verbal experience as void of intelligence. He proved through his detailed research of mother/infant interactions that the mother's ability to attune is both complex and fundamental in developing the child psychologically and relationally.

I believe there is great value in understanding these subtle aspects of our work more deeply because they tap into something at the very core of the arts therapy encounter; a form of pure improvised creative expression. It seems akin to that which the child evokes within the mother: an intuitive multimodal response; it is vibrant, visceral. It is alive in all non-verbal relationships and all time-based art forms. It is possible that this essential aspect is the seat of the dramatherapeutic relationship and key in challenging the thought-based hegemony in intervention choice. Ours is the arena to challenge such ideas for the sake of our non-verbal clients, for the intuitive intelligence within our practice, and for the sake of art forms and human experience that can't fit into categorised structures.

In order to understand the pre-verbal domains in dramatherapy we must examine the idea that artistic work at its purest is a mutlimodal experience that transcends form and works beyond categorisations, thus avoiding the 'superficial act of generalisation' (Levine 1992, p. 18).

Our ability to navigate the multimodality of our work and our art is, I believe, a crucial key to reaching the deepest layers of our experience as therapeutic companions and artists. As more is expected of us academically and clinically we must proceed cautiously, we must balance our deepening cognitive concern within the arts therapies with a deepening embodiment of the non-linguistic, boundary-less depths of our practice. Without this parallel process the arts therapies move more onto the pages of our books and away from clients who often are silenced because they present little in terms of a linguistic challenge. We must be aware of our unconscious propensity for linguistically led approaches. And we must claim recognition and understanding of the corporeal and interpersonal perspicacity within our practice.

> There is really no such thing as the 'voiceless'. There are only the deliberately silenced, or the preferably unheard. (Arundhati Roy, The 2004 Sydney Peace Lecture)

Let us not unwittingly assume that instinctively driven therapeutic processes can be left unexamined. We should not assume that literacy resides only within the verbal domains. It was Lindkvist's aim to give voice to those 'deliberately silenced, or the preferably unheard', the very clients that embody and represent the surreptitious wonders of the pre/post-cognitive. As we give voice to each of the hidden corners of our work, we give voice to some of the most furtive aspects of human experience and consequently the most radical art forms.

References

Bateman, J. (2008). *Multimodality and Genre*. London: Palgrave Macmillan.

Costeloe, K. et al. (2012). Short term outcomes after extreme pre-term birth in England. *BMJ, 345*, e7976.

Dissanayake, E. (2000). *Art and Intimacy, How the Arts Began*. Seattle, WA: University of Washington Press.

Erikson, E. H. (1950). *Childhood and Society*. New York: W.W. Norton.

Geurts, K. L. (2002). *Culture and the Senses*. Berkeley, CA: University of California Press.

Grotowski, J. (1968). *Towards A Poor Theatre*. London: Methuen.

Hammond, D. (2016). *My NHS Dementia Unit is About to Close and I Fear for My Patients*. Available at: The guardian.com. Accessed 24 June 2016)

Langer, S. K. (1967). *Mind: An Essay on Human Feeling*. Baltimore, MD: The John Hopkins University Press.

Levine, S. K. (1992). *Poiesis*. London: Jessica Kingsley.

Lindkvist, M. R. (1998). *Bring White Beads When You Call on the Healer*. Worcestershire: J. Garnet Miller Limited.

McCluskey, U. (2005). *To Be Met as a Person*. London: Karnac Books.

Meltzoff, A. N. & Borton, R. W. (1979). Intermodal matching by human neonates. *Nature*, 282, 403–404.

Nind, M. & Hewett, D. (2005). *Access to Communication*. London: David Fulton Publisher.

Oxford University Press. *Oxford Living Dictionaries* (2017). Available at: https://en.oxforddictionaries.com/definition/attune. Accessed 13 May 2017.

Pearson, J. (1996). *Discovering the Self Through Drama and Movement*. London: Jessica Kingsley.

Porter, R. (2014). Movement with touch and sound in the sesame approach: Bringing the bones to the flesh. *Dramatherapy*, 36(1), 27–42.

Prince, M. & Jackson, J. (2009). *World Alzheimer's Report*. Alzheimer's Disease International.

Reddy, V. (2008). *How Infants Know Minds*. Cambridge, MA: Harvard University Press.

Smail, M. (1999). *Movement with Touch*. London: Sesame Institute.

Stensaeth, K. & Trondalen, G. (2012). Dialogue on intersubjectivity with Colwyn Trevarthen and Stein Braten. *Voices Journal*, 12(3).

Stern, D. N. (1985). *The Interpersonal World of the Infant*. New York, NY: Basic Books.

Stern, D. N. (2010). *Forms of Vitality*. New York, NY: Oxford University Press.

Trevarthen, C. & Malloch, S. (2009). *Communcative Musicality*. New York, NY: Oxford University Press.

Wethered, A. G. (1993). *Movement and Drama in Therapy*. London: Jessica Kingsley.

11

Bearing the Unknown

Sophie Lasek and Laura Francis

This chapter is an account of our experiences of training as dramatherapists at the Royal Central School of Speech and Drama. Now, six months after graduating, we have begun the process of piecing together this shared expression of the student experience of becoming a Sesame-trained dramatherapist. We began to explore how much was individual and how much was shared about our experience. We are mindful that we are two voices of hundreds of student experiences and that this chapter is not a comprehensive account of everything we learned or a critical reflection of all elements of the Central training.

The first term was largely experiential. Through studying the course strands of Drama, Laban movement, Myth, and Movement with Touch and Sound, we obtained first-hand experience of how dramatherapy can enable people to explore and work with their unconscious material. There were concrete elements of being a dramatherapist which we learnt, including the Sesame structure of sessions, the symbolic content of stories and the importance of confidentiality. However, there was a pedagogic approach in which the tutors did not merely impart knowledge and information on how to be and what to do as a dramatherapist, but encouraged us to focus on reflective practice and our own process. We realised that a critical understanding of dramatherapy was not wholly sufficient, which meant we each encountered the feeling of 'not-knowing' how to be a dramatherapist. This chapter focuses on our individual encounters with this feeling and how we began to understand the nature and significance of this particular kind of not-knowing. By understanding what was shared in our processes, we have reflected upon how much the journeys we went on mirror the journeys of change and healing which we hope to facilitate for our clients. By reflecting on the way becoming a dramatherapist has changed us, we have found a way to articulate it as a process of change.

Sophie: Becoming Ready to be Surprised

The first term finished with a critical reflective essay of how moments of our experience informed our understanding of the Sesame Approach to Drama and Movement Therapy. Reading back over my essay, I had reflected on how I felt about not being able to know how to respond to clients at this early stage of training. I wrote about two moments in a Myth session and in a Movement with Touch and Sound session where we were to connect with a fellow student as a client on a one-to-one basis. In the Myth session we created an image for how the client may have been feeling, and in the Movement with Touch and Sound session we attuned through movement to connect (Stern, 1985; Porter, 2013). During these moments, my ego was cognitively telling me how to be competent and I became unnecessarily panicked and desperate when I did not know what to do in response to clients. Geller and Greenberg state that therapeutic presence in psychotherapy 'involves a simultaneous awareness of what the client is experiencing, the therapist's own in-the-moment experience and the relationship between the two' (Geller and Greenberg, 2012 in Hougham, 2013, p. 101). These experiences in my first term were centred on how I felt I should have been reacting as a therapist, rather than an in-the-moment experience relating to both the client and myself. The desperation I felt in wanting appropriate ways of responding to come to me was linked to my lack of therapeutic presence in those moments. Hindsight has now allowed me to realise that after three months of training, I was not ready to trust and appreciate the emptiness inside of me when working with clients and I was therefore not in a place to offer real therapeutic presence.

The second term of the course marked the start of a new stage of our training as we started our first placements working with clients. Before training, I had worked for a dynamic and people-focused business where staff coaching and development was key to our work. Therefore, it was a shock to realise quite quickly that the placements we were embarking upon would be supported by our placement supervisors, but led mostly by ourselves and our own learning. At the time, I questioned the efficacy of such an approach and wondered why we were being 'thrown in the deep end' as a teaching method. I remember feeling as though I wanted to take the teaching staff and my supervisor's brains out of their heads to put into my own. I clutched desperately onto my session plans and asked my supervisor to give me some answers and some tried-and-tested, effective ways to respond to clients. This was not given to us. We were met with answers which reflected our questions back to us. Not knowing what could happen in a session and, in turn, not being able to have a plan of action induced a fear in me; it felt as though if I had nothing to bring, I had no way to help, exacerbating the helplessness the client may have been feeling. Essentially, not-knowing felt unsafe. I continued to want to understand my clients in a cognitive way, to read their case histories thoroughly and to have something tangible with which to set goals and achieve something palpable in therapy sessions. The anxiety of not being able bear being open to the unknown means that I am not able to really listen to clients when entering an encounter with them.

In our third term, I completed my second placement working with a group of children who had social, emotional and mental health needs. My supervisor questioned me on my consideration that dramatherapy gives children the opportunity to play out what they want from life. I also explored my personal need to want to make things right for the children in our group. My supervisor acknowledged for me that many of the children who we work with do not have the power to change their lives for the better. He encouraged me to question whether therapy was about making things better, or joining our clients in how wrong things are. So, alongside my not knowing, I was also wondering what drama-therapy was, how it helped people and asking questions about whether I could ever possibly know what making things better for clients meant anyway.

At the time I assumed that this fear-inducing, anxiety-provoking 'not-knowing' was not what our placement supervisors and prepara-tion for clinical practice sessions were encouraging us to embrace and that I had got it wrong somehow. However, I understand now that the course team could not simply impart to us in a lecture or textbook what they meant by being open to the unknown. However difficult it was, by remaining open to trying to find 'answers' within myself and trusting in the course team who had belief that I was on the right track, I learnt how I and, in turn, my clients, find ways to bear difficulty, tension and anxiety. I began to learn about the fruitfulness which can arise when we, as therapists, stay with our clients' unknown, untold stories – their unknown, repressed, complicated and destructive feelings, and their unknown unconscious material. Again, my supervisor on my second placement brought my attention towards the value of staying with the conflict of seemingly opposing feelings, as, for example, the conflict of loving an abusive father. He made me wonder what might happen when we allow clients to explore their conflicting feelings and what could arise when their paradoxical feelings are witnessed and shared in dramatic role with their therapist. This coincided with my personal discovery of what staying with the tension of opposing feelings can bring about, as I wrote my analytical psychology essay over the summer on my own expe-rience of this.

It was an intense year of self-discovery and my unconscious had been thoroughly rummaged, noticed and prodded through individual Jungian analysis, group dramatherapy, experiential sessions on the course, reflec-tive essays and supervision. In my essay I explored the Jungian concept of the shadow which exists within our individual and collective unconscious. It is the 'hidden, repressed, for the most part inferior and guilt-laden personality' (Jung CW9 in Storr, 1998, p. 422). Johnson (1991) describes the integration of shadow using a seesaw analogy where one side of the seesaw holds desired characteristics and the other everything we have repressed. The seesaw must be balanced for us to be in equilibrium and it may break if too heavily loaded on one side, equating in neurosis, psychological breakdown or shadow bursting into consciousness when we least expect it (Casement, 2006). Up until starting Jungian analysis when I began the course, I largely denied and avoided the existence of anything dark within me and was also living with anxiety which seemed unexplained. My seesaw was off-balance by only acknowledging positivity. I was resistant to having a shadow as I thought that it would dilute my joy and positive outlook. However, I slowly realised that integrating and holding shadow qualities did not burden me or dilute any happiness, it actually began balancing out my psyche so it was not straining at the fulcrum. I began to feel more peaceful within myself.

Jung wrote how the conscious ego and unconscious shadow, and all psychological pairs of opposites, must be in balance with each other in line with the seesaw metaphor. Johnson summarises: 'to make light is to make shadow, one cannot exist without the other' (1991, p. 17). If we do not acknowledge the existence of opposites in this way, the neglected side will attempt to create equilibrium by compelling individuals to compensate for the imbalance, sometimes through uncharacteristic behaviours or neurotic thinking (Huskinson, 2004). Insights such as this made me realise that the intense fear of losing my loved ones was probably compensating for not acknowledging that my feelings cannot exist without their opposite being constellated; I cannot love as deeply as I do without fearing loss just as much. My anxiety gradually subsided once I began to simultaneously hold in one hand the joys of life, and in the other their opposite, life's sufferings. Ancient China called the honouring of opposites the Tao which is 'not a compromise but a creative synthesis' (Johnson, 1991, p. 48). Johnson (1991) and Monbourquette (2001) both write that one of the first steps in integrating one's shadow back into consciousness is to endure the collision of seemingly irreconcilable opposites and to embrace the unpleasant paradox we then face, rather than living with contradiction. 'Those who persist in this uncomfortable state will see their deep self, their Self, taking charge of bringing these poles into harmony; the opposites will show themselves to be complementary' (Monbourquette, 2001, p. 60), much like the Tao.

Reflecting back now, I wonder about what darkness and difficulties my clients held which I was unable to acknowledge or listen to until I found more balance within myself. At the time, I was struck how important it suddenly seemed to stay with clients' tensions and conflicting feelings and to compassionately value the difficulties in their lives. I felt more understanding of how important it was to give their shadows space to be listened to. However, the shadow and everything we suppress because it is just too painful to bear is, by its very nature, hidden and repressed. I think back to my first placement where I described earlier wanting to pick the brains of 'those-who-knew' on our course team and to have discernible understanding of clients. When working with unconscious material, we cannot know. I realise now that 'those-who-knew' knew the importance of not trying to know everything, because we can never fully know. Similarly, the course team encouraging us to embrace fear-inducing, anxiety-provoking 'not-knowing' was part of our process of being able to persist in an uncomfortable state in order for us to find some balance or let something new emerge. I began to value the myths, folk tales and stories we tell in dramatherapy sessions for their capacity to hold the balance of dark and light for our clients and to have the most ostracised parts of themselves heard and respected. Dramatic metaphor offered the safety of exploring these areas of the Self which can be so difficult to face. Similarly I began to value the oblique nature of the Sesame approach more; our clients often do not know what is going on for themselves and how repressed trauma is playing out in their lives. We therefore cannot aim to completely know what is going on for clients, which is why we often stay in the oblique realm of metaphor to enable processing to continue.

Our fourth and final term approached and even though I sensed a need to stop anxiously protecting myself with thorough, meticulous session plans and start encountering clients in sessions with openness, it was still difficult. However, I was given no choice in one of my final placements working with adults with autism. The group I worked with was unpredictable and most of the adults did not use verbal language. If I had gone into sessions with a plan, I would not have been attuning to clients and the sessions may have lacked any meaning or relevance to them. It would have been a clunky attempt to compel people to do drama activities.

Instead, the pace of these sessions was slow and patient; we worked with Veronica Sherborne's (1990) developmental movement and Movement with Touch and Sound which formed the basic structure of the sessions. The space in the sessions which I ceased anxiously filling by persevering in the discomfort of the unknown allowed me the opportunity to experience what happens when you let the client make choices. I realised that I could be and even needed to be surprised by what happened. It was not until I had embodied, lived experiences of how surprising moments are the moments which bring about change, healing and new imagined possibilities for clients that I could begin to trust myself to abandon plans and be open to fresh encounters.

Just as this placement with adults with autism drew to a close, I began running a dramatherapy group on an acute inpatient psychiatric unit. The nerves I experienced were like no other: again, I was not able to plan, I often did not know who was going to come to the session until 10 minutes beforehand, or if I had got to know someone in the group over a few sessions, more often than not they would be discharged. I had learnt the value of not going in with a scrupulous plan and also knew that because of my nerves, if I had a plan, I would have stuck to it. Plans protected me from feeling like I wanted the ground to swallow me up in an escape from the difficulty of not knowing what would be brought for me to hold and work with and whether I could or not. I would ritualistically read a section from Forrester and Read Johnson's (1996) chapter on extremely short-term dramatherapy in acute psychiatric settings. This assured me that sharing spontaneous sounds and movements would allow pertinent images to emerge and evolve into clients' exploration of their identities and feelings around being sectioned in a psychiatric hospital. Forrester and Read Johnson were right, and they were right, too, that this type of group would create unity, cooperation and equanimity. Week after week, I learned this for myself, it became embodied within me and I completely trusted that drama and creative expression could transport what the clients brought through the session with respect, compassion, empathy and containment. This experience seemed to clarify, finally, what the course team had meant about being 'okay with the unknown' and 'being with the client'.

Hindsight and reflection has enabled me to understand just how important this experience of learning how to be a dramatherapist from within myself was, as Marian Lindkvist (1998) outlined. I understand why questions I asked were reflected back to me and feel grateful to be in a profession which is so connected to something which lies deep within us all and is core to being a human. Being 'thrown in the deep end' back in January 2015 was a careful, considered, well-held and completely necessary process. The disorientation which we all experienced when the course and our placements started was essential to our process of moving from our heads and rational comprehensions and into our feelings and bodies. This helped me find the balance I needed within myself through integrating my shadow and becoming able to bear the tension of paradox. I was then able to become more familiar with my unconscious and could start to move past fears of the unknown. Thus, I was enabled to be a responsive dramatherapist who trusts I can be with clients and what they hold, known and unknown.

Laura: Letting Go to Let the Unknown In

Looking back to my encounter with the unknown at the beginning of the course, the image came to my mind of Alice in Wonderland falling down the rabbit hole. Yet when I watched this moment in the 1951 Disney film again recently (Walt Disney Productions, 1951), I saw that Alice does not seem terrified. This was not the kind of falling I experienced. Encountering the unknown was a constant background sensation of groundlessness, with sudden intense ruptures of panic. In a Drama session, I facilitated my fellow students working with puppets, and in one moment the puppets all turned to face me. I froze and could not respond. On another occasion, when I facilitated my Myth session, someone again turned to me, and I could not respond. I did not know how to. I felt like there was nothing inside me. Another moment from a Drama session haunted me. We each made a paper house, and I then spent all my time trying to draw other people out of their houses to play. At the end of the session, I looked back at my own house and felt I had abandoned it. I was shocked, and began to realise that I needed to get back in touch with my own inner experience to enable myself to be able to respond to the world outside.

So began a bittersweet process of deep exhilaration as I became more aware of feelings and sensations inside my body, mixed with grief at how out of touch I had previously been. There was never a moment on the course when I regretted having taken this path, yet, confusingly, part of me still needed to mourn the life I was leaving behind. It also felt all too easy to play out the letting go process as a pattern of self-destruction. The 'knowing' I wanted to be a dramatherapist had been hard won and tested on every step of the path towards starting the course. Yet now I was being asked to let go of the preconceptions of what I thought being a drama-therapist was. I felt angry towards myself for not knowing, and afraid that I did not know how to be myself anymore.

I was being confronted with parts of myself that were resisting the process. In retrospect, this was a powerful insight into how the process of letting go might feel for clients, and how, even if change is longed for, we still hold on so tightly. With one client I worked with on placement, I felt that if only we could make it over the threshold into the therapy room, we could start the work. Gradually I saw that what was happen-ing in our process outside the room, which could have been labelled 'resistance', was an expression of the coping mechanisms they had used to survive. Therefore, our work was not to get through this resistance as quickly as possible, but to work with what was present. As Jung said, 'we must be able to let things happen in the psyche' (Jung and Wilhelm, 2010, p. 90) and I was slowly learning to let go enough to come into alignment with this.

The course was an invitation to drop down into a deeper knowing of the whole, known and unknown, conscious and unconscious, which Jung calls the Self (Storr, 1998). We were learning to respond to and from there, not from ego. I was beginning to realise how as a dramatherapist, the act of stepping over the threshold into the unknown, onto the empty stage, is one we need to learn to bear again and again, in each moment of each session through all the years of our practice, because our task is to accompany our clients to do the same. Through participating in drama-therapy sessions day after day, I was internalising the strong containment of its ancient ritual form, the time, the place, the tools, the rhythm of our practice. I was discovering that if I could let go of what I thought I knew and what I thought a dramatherapist was, there could be enough space for my own way of 'not-knowing' to emerge.

For me, this was a journey that happened in my body. The first Movement with Touch and Sound session was a turning point. I left the session full of feelings of safety, wholeness and freedom, and with a clear intention to dedicate myself to learning how to do this practice. Another turning point came in a session where we were invited to remember what had inspired us to start the course, and I reconnected with the burning intention I felt inside to do this work. I became increasingly aware of how not-knowing was a different experience when I could keep in touch with an embodied sense of being safe and held. The terror of the unknown had been that, if as a therapist with a client I reach a point where I feel I have nothing to give, I would be confirming that their situation is hopeless and making it worse. Yet on my placement working with young people with autism, with one client I was slowly learning how to face the fear of doing 'nothing' that was present within our sessions. By actively staying present and embodying a sense of safety, in one session we took the step over a threshold, and instead of there being nothing there, it felt we entered a shared space, where I was not being moved by my thoughts, and we were both responding from somewhere else, within the relationship.

I was beginning to understand attunement (Stern, 1985; Lindkvist, 1998), how to feel safe enough to respond to the client and what was there in the session, without having to know what it was. Rather than checking with my ego that I would be safe, I was learning that a core part of the role of a dramatherapist is to actively trust that the client and I will both be safe, whatever happens, and how in this way we stand in for the part of our clients that feels safe enough to stay with their experience, without separating, projecting, splitting, or pushing it into psychopathology. By learning to trust what I experienced in my body during sessions, I began to understand these feelings within the context of the relationship with the client, of how they were speaking of the client's experience through somatic countertransference. Lindkvist said to 'never mind the meaning, just follow the patterns' (Lindkvist, 1998, p. 40) and I was learning how to follow whatever the client was bringing, without an ego-centred intention to change or get rid of it, which would have been rejecting those parts of them. In this way I was discovering how to hold the unknown, not by consciously or cognitively knowing it, but by seeing and holding it with compassion. I became more aware of my breathing and how this could help me stay with what I was experiencing in my body. During the last period of the course images of shapes emerging from underwater and whales came to me, as did the image of a free diver. This image symbolised for me how active relaxation was the key to being able to dive down deeper and deeper, breath by breath, into these unknown, terrifying and astoundingly beautiful places that it is impossible to survive in. Perhaps this was not so different from Alice's fall after all, but I had just learnt my way to do it, to feel safe enough to let go.

Towards the end of the course, I also began to understand how knowing can only happen in relationship. As we learnt to become dramatherapists, we met in our circle of students again and again. With clients, we meet in the session again and again. When I reflected on a session with one client where we had sat opposite each other, rather than seeing it through my eyes I suddenly saw a wide view of the room, with myself in the picture too, and saw how our positions suggested a power dynamic where both of us had knowledge the other was seeking. In the next session, we literally worked side by side, writing and drawing together, and an outpouring of rich material emerged. I felt this change of position expressed how it is by being in relationship together that we find a way of knowing how to stay with whatever needs to pass through.

I was also learning how story and symbol can give creative space and form to the unknown, without having to know it reductively, or conquer its power, or make dual its paradoxes. I began realising how stories were not only forms to explore in sessions, but how their patterns were also reflected in therapeutic relationships with clients. With one client I was devastated when I realised I was playing out the role of a witch, but by reflecting on this within the roles of a story, I was able to feel safe enough to work creatively with the transference and countertransference at play. The story and its symbolic images were safe containers within which to bring awareness to these powerful patterns. We were both held within its form of knowing, the archetypal imagery that had been passed down the generations, and had survived across continents because of its resonance and the paradoxes it could hold within it. A story that held us all throughout the course was Ali Baba and the Forty Thieves, with its magic mantra 'Open Sesame!' from which Lindkvist named the Sesame approach to drama and movement therapy. In doing so, she placed the power of story and symbol as a form of knowing at the heart of our practice. I also increasingly see how the story reflects the journey of becoming a dramatherapist, and that same journey we intend to accompany our clients on, of learning how we can feel safe enough to step over the threshold into the unknown, the dark cave of the unconscious, where not only will we find suffering, but also the jewels that are the patterns of our healing.

Conclusion: The Shared Experience

We have shared experiences from our individual journeys. We realised emergent themes including the importance of having the capacity to stay with conflict, to hold what we do not know and will not know and to work with being open to surprise in sessions. We both slowly learnt that we did not need to know everything about our clients and what they bring to session to respond to them with compassion. Being able to stand here now and look back, we can reflect on the themes of time and change in the process of becoming a dramatherapist. At the end of the course we have earned an initial understanding of being a dramatherapist, but it is interesting to consider whether this is a linear process or one of circumambulation. Is becoming a dramatherapist a singular happening, after which everything is irrevocably changed, or is this process a continual circular journey? When we were training, we had to keep crossing the threshold into the unknown again and again to build up our trust that we would be able to survive and bear what lay beyond. We needed hope and courage to do this. Now we both realise this process is actually never ending and that every time we step over the threshold and face the fear of the unknown it is not that it gets easier, but instead our trust in our own capacity to meet whatever we find increases. It is actively staying with this process of encountering new thresholds with openness that enables us to keep developing as dramatherapists. Chapter 1 of this book outlines that praxis requires a willingness to be 'meaningfully diverted, surprised, shaped and shifted'. We have come to realise that surprise is key to dramatherapy practice because we are working with the unconscious; surprises are surprising because they are initially hidden. If we feel we know what is going to happen going into an encounter and have a planned idea for how to respond, then we are not open to anything new and cannot provide the space our clients need for change to occur. In this way, we wonder if holding the possibility of surprise in dramatherapy is the way we hold the possibility that life can be different, having learnt to trust this by experiencing it ourselves.

References

Casement, A. (2006). The shadow. In R. K. Papadopoulos (Ed.), *The Handbook of Jungian Psychology: Theory, Practice and Applications*. Oxon: Routledge.

Forrester, A. M. & Read Johnson, D. (1996). The role of dramatherapy in an extremely short-term In-patient psychiatric unit. In A. Gersie (Ed.), *Dramatic Approaches to Brief Therapy*. London and Bristol: Jessica Kingsley.

Hougham, R. (2013). 'Rehearsing the unrehearsed': Reflections on the concept of presence in dramatherapy and performance training. *Dramatherapy*, *35*(2), 99–107. Available at: http://www.tandfonline.com/doi/full/10.1080/02630 672.2013.823787#tabModule. Accessed 15 December 2014,

Johnson, R. A. (1991). *Owning Your Own Shadow: Understanding the Dark Side of the Psyche*. New York, NY: HarperCollins.

Jung, C. G. & Wilhelm, R. (2010). *The Secret of The Golden Flower: A Chinese Book of Life*. San Diego, CA: Book Tree.

Lindkvist, M. (1998). *Bring White Beads When You Call on the Healer*. New Orleans, LA: Rivendell House Ltd.

Monbourquette, J. (2001). *Befriending Your Shadow: Welcoming Your Unloved Side*. Ottawa: Novalis.

Porter, R. (2013) Movement with touch and sound in the Sesame approach: Bringing the bones to the flesh. *Dramatherapy*, *36*(1), 27–42. Available at: http://www.tandfonline.com/doi/full/10.1080/02630672.2014.926957 #tabModule. Accessed 19 December 2014.

Sherborne, V. (1990). *Developmental Movement for Children: Mainstream, Special Needs and Pre-School.* Cambridge: Cambridge University Press.

Stern, D. N. (1985). *The Interpersonal World of the Infant.* New York, NY: Basic Books.

Storr, A. (1998). *The Essential Jung: Selected Writings.* London: Fontana Press.

Walt Disney Productions, Armstrong, S. & Carroll, L. (1951). *Walt Disney's Alice in Wonderland*, Racine, WI: Whitman.

12

Mythic Place

Marianna Vogt

Introduction

In this chapter I argue that relationship to place is psychologically significant and can be strengthened using the Sesame Approach to Drama and
Movement Therapy. My personal experience has been that connecting to
place is as important as attaching to people. My clinical practice as a dramatherapist shows that I am not alone in this. I have seen in myself and in
my clients that a chronic sense of dislocation can be ameliorated through
dramatherapy work, most significantly through myth- and storytelling,
which is a keystone of the Sesame approach. Because my theory was born of
personal experience, autoethnography has been important to my research.
Additionally, I support my argument with examples from my clinical work,
and the written work of philosophers, geographers and anthropologists.

The essay is divided into sections: 'What Is "Place"?', 'Why Does Place
Matter?', 'Making Place with the Sesame Approach' and a conclusion and
concluding questions.

What is 'Place'?

'Place' is a spot, generally in geographical space but also in time, emotion
or thought that has been endowed with meaning by a person (or people),
and which that person (or people) knows and understands intimately.

It is the opposite of 'space', which is what exists between 'places' and where we find the unknown, potential and limitlessness. 'Space' is what we move through; 'place' is where we are still (Tuan, 2011; Cresswell, 2004).

'Place' is boundaried 'space'. People apply boundaries to manage small parts of the infinite in all kinds of ways. We have defined the reaches of our solar system (even if we're still not sure about Pluto), mapped out political borders, named streets and built garden fences.

We don't just make 'places' by delineating parts of physical 'space'. As I write, I am putting my thoughts into 'place'. 'What is "place" (or time or life)?' is an impenetrable question. It's too big to grapple with. But by closely interrogating small parts of that question and by looking to the definitions that other thinkers have applied to the question before me, I am moulding my idea into a form that does not overwhelm me and into an argument that others can follow. I am moving my idea out of the vastness of 'space' and putting it into the specificity of 'place'.

'Place' is where we know and where we are known. As Yi-Fu Tuan, one of the most important philosophers on 'place', says, 'When space feels thoroughly familiar to us, it has become place.' (Tuan, 2011, p. 73) It is by interacting with and thereby thoroughly familiarising ourselves with areas in 'space' that we create 'place'.

Many areas are both 'space' and 'place' because what is 'place' for one person is 'space' to another. Consider London: returning there on a late flight in August, I looked down at the approaching city. It was vast, and glittered brashly against the night sky. I could conceive of nothing except its enormity. Its glow extended beyond my vision. As we flew lower I saw pairs of lights move in the pattern of streets, each pair a car holding a person or people. Shortly before landing, I was able to distinguish building lights from street lights. Each house and each office was filled with more people still. My home of many years felt far too big for me to know, except in abstraction. Like that, London is 'space'. But within the 'space' of London, there is a lot of 'place'. Each of the estimated 8.3 million inhabitants (Office of National Statistics) creates their own 'places' through the acts and interactions of life. My 'places' in London are my neighbourhood, my flat, my balcony, my bed. Less domestically, they are the institutions I work in, the parks I run in, the shops I shop in, the streets I know.

I create these 'places' by bestowing value to them, knowing them intimately through repeated action within them, and by claiming them as mine. The Persian butcher in Nag's Head Market, for example, is *my* butcher because according to my values he is one of the best in the area. (This is bestowing value.) I make his shop *mine* by buying from him often and thus fostering a relationship between us (knowing intimately through repeated action), and by calling him *my* butcher (claiming ownership). 'Place' is similarly created and maintained daily by 8.3 million Londoners, each of us saying, in 'places' large or small, solid or fleeting, 'I am not a stranger here.'

'I am not a stranger here' is a claim most contemporary, highly mobile humans must repeat to themselves and others with a frequency unnecessary in more settled societies. Before people became as mobile as they are now, they spent much more time in 'place'. 'Space' existed over the next river where a different group of people lived, in the woods or on the plains that people had not yet claimed away from animals, and of course in the imagination. But people's range of movement was more limited and they spent less time in the unfamiliar (Diamond, 2012). Now, 'space' can dominate. It is not unusual for people to move from city to city or country to country in search of work, safety, family or adventure. (Such movement affects even those who don't move. Immigration and emigration change the 'places' of the people who stay put.) These travels through 'space' are stimulating and full of possibilities, but are often accompanied by a sense of danger, a barrage of new information and a recognition of the enormity and unknowability of the world that, without anchor, can devolve into meaninglessness and end in exhaustion.

'Place' is where we are still. 'Place' is where we know, and don't need to know. 'Place' is what nurtures and restores us. 'Place' is where meaning doesn't flit away and so doesn't need to be caught. 'Place' is where I am. It is where I can be lazy, germinate in fallow earth, and 'live intensely, like a hare listening' (Renard, 2008, p. 268). Only outliers can navigate 'space' without 'place' to retreat to.

Why Does Place Matter?

I grew up with an American mother and a German father, commuting to American schools from a German village, speaking in mixed idioms with a mixed vocabulary, viewed by my friends in the village as The American and by my classmates as The German. My mother comes from a Scottish/English immigrant background and my father's parents were displaced by war (and choice; they could have stayed in the East but decided not to) from East Prussia to what became West Germany. I spent some summers with my grandparents in Michigan, USA. My parents are keen travellers and as a family we frequently visited France, Belgium and farther-flung countries. For eight years we spent two weeks every summer on the tiny island of Sark in the English Channel. On Sark, I formed intimate relationships with its cliffs, beaches, hills and oceans, and felt more in 'place' than I have before or since. Knowing Sark is there still comforts me, despite not having been in 18 years.

When I was 16, my family and I moved to the United States because of my mother's job. I spent a summer in the suburbs with them and went to university in the autumn. There I was, at 16, the youngest student. Again, I was viewed as German, this time in a historically Jewish university where some of my dorm-mates came from families so traumatised by the Holocaust that they couldn't even buy German coffee makers. I dated the son of a Holocaust survivor whose sister had committed suicide. I felt guilty. I felt foreign. I felt profoundly lonely. (The relationship was not a good one.) I missed Europe, I hated America, and started reading Kierkegaard, Sartre and Schopenhauer which didn't help things. I spent a term abroad in Kingston, Jamaica studying Jamaican folk dance, where I felt guilty for being white instead of being German. Following graduation, I moved to different cities in the United States, then to Brussels and now I live in London. I haven't felt completely 'in place' in any of these places, but the places where I feel most comfortable are those that have large immigrant populations (like London and New York) or an intrinsic identity crisis due to bilingualism (like Brussels).

I value my experience between 'places' and cultures. Because of it, I know that perspectives, interpretations of these perspectives and therefore reality are different for different people and cultures, and that reality can be different for that same person (or culture) when they (or it) views it from different 'places'. This is invaluable to my work as a therapist.

The downside to this history has been a negotiation with depression that started when I was a child. Initially, my depression was marked by terror at the impermanence of everything; a sense of impermanence that left me unable to sleep because I thought the world might disappear forever if I did. Later it manifested as nihilism: I quickly lost faith in the meaning or permanence of things, and still often lack lasting faith in the meanings I bestow.

However, my frequent uprooting and sense of impermanence has been as much a source of freedom as anxiety. As Doris Lessing (2013) said to interviewer Terry Gross, after describing a childhood spent between- and out-of-'place': 'Now, if you've had that childhood, you're never going to belong anywhere. You are free to move anywhere you like and feel happy there.'

Lessing highlights a real advantage, but arriving at the freedom to 'move anywhere and feel happy there' is not easy for many people who have had out-of-'place' starts in life or whose sense of 'place' has been severely disrupted. Roger Cohen, *New York Times* political columnist and family memoirist, observes of his own and other diasporic families: 'If you dig into people who are depressed you often find that their distress at some level is linked to a sense of not fitting in, an anxiety about where they belong: displacement anguish.' (Cohen, 2013)

Recently, my depression is defined by exhaustion. I am constantly moving and constantly busy. When my life is defined by transition, I am free of the feeling that there is somewhere (or someone) I should be. This is tiring. I am interested in 'place' because I need a respite from 'becoming' and a chance to 'be'. I need a vacation.

But packed into every holiday bag, of course, are all the neuroses you meant to leave behind. On a recent hiking holiday on Gran Canaria, my husband and I stayed in a tiny village with one bar on its one square, which is where we finished most of our hikes. We took off our boots, shelled peanuts, drank beer and watched the people, who in late March were mainly locals. My husband was fascinated by the old men and women whom we saw every day, sitting in the same place with their walkers and shopping, nodding to people who passed, sometimes talking but mainly seeming to be doing nothing. He wondered: Can you imagine a life like that? Just sitting and waiting? I said: They're not waiting, but being.

I didn't mean it as a profound observation, but it has stuck with me. If you are 'in place' you can *be*, instead of wait, like the villagers in the square who belong there. I, on the other hand, found it hard to sit still even after day-long hikes and a couple of beers. I was intensely aware of being a tourist, not belonging, sounding and looking different, anxious about the next words I'd have to speak in my appalling Spanish. I felt differently while hiking, surrounded by rocks instead of people. But I wanted to be able to be still at that bar too, or anywhere.

How can I drop the jittery, hungry habit of anticipation and learn how to *be*? By making the 'place' to do it. I am now often calm and content without effort, but when I find myself again edgy and off-balance, I bring myself back into 'place' with intentionality. In the following section, I define four steps to 'place'-making, which can be practised with intentionality, that have been useful not only to me, but also to my out-of-'place' clients.

Making Place with the Sesame Approach

People with a fragile sense of 'place' can strengthen their relationship to 'place' through the three steps outlined in 'What is "Place"?': (1) Bestowing value/meaning, (2) Knowing intimately through repeated actions and interactions and (3) Claiming ownership. A deeper practice of 'place' adds a fourth step: (4) Telling stories, which incorporates all three of the previous steps. (These steps do not have to be practised in any particular order.)

I see many clients who suffer from a sense of dislocation and have benefited from practising these four steps. This is likely because I work in London among a population high in migrants and immigrants. Many clients, though, do not have a problem with 'place' or may need to explore their relationship to 'space' and its unbounded potential for newness and adventure – I suspect that such a therapy might attract the teenagers of that tiny Canarian village, or anyone else who has never left home but who has longed to. It is important to remember this and not to project a problem or fascination with place onto clients.

If client and therapist decide together that strengthening the client's relationship to 'place' is an appropriate intervention, they must start by exploring the nature of the disruption to the client's relationship to 'place'. Every client is different, but I propose that tenuous relationships to 'place' generally fall into two categories: (1) not being present, lack of awareness of present surroundings and/or doubt in the permanence and reliability of 'place' or (2) missing a sense of having a 'place' on the timeline of human experience. I discuss how I work with the first situation under the subtitle 'Proving the Presence' and present techniques for working with the second under 'Place-Makers and Myth-Makers'.

Proving the Presence

Some clients may lack awareness of connections they already have to 'place'. In this case, a therapist can bring a client's attention to these connections by encouraging observation of the environment and of how the environment affects the client emotionally, physically and intellectually. Movement can be brought into the client's observations of the therapy space (gradually becoming 'place' as the relationship between it and the client strengthens) by inviting the client to move in response to a point or object in the room. It is helpful to have movable or flexible objects to work with (indeed, the therapist can be such an object) so that the client can easily observe the impact they have made on the environment, and in turn react with another response to the change they have occasioned. Following a series of interactions, it is valuable to name what the client has done in order to acknowledge the reality of the client's connection with the 'place'. This does not require analysis or even naming of feelings. The client should merely list what they did, for example: 'I hit the wall and the clock shook. I tapped the balloon and it sank.' The simplicity of this task is part of the attraction. The touch and impact between client and environment and client and therapist doesn't need to be proven or analysed, it just needs to be done and, importantly, acknowledged.

Stamping, a favourite technique of Sesame's founder Marian Lindkvist, is another useful tool to make a client aware of their connection to their environment. A client's fierce stamp almost forces them to recognise contact with the supporting ground, and is an assertion of their presence in the world, in a 'place'.

All this stamping etc. might sound like a lot of work, and not appropriate to finding 'place' if 'place' is where we are still. Testing the world and our presence in it, though, builds trust that it and we are there. Without trust, it is difficult to rest. I have seen many of my clients find moments of calm through testing their surroundings, for example, in sessions where I encourage them to explore their relationship to gravity. In these sessions, I begin by asking clients to focus on the points of contact between their bodies and the ground. I invite them to use this touch as a starting point from which to consider the relationship between them and the floor. I ask them to notice and test how the ground supports them, what it is like to fall against it, the walls or other objects in the room, and what their reaction to this pull and support is. When clients and I have worked with gravity in this way, the sessions have often become very still and have seemed to be about pausing rather than working.

Again, it is useful to name the connection to the environment that was made. Art-making, including storymaking, can be an expanded version of naming the experience of a session or of naming, ordering and balancing experiences of a lifetime. I often end sessions by inviting my clients to make marks on paper. One young client of mine regularly spends the last several minutes of his sessions drawing while I tidy up the room. Sessions with him generally involve personal and role play with extremely violent imagery. His end-of-session drawings fall into two categories: pictures with imagery that mirrors the session, a man with an aimed gun and bleeding head, for instance, or pictures with images that balance the session: a house with flowers and sunshine after a role play full of murder. The first type of image names the experience, the second balances it.

Place-Makers and Myth-Makers

A step beyond naming and balancing is to synthesise the experience of the session, and ultimately the experiences of a lifetime, into a coherent and tolerable narrative. This is where storytelling comes in. Using narrative to heal is of course not unique to dramatherapy or to a practice of 'place'. It is a technique that runs through many psychotherapies. But if 'place' is about presence, interaction and connection, storytelling is very useful to a practice of 'place', for as dramatherapist Alida Gersie says, 'narrative bridges the inevitable discontinuities in presence and shared experience' (Gersie, 1997, p. 202). Tuan, too, sees the formalising effect of art (and storymaking is art) on experience as an important aspect to the experience of 'place':

> images of place … are evoked by the imagination of perceptive writers. By the light of their art we are privileged to savor experiences that would otherwise have faded beyond recall. Here is a seeming paradox: thought creates distance and destroys the immediacy of direct experience, yet it is by thoughtful reflection that the elusive moments of the past draw near to us in present reality and gain a measure of permanence. (Tuan, 2011, p. 148)

People have been making art from experience since at least as far back as the Lascaux cave painters. Perhaps the greatest bodies of ancient, cumulatively created art are myths. Like one client can use art to formalise their experiences of one session, whole cultures have, in myths, formalised collective experience. Through them we are granted the '[privilege 'to savor experiences that would otherwise have faded beyond recall' (Tuan, 2011, p. 148), and to understand our own similar psychological experiences in transpersonal context.

Experiencing the myths of a particular 'place' can deepen a person's relationship to it. Whenever I have moved, I have sought out the stories of my new home to better understand it. This, combined with the daily relationship-building and meaning-bestowing that constitutes a practice of 'place' based in the present, helps me start to feel in 'place'. When I arrived in London, for example, I lapped up Peter Ackroyd's *London: The Biography* (2000), sought out literature and folklore about the city, and read up on myths about the British Isles. Through these stories, I started to feel connected not only to the city's present, but to its real, fictitious and mythical past. (Oliver Twist walked past my house on his way into London!) Joseph Campbell says his 'grand introduction' to Native American mythology was as a child playing in the woods:

where the Delaware Indians had lived, and the Iroquois had come down and fought them. There was a big ledge where we could dig for Indian arrowheads and things like that. And the very animals that play the role in the Indian stories were there in the woods around me. (Campbell, 1991, p. 13)

Being in that 'place' led him to myth. Anthropologist Keith Basso cites Laguna Pueblo poet and novelist Leslie M. Silko in his writing on the importance of 'place' to the lived mythology of many Native American traditions:

The stories cannot be separated from geographical locations, from actual physical places within the land ... And the stories are so much a part of these places that it is almost impossible for future generations to lose the stories because there are so many imposing geological elements ... you cannot live in that land without looking at or noticing a boulder or rock. And there's always a story. (Silko in Basso, 1996, p. 64)

Knowing the history and myths of a 'place' deepens our sense of belonging to it, even as our daily intimate actions within a 'place' can strengthen how its myths resonate and live in us. By living, we are always creating or recreating stories.

Stories of the past and stories created in the present strengthen attachment to place. But neither is the future insignificant to our sense of 'place'. Samuel Scheffler, New York University professor of philosophy, notes that:

However self-interested or narcissistic we may be, our capacity to find purpose and value in our lives depends on what we expect to happen to others after our deaths. Even though we as individuals have diverse values and goals, and even though it is up to each of us to judge what we consider to be a good or worthy life, most of us pursue our goals and seek to realize our values within a framework of belief that assumes an ongoing humanity. Remove that framework of belief, and our confidence in our values and purposes begins to erode (Scheffler, 2013).

Scheffler focuses on the ongoing existence of people, who are not insignificant to a person's experience of 'place' since hardly anyone lives somewhere completely devoid of other people. But I think we similarly need faith in the continuity of 'place' itself to maintain 'confidence in our values and purposes' (Scheffler, 2013).[1]

This is why I am terrified by climate change and rising sea levels. It's probably why my relatives keep asking when I will have children. We, like all other life forms, have an instinctive need for our species to continue, and the thought of the annihilation of our kind, whether species or family, is not just the fear of death, but terror at the complete loss of meaning.

Still, story comforts. Bedtime stories are a balm to childhood dread. Insomniacs look to novels or newspaper apps to distract their pinging minds. Poems soothe by putting into form and rhythm our greatest fears, among which must be 'Not to be here,/Not to be anywhere,/And soon' (Larkin, 2003, p. 190).

Scientists are storytellers too, though we have a tendency to place their work in a realm apart from, and often above, narrative and myth. Medical researchers, in their chase for immortality and against the marks of ageing, are working from the old story of the Fountain of Youth and contributing their own take on it. David R. Montgomery, professor of geomorphology at the University of Washington, USA, says of Great Flood myths:

> Like most geologists, I once dismissed these accounts as imaginative fantasies … however … many geomyths are in fact grounded in events that actually happened … Now geomythology is reweaving empiricism and symbolism, ferreting out kernels of fact buried in fable. Humans have always toiled to make sense of the world and our place in it. And for most of our history as a species, oral traditions were the only way to safeguard knowledge for posterity. In this sense, science can be seen as an extension of folklore – a new way to pass on the same stories. (Montgomery, 2015)

Basso writes 'the country of the past transform[s] the country of the present' and also of the future because 'remembering often provides a basis for imagining' (Basso, 1996, p. 5). Through stories we not only connect, but innovate.

---

[1] For the western Apache, 'place' holds meaning and history; when the bluff is gone, the story that happened there is too.

What role do mythic 'places' play in psychological health? Sometimes, for some people (I am one), personal meaning boundaried by the present is not significant enough to turn 'space' into 'place'. This might not be true of all the 'places' we need in our lives, maybe just for the most important ones at the most important times. It is why Catholic churches are built on ancient sites of worship, why people flock to Stonehenge for solstices as they imagine their neolithic ancestors did, and explains the phenomenon, which I have seen in my own family and which was recounted to me by several friends with recent immigrant backgrounds, of elderly family members determined to return to their country, city or village of origin before dying or to die. Sometimes, some people need a 'place' that has been endowed with meaning by generations of people on (or from) which to make sense of their own narratives and beliefs. The person who is attracted to such 'places' inevitably endows them again with personal meaning and connection, continuing the cycle. Myths, like these old important 'places', are the bedrock on which new stories can be told and lived out.

Campbell claims that reading myths is enough to participate in 'the rapture that is associated with being alive' (Campbell, 1991, p. 5). In Sesame dramatherapy sessions, stories are told, which provides a more immediate experience than story-reading, and myths are enacted, which brings stories into the body more directly still, further heightening 'the *experience* of meaning' (Moyers in Campbell, 1991, p. 5) or 'experience of *life*' (Campbell, 1991, p. 5) that myths facilitate.

Conclusion and Concluding Questions

Making 'place' is making sense – it allows us to know and trust some small part of this overwhelming universe. We make 'place' by projecting aspects of ourselves and our needs, whether individual or collective, onto space. The exploration of 'place' in this essay is not just heavily influenced by autoethnography, but is written from a very anthropocentric perspective. How could it be otherwise? I am a person writing about people, after all. But there are traditions (many Native American cultures among them) that encourage humans to allow places to project themselves onto people, and claim that this is where stories come from, not from the minds of humans. This is an understanding of 'place' I would like to explore further, especially looking at the psychological fallout of losing this kind of relationship to place. Physician and addiction specialist Gabor Maté writes compellingly about this in his book *In the Realm of Hungry Ghosts* (Maté, 2008).

I am also interested in looking at how nomadic people understand 'place'; at how a path, a line moving through space, can be 'place' and how forcible settlement can be a form of traumatic dislocation. (Isabel Fonseca writes of this in *Bury Me Standing: The Gypsies and their Journey*, Fonseca, 1995)

I am continually informed by my theories on 'place' in my clinical practice, and would like to put together a more formal study of how working with relationship to 'place' benefits (or not) different populations. Such a study could have timely practical implications, considering the current refugee crisis in Europe.

I am curious about people who have spent their whole lives within a small perimeter. This essay has focused on people who move a lot, but what about those who don't? Last summer, I visited an acquaintance in Augsburg who pointed out to me the different flats where he and each of his children had been conceived, all of which he could point to from one spot in one street. This was in the oldest part of a town that has been around for more than 2000 years. What does 'place' mean to him?

There are a lot of places to go from here.

References

Ackroyd, P. (2000). *London: The Biography*. London: Vintage Books.

Bachelard, G. (1994). *The Poetics of Space*. Boston: Beacon Press.

Basso, K. (1996). *Wisdom Sits in Places*. Albuquerque: University of New Mexico Press.

Campbell, J. (1991). *The Power of Myth* (with Bill Moyers). New York: Anchor Books.

Cohen, R. (2013). The quest to belong. *New York Times*, 18 November 2013, A39.

Cresswell, T. (2004). *Place: A Short Introduction*. Malden, Oxford & Victoria: Blackwell Publishing.

de Certeau, M. (1988). *The Practice of Everyday Life*. Berkeley, Los Angeles & London: University of California Press.

Diamond, J. (2012). Setting the stage by dividing the space. In *The World Until Yesterday* (pp. 37–76). London: Penguin.

Eliot, TS. (1963). *Collected Poems*. London: Faber & Faber.

Farrell, H. M. (2014). Sunday dialogue: Treating mental illness. *New York Times*, 4 January 2014, SR2.

Fonseca, I. (1995). *Bury Me Standing: The Gypsies and their Journey*. London: Vintage Books.

Gersie, A. (1997). *Reflections on Therapeutic Storymaking*. London and Bristol, Pennsylvania: Jessica Kingsley.

Larkin, P. (2003). *Collected Poems*. Victoria and London: The Marvell Press and faber and faber.

Lessing, D. (2013). Fresh air remembers 'Golden Notebook' author Doris Lessing. NPR's Fresh Air with Terry Gross, 18 November 2013. Available at: www.npr.org/2013/11/18/245955408/fresh-air-remembers-golden-note-book-author-doris-lessing. Accessed 6 February 2014.

Lindkvist, M. R. (1997). *Bring White Beads When You Call on the Healer*. New Orleans: Rivendell House Ltd.

Martin, C. (2015). On being. Available at: www.onbeing.org/program/transcript/7194#main_contenthttp://www.onbeing.org/program/transcript/7194#main_content. Accessed 18 May 2017.

Maté, G. (2008). *In the Realm of Hungry Ghosts*. Toronto: Vintage.

Montgomery, D. R. (2015). The real landscapes of the great flood myths. Nautilus, *25*. Available from: http://nautil.us/issue/25/water/the-real-land-scapes-of-the-great-flood-myths. Accessed 18 May 2017.

Office of National Statistics Online (n.d.). Available at: http://www.ons.gov.uk/ons/rel/regional-trends/region-and-country-profiles/region-and-country-profiles---key-statistics-and-profiles--october-2013/key-statistics-and-profiles---london--october-2013.html. Accessed 6 February 2014.

Oxford English Dictionary (1970) Vol. VIII, 2nd ed. London: Clarendon Press.

Renard, J. (2008). The Journals of Jules Renard. Ed. and trans. L. Bogan and R. Roget. Portland and New York: Tin House Books.

Scheffler, S. (2013). The importance of the afterlife. Seriously. *New York Times Online* Opinionator Blog 'The Stone', 21 September 2013. Available at: http://opinionator.blogs.nytimes.com/2013/09/21/the-importance-of-the-after-life-seriously/?_php=true&_type=blogs&_php=true&_type=blogs&_r=1. Accessed 27 January 2014.

Tuan, Y-F. (2011). *Space and Place*. Minneapolis & London: University of Minnesota Press.

13

Refugees and Resilience

Enda Moclair

This chapter uses an evidence-based case study to describe dramatherapy work with Syrian refugees who had escaped the conflict in their homeland into Southern Turkey during 2011–2015 and recommends an integrated approach which draws specifically on aspects of the Sesame Approach to Dramatherapy. The Sesame approach works to integrate and develop connections between the physical, emotional and mental aspects of the psyche and bring these functions into balance through imagination, drama, movement, music, poetry and art. In the humanitarian world, cognitive behavioural therapy (CBT) has become a popular approach offered to those fleeing traumatic circumstances and enduring adversity. It focuses on goals and problem solving and is easy to deliver. This chapter argues that a broader repertoire of dramatherapy reaches and engages a wider community in deeper, more culturally attuned ways. It draws on the work of Papadopoulous (2002, 2007) to look at ideas of trauma, resilience, adversity-affected developments and 'home' and brings together ideas from dramatherapy and the notion of emotional and social capital. These psychoanalytical terms address the promotion of inner resiliencies such as empathy, compassion and interconnectedness within and between people who struggle to both mourn the loss of home and search anew for identity and place in the world (Alayarian, 2007). Such ideas, combined with drama and different art modalities, can inform culturally sensitive therapeutic practice. The chapter concludes with recommendations for dramatherapy and creative expression to be commissioned by international aid donors and the humanitarian NGO community in working with the displaced and vulnerable.

Context

The conflict in Syria began in 2011 and as it escalated many thousands of Syrians were caught up in the ensuing fighting, fleeing Syria into neighbouring countries. Turkey has hosted nearly 3 million displaced Syrians since March 2011 and continues to receive more as the situation becomes more protracted. The bedrock of all community-based psychosocial work is the recognition of the affected community's capacity for recovery, resilience and future rebuilding and development. To support refugee needs many NGOs began supporting community psychosocial activities and services through community centres in southern Turkey.

My initial overall aim, in the role of a Sesame-trained dramatherapist and training facilitator, was to co-create a restorative and therapeutic environment with the community centre care staff and to develop psychosocial activities for children, youth and adult groups. This required training psychosocial care teams to work with displaced Syrians of all ages through three community centres and to design and develop psychosocial services (PSS) that would support resiliencies and coping strengths. The PSS care teams were a mix of Syrian and a few Turkish staff, neither with previous experience of working therapeutically, and most of whom had themselves fled the conflict inside Syria and were themselves refugees.

While the basic needs of the refugees living in camps are largely met by Turkish government support, the majority of those living outside the camps are unregistered and ineligible for government assistance. Uncertainty in terms of legal status, language barriers, lack of job and schooling opportunities, loss of traditional roles and exploitative work and wage conditions are daily challenges. Many Syrian families find themselves unable to provide for themselves, and are forced to resort to negative coping mechanisms, including early marriage and child labour. Mental health and psychosocial pressures were reported to be increasing due to growing hostility from the host community members who often felt Syrians were getting preferential treatment:

> *Every place we are hearing that 'you are Syrian why don't you go back to your country, why did you ruin your country? Why don't you go fight in your own country? Why don't you leave our country?* (PSS Care Team member, April 2014)

Syrian staff who had escaped conflict themselves were often working all day in the centres providing services to other displaced Syrians. They would then go home to accommodation often overcrowded with displaced family and friends. The need for debriefing and assessment for these staff felt a priority. I was concerned that the unconscious organisational busyness and reactive firefighting, often commonplace for humanitarian organisations, could undermine the very processes we were trying to give space to, and deny the conditions that a therapeutic space requires. Addressing this challenge required a systemic assessment of stressors. The overall outcome of the assessments found that the majority of staff responding to the ongoing humanitarian crisis had themselves gone through multiple traumatic experiences. They too were living with uncertainty and facing complex and challenging social circumstances along with the ongoing distress and concern for family members and friends still in Syria.

Trauma and Resiliencies

The daily challenges of living with loss, grief, anxiety and uncertainty are inherent in the lives of refugees. Although some may have been able to experience such violations without developing serious psychological symptoms, for others the accumulated impacts of trauma are too much to bear. Unhelpful assumptions about displaced people only compound these problems. Critical incidents such as fleeing one's home and struggling through the extreme challenges of relocating to another country are often assumed to be traumatic events for all people, who will all be in need of support. However, having endured life-changing challenges, people fleeing conflict can also be resourceful and resilient, and if they can connect to enabling conditions the majority can manage this with little or even no support. Papadopoulos (2007, p. 302) describes the 'tendency by mental health professionals to approach the state of being a refugee as if it were a psychological, or indeed a psychopathological, state'. He offers a framework that encourages and enables therapists to avoid such assumptions and to work together on resiliencies and adversity-affected developments. He notes that whenever one thinks of psychological inter-action with refugees, the first association tends to be with trauma rather than with 'home'. 'Yet loss of home is the only condition that all refugees share, not trauma.' (Papadopoulos, 2002, p. 9)

By recognising and redefining the centrality of 'home' for refugees, Papadopoulos advocates its centrality as a theme for both refugees and those working with the therapeutic care of refugees: home as a place where trust can develop and tensions can be held and contained, includ-ing joys and sorrows, hopes and disappointments, love and discord, collaboration and competition. Papadopoulos also identifies home as central to personal and family wellbeing and describes the centrality of loss of home to refugee experiences as 'nostalgic disorientation' (Papadopoulos 2002). This refers not just to the loss of home, but to the bewilderment and complexity of loss that displaced people can experience. He talks of the phase of 'frozenness' that can occur when people withdraw, as well as the different kind of reactions experienced at this loss: from depression to anger and apathy. He further notes the shared 'themes of these conditions are a deep sense of a gap, a fissure, a hole, an absence, a lack of confidence in one's own existence and consequently in reading life' (Papadopoulos, 2002, p. 18). This state of frozenness, while *transitional*, can often be mis-diagnosed as traumatic dissociation and emphasises the need for therapists to distinguish between human unhappiness, psychological disturbance and trauma. The shattering of this internal compass raises the questions of where and what is home? Where was it? Where might it be?

This complex question of the problem of home therefore requires the development of an integrated approach that enables what Papadopoulos terms 'therapeutic witnessing'. 'Therapeutic witnessing' describes the sharing, hearing and honouring of stories and experiences of refugees and is a key step in nurturing social capital. The sudden disappearance of the familiar and displacement from everything that constitutes 'home' and normality is accentuated and amplified through the experience of being unseen and often unwanted in the new host country.

> *Since we fled from Syria our wounds are getting bigger, wound over wound. We don't feel relief, we don't feel welcome.* (PSS Care Team member, April 2014)

Papadopoulos makes an important distinction between resiliencies – strengths that were always there – and adversity-affected developments as newly acquired strengths which can arise in the face of stress. Furthermore, he recognises two distinct characteristics within trauma. The first is a wounding of the psychological immune system, a 'rubbing in' that marks us and lingers negatively through the rest of our lives. The second is a 'rubbing off or rubbing away' which contributes to the acquisition and development of new adversity-affected developments. This brings into view the old adage known as the 'miracle of suffering'. Despite the wounding, pain, disruption, loss and confusion of their experiences, new values, perspectives, adversity-affected developments and revitalised resiliencies are able to emerge. Papadopoulos sees a duality in trauma work: being aware of the pain, dislocation and vulnerability of refugees as well as bearing witness to their own awareness of their inherent resiliencies and adversity-affected developments. To what extent might the wounding be able to activate self-healing mechanisms? And how might dramatherapy contribute to enabling refugees to bear witness and connect to inner resiliencies and adversity-affected developments that promote emotional and social capital, and reform an inner sense of home in the absence of the one they have physically left behind?

Creativity and Resiliences

The inner and outer fragmentation that people experience in fleeing conflict and losing and leaving home cannot be captured, reflected or honoured by conscious rational thoughts and words alone. Working with Sesame's Approach to Drama and Movement Therapy and different creative modalities can enable a deeper dialoguing and therapeutic witnessing within individuals and groups by virtue of its footing in Jungian psychology. It is also helpful in working with memory that is not always accessible to consciousness. Stuart Turner (1989) notes interestingly how 'modern (dual-representation) theory of traumatic memory has identified a part of memory that is not available to consciousness, and how it is this type of memory that leads to many of the emotional problems after trauma' (Turner, 1989, p. 172).

This is where art, music, drama and movement therapy enable a more embodied means of connecting with the unconscious than the problem/solution orientation of CBT. Creative expression can enable and empower groups to contain and capture the complexity and confusion of their experiences, particularly non-literate groups or when emotional literacy has not been taught. It can also be valuable when values of stoicism are prevalent and when the language does not lend itself to specificity. This is an important consideration as words for specific emotions and their qualities can tend to be very general in different languages such as 'mental health' and diagnosis in Western therapeutic discourse. This was particularly relevant as discussing mental health wellbeing in Syria is a taboo subject, with most people preferring to address issues arising through and within the family rather than seeking outside help. Talking about such issues directly is uncommon, particularly for males.

> We have a saying, 'If you are not wolf the wolf will eat you'. So if you are not strong or you show weakness you will not be able to protect yourself or your family. (PSS Care Team member 2014–2015)

The Sesame approach, with its emphasis on non-verbal expression and embodiment, is particularly adaptable to such challenges in multicultural contexts as working with myth, drama and creative expression draws on local cultural resources that can contain and express what words cannot. This approach enables an exploration of and connection to inner and collective resiliencies, to bear witness to and strengthen adversity-affected developments in responding to both complex personal issues and collective distress and crisis. Richman describes the non-verbal characteristics of functioning as aesthetic and creative and notes how traumatic memories generally lack verbal context and narrative, often encoded in the form of sensation and images. She suggests 'music dance and art therapies are all designed to access the sub symbolic system directly' (Richman, 2014, p. 94).

Case Study – Promoting Resiliencies

The integrated approach I developed highlights the centrality of creativity and spontaneity in the cultivation of emotional and social capital resiliencies and includes a potential in empowering participants to measure the adversity-affected growth that supports healing and growth. It describes the interplay between: 'home'; qualities of trauma; and the role of dramatherapy and creative expression in enabling a deeper therapeutic witnessing by appreciating the influence of culture, values, language and experiences of education when responding to the needs of those in distress and crisis. In order to support and resource staff to develop the confidence and competencies to facilitate drama and arts-based psychosocial activities with other Syrian refugees accessing the services provided by the community centres, the PSS care teams had to first undergo their own, parallel therapeutic and experiential process. In doing so, they would indirectly encounter and work through their own experiences and discover their own resiliencies and adversity-affected developments as well as being able to trust the role of the creative process in working therapeutically with others while avoiding direct therapy.

I decided to begin the year-long work with the PSS care teams by focusing first on 'discovering' key resiliencies through art and poetry and not retelling difficult stories. My aim was to establish safety, through ritual and play. This was important both in developing the trust between and within members and because many people in the care teams were very fragile. Some were still in transit, internally and externally, and the solid ground of safety and trust was needed before any deeper work around adversity-adapted developments could begin. Some had experienced torture and the emotional affects accessed through the taking on of different roles required more psychological strength before they could step out and inhabit other roles without being overwhelmed. The therapeutic relationship, as in any culture, is influenced to varying degrees by the currency of core values informing relationships and in particular those around: patriarchy, gender stoicism, equality, status and hierarchy. The mostly 'rote' education system in Syria further impacts and influences therapeutic interventions. Paying attention to people's experience of learning, to how they learned to learn at school, the values of the education system and how it has been affected by conflict were integral steps in enabling the PSS care teams to appreciate the role of values on therapeutic relationships within the culture. This is an important consideration as education by rote tends to promote competitive learning and not cooperative learning which in turn affects the quality of emotional and social capital. Furthermore, with rote educational approaches critical thinking and creativity are rarely promoted and creative expression is considered something mostly for children. The initial reactions by the majority of the PSS care teams to using drama and art were that they were no good at either: too shy to act as they hadn't created art works since childhood. These responses were also accompanied by feelings of embarrassment and low self-esteem. For the first month we played a lot using action methods to promote trust, connection, ensemble and spontaneity between the care team members. Amplifying self- and collective awareness of resiliencies through embodied story work and methods and techniques drawn from dramatherapy proved a helpful intervention for developing emotional capital and restoring and nurturing self-esteem, connecting to self and connecting to others. Once the team members had a stronger sense of their core resiliencies within themselves and were connected up to more of these inner strengths, then the more delicate work around acceptance, loss and identity, adversity-affected developments, could begin.

Initially, each session explored an activity beginning with a different calibration of warm-up and bridging exercises and then working with emerging themes though a variety of art forms. Reflecting on the experience afterwards using a different creative modality helped deepen expression and encourage unconscious qualities to surface. It seemed to enable participants to connect with a deeper resonance of what was significant for them as well as considering whether such an art form would be culturally appropriate. For example, visual art work was considered appropriate and accessible for most. As in many cultures, activities that promoted interaction and physical contact between genders were initially encountered with resistance and considered inappropriate, For example, dance and movement were deemed not suitable by the group for youth or adult women but were considered helpful for children. Drama was initially considered a sensitive area by the PSS care team particularly depending on the story being dramatised. Poetry was valued by both genders and considered appropriate for all ages though children were not considered able to use this form. Developing trust in different art modalities was therefore not a linear process but required indirect circling, attunement and intuitive facilitation. Working with image theatre, tableaus, single scenes drawing on Image Theatre sculpting and embodiment contributed to the development of a team language and seemed to capture and express, often better than words, people's experience. After the second month I began to introduce storytelling as a means of introducing the form and enabling members to experience the capacity in stories to promote connection, communication and relationship between members. 'The capacity to recognise, value, help and be helped by those perceived as "other" is what we mean by emotional capital.' (Papadopoulos, 2002, p. 75) We began with storytelling using general, resonant words e.g. door, teacher, dinner. Later, the sharing of more personal stories contributed further to developing emotional and social capital. Deeply personal stories only get told when they are ready to be told (Kaufmann, 2006). Often, our stories are strangers to us and need time to come 'home'. Aspects of the story may have been exiled to the unconscious or the past, or we may have become used to seeing and telling only a particular version. Creative exploration and expression enables stories to surface safely and float naturally, in an environment of shared trust. As the group community is engaged in a similar exploration, this contributes greatly to our courage, motivation and perseverance to stay and bear witness (Moclair, 2011).

Particular to the Sesame approach is the helpful use of dramatising myths drawn from the local culture that contain resonant themes while allowing distance to subjective experiences. When participants began to feel comfortable with a wider range of expression, I introduced myths. I sourced local myths that held relevant themes such as 'home' and adapted myths from other countries to the context to be enacted and explored. One German myth, the Four Musicians of Bremen, adapted to include local place and character names – the Four Musicians of Aleppo – contains general themes of rejection, alienation and migration and was explored and played out with high energy by the group. Such symbolic stories offer containment and opportunities to obliquely explore resonant but often banished and buried themes. The indirectness seemed to make it easier for participants to get up and act. Initially hesitant, most participants delighted in the safety, freedom and range of possibilities that playing a character in a myth story afforded them. Once this had entered the group repertoire and become valued, the transition to dramatizing personal stories became easier. The dramas enabled participants to experience authentic expression, something previously out of bounds for many, and to reflect on personal issues, and give themselves permission to try out and practise new roles in safe and non-judgemental ways. These dramas contributed to the recalibration of old values and the emergence of adversity-activated developments and new roles that helped contribute to and constitute identity renewal. The 'co-creation' and shared leadership aspects of the group work was critical in affirming individual and collective resiliencies and enabling group members to experience their stories and ideas as invited, respected, heard and valued, all ingredients of 'therapeutic witnessing'. For most this was a new way to behave and work together that they began to value. For others, being invited to participate and share their ideas and actions was still too threatening and I had to find ways and opportunities to promote their confidence to do so. Working with rigid and stereotypical roles necessitates a strong, trusting group and safety and spontaneity are essential for authentic and creative expression, as they can 'hold' the group during such periods of fragmentation and transition. Developing feedback strengths was another important development. Few in the group had experienced the giving and receiving of feedback in their work and family lives as positive, constructive or intended to contribute to learning and development. Most had experienced it as rebuke and control, involving degrees of shame, coercion and loss of face. In cultures with high power distance and low risk tolerance, authentic communication can be fraught with danger, especially with those of higher status/power. The last art forms, and the most powerfully experienced and appreciated by the care team group, were the dance and movement sessions. Initially considered a 'no go' art form at the beginning of the year, the group members spoke of the freedom and joy in being able to move and dance according to how their bodies wanted to, not by following traditional dance moves. They spoke of the feeling of connectedness in witnessing others in the group move and express themselves with no self-censorship or sense of shame.

A key theme that emerged for the team from this work was around hope and spirituality. The inner landscape mirrors the outer, the safety and centrality of homes as well as community resources and places of spiritual worship. Beliefs and practices that are integral to home are specifically targeted, smashed and turned to rubble during conflict such as this, something I have witnessed elsewhere working in other war-afflicted countries. The deliberate intention of the oppressor is to break people's sense and sources of hope and of spiritual redemption. Home is gone. Former neighbours are now enemies. Flight or death is the choice for so many. The imagination for a better future, like the soil that used to produce crops that sustained, and a contributing factor in the conflict, can also dry up and wither. The group spoke of the good relations between different ethnicities and religions before the war and expressed disbelief and sadness at what had happened. One group member shared in one session how life in his valley between different faiths prior to the conflict had been characterised by goodwill and reciprocity for many years. However, as the conflict crept closer this cooperation fragmented and surrounding villages, previously experienced as safe, were no longer so, to the point that he felt encircled by hostile villages and trapped in what had been home. Home was now a prison from which he and his family had to escape.

This spiritual shattering for those coming from a strong faith background can be a significant part of the trauma endured by those fleeing upheaval and conflict. Also the use of torture, which deliberately and explicitly attacks the body, where memory is stored (van der Kolk, 2014) can further contribute to an internal shattering and loss of hope. Especially for the less resilient or fortunate, this can be such a profound shattering of the sense of 'self' and sense of where and what constituted 'home'. Much of the work around hope within the group combined practising self-soothing and mindful body work with identifying and amplifying 'hopes', embodying and exploring them with dramatherapeutic exercises as well as with psycho-education that helped them be aware of what was happening within themselves and others.

Measuring Awareness of Resiliencies and Adversity-Affected Developments

Very helpful for members in concretising their resiliencies and recognising adversity-affected developments, welcoming them 'home', was being able to reflect back on the year-long work together. This was enabled by use of a holistic resilience baseline with the PSS care teams that began at the start of the year that mapped how they saw their resiliencies then. At the end of the year each member returned to this baseline and used non-verbal creative expression and words to evaluate once more their resiliencies, areas of growth and development emerging from the challenges of their difficult experiences. This places members at the centre of attuning to their own developments and healing. It helped them to tolerate some of the uncomfortable dissonance and resistances that arose over the year as they deepened their self-awareness and engaged with the psychological defences that arise to protect us through times of adversity and chronic stress.

The brief testimonies expressed within the group during their final reflections on what areas of growth/personal development resonated for them at the end of the year together in early 2015 and shared below, with permission from the PSS care team members to publish here, capture both some of what seemed to be less meaningful developments and insights for some along with some of those that were more meaningful:

"Before I was trusting but now I don't trust so easily"

"I am strong like a tree, deep roots but despite that just like the tree I have faced many bad times like the tree faces: snow, rain. I feel I am facing everything and all the challenges of life and I stay strict and strong against all the conditions and bear fruit"

"In my relations I still have the same emotions but now love is in a new shape, smaller"

"*Through this year I discover the treasure inside myself*"

"*We are all feeling the pain in your heart, speak out more, you are loved, it's not shame to share*"

"*When I reflect, and saw how we moved and danced, I felt the journey was like the journey of life, we face new lives through the seasons, people come and people go, while we dance accordingly*"

"*Some things from this war I cannot and will never accept. That he died fighting for freedom and us, and is now in heaven helps me accept*"

"*People from my country are carrying the same sorrow and grief that I am holding in my heart and this is hard and every time I am hearing what someone has been through, I am going through. I feel I am holding everything and this gives me the confidence that I am strong. Look at us! We haven't collapsed*"

Residing within the above are testimonies of both existing resiliencies and of adversity-affected developments discovered and witnessed over the year. These include themes of acceptance, endurance, of finding hope, of finding ways to live with loss and grief, as well as discovering more of self, discovering strengths and fortitude within self and others. Reflecting through different forms highlights the importance of 'witnessing' and honouring these connections so that the small slivers of adversity-affected developments could concretise, gain awareness and value, alongside existing resiliencies.

Conclusions

There is a tendency currently, in the media, the humanitarian aid community and in refugee discourse in general for refugees to be considered traumatised by their experiences and for humanitarian response programmes to tailor supports and interventions to address such 'refugee trauma'. While undoubtedly people suffer and survive cruel and degrading experiences they can also be strengthened by and through their exposure to adversity.

The experience of working with the integrated and systemic approach described in this chapter highlights the cultural sensitivity and adaptability of Sesame's indirect, drama- and arts-orientated therapeutic process. It describes how it can contribute to healing by bringing to the surface of conscious awareness resiliencies, adversity-affected developments and feelings which have been unacknowledged, not 'seen' and often internally repressed, denied or displaced so that they can be creatively integrated into the personality. Resilient people more often have a need to prove that adversity can be overcome: they do not want to be identified as victims but survivors. 'By making use of adversity as its base rather than trauma, Adversity Affected Development makes the subtle but important differentiation between being exposed to adversity and being traumatised.' (Papadopolous, 2007):

> We wanted to be free but they didn't hear us but bombed us instead. But strangely ... war also brings out the best in us. (PSS Care Team member, December 2014)

Exploring and expressing what words often are unable to do through drama and art was necessary for several reasons. The care team members initially struggled to see adversity-affected developments as growth. They were out of sight, unseen amidst the fog of their 'nostalgic disorientation'. Furthermore, trauma can affect the part of the brain that processes language, so drawing on image and symbol enables expression and narrative to emerge that can help people make sense of their experiences. It does so in ways not accessible to conscious talking approaches to therapy. Dramatherapy enables engagement of the whole person at a level deeper than speech. Drama and the creative arts also have physical components and thus provided opportunities for catharsis and for the release of kinaesthetic tensions and body memories. Creating art, embodiment, poetry, music and drama are therefore integral to 'restore continuity and facilitate integration of dissociated states and splits in experience by reuniting affect, cognition, and perception turned asunder by traumatic experience' (Richman, 2014, p. 95). Furthermore, cultural differences in the expression and perception of pain and the range and depth of language used to describe it can make this work more challenging. This is the case particularly where mental health problems carry a stigma and emotional expression is not taught but more often is taught to be avoided, particularly for males.

Yet CBT continues to be the main form of therapy offered by humanitarian organisations to children and adult refugees. CBT's emphasis on problem solving, while meeting the needs in some people, will be less helpful with others as it largely avoids the unconscious and creativity of a person. Furthermore, a model for trauma treatment as predominant as CBT, employed by international non-governmental organisations (INGOs) across cultures, risks globalising a set of assumptions around mental health and wellbeing based on Western models of pathology. In emphasising positive thinking, CBT can also distance people from addressing the political sources of their suffering which can contribute further to their experience and sense of disempowerment. The Sesame Approach to Dramatherapy, working obliquely with image and symbol, recognises, however, that it is from the unconscious that images and symbols rise, with the potential to enable the survivor to make sense of their complex experiences. Symbol formation is at the essence of artistic creativity and it is through artistic expression that trauma can be symbolically represented and witnessed. This oblique route draws on Jungian insights which recognise the need of the unconscious to express symbolically, through images and not words, via drama, creative expression and movement, in order to surface into consciousness. Using drama to inhabit and explore different roles, and creating art works during the group sessions, gave opportunities for members to explore, discover, take risks and reflect, and for new perspectives, insights, ideas and reframing to open up. This enabled their relationship to experiences of losing home and being displaced, fleeing conflict and their new lives in Turkey to begin to shift from victim to survivor. It helped people discover and recognise that adversity can lead to growth and contribute to the restoration of hope as well as new inner resources. They were able to create and express the losses endured, the shame and humiliations experienced, and the hopes yearned for, through the language of symbol, image and embodiment. Such therapeutic witnessing enables connections to be organised and re-established with what was lost, for self-esteem and adversity-affected developments to be recognised and grow, for acceptance and mourning to have 'permission', for the internal compass to begin pointing homewards. Developing the resilience of reflection, supported through an approach that places the person at the centre of recording, recognising and gauging both their challenges and their own incremental growth of adversity-activated developments in the face of such challenges is very helpful.

The strength of the Sesame approach that focuses on resilience, adversity-affected developments and home, explored and expressed and enabled through drama and art, is that:

> the body speaks, dances, sings and enacts scenes not in order to deny its fragmentation but to reveal it. Such revelation is also a transformation, a gathering up of the disjointed parts into a unity of signification. This unity forms what we might call a 'fragmented totality', a way of being a self that neither falls apart into difference nor escapes into an idealized identity. (Barba, 2010, p. 68)

People are displaced and become refugees as a result of socio-political and environmental circumstances. The current instabilities and inequalities within the global system have placed already strained agencies at breaking point. Funding for delivery of relief items and response to refugees' material needs is more often given more value and focus by donors and humanitarian organisations than approaches that support people's inner as well as outer wellbeing. As it is likely that the inequality and resultant instability and stressors of the current global system will lead to greater volatility, conflict and the displacement of more refugees, the need for a more nuanced, creative, community-based, culturally attuned and diverse response, as enabled by the Sesame approach, by NGOs in supporting resiliencies and adaptive development strengths only increases.

References

Alayarian, A. (2007). *Resilience, Suffering and Creativity – The Work of the Refugee Therapy Centre*. London: Karnac Books.

Barba, E. (2010). *Performance in Place of War*. Chicago, IL: The University of Chicago Press.

Kaufmann, P. (2006). Magic Threes, Creative Expression Workshops, Phnom Penh.

Moclair, E. (2011). *Stoking the Embers Within: Working with a Whole Person Learning Approach in Cambodia*. Phnom Penh: VBNK.

Papadopoulos, R. K. (2000/2002). *No Place Like Home – Therapeutic Care For Refugees*. London: Karnac Books.

Papadopoulos, R. (2007). Refugees, trauma and adversity-activated. *European Journal of Psychotherapy and Counseling, 9*, 301–312.

Richman, S. (2014). *Mended by the Muse – Creative Transformations of Trauma*. London: Routledge.

Seyderhelm, A. (2016). The Role of Therapeutic Storytelling in Early Years Loss And Bereavement. http://www.huffingtonpost.co.uk, April 2016.

Sidoli, M. (2000). *When the Body Speaks*. London: Routledge.

Turner, S. W. (1989). Working with survivors: The Medical Foundation for the Care of Victims of Torture. *Psychiatric Bulletin, 13*, 173–176.

Van der Kolk, B. A. (2014). *The Body Keeps the Score: Brain, Mind, and Body in the Healing of Trauma*. New York, NY: Penguin Books.

WHO – Mental health, resilience and inequalities – WHO/Europe, www.euro.who.int, *2009* www.freedomfromtorture.org/sites/default/files/documents/Summerfield-PsychologicalResponses.pdf.

14

The Jung Connection

Mark Saban

In this chapter I try to explore several links, some apparent and some rather better hidden, between Jungian psychology and theatre. These fruitful interactions have the capacity, I think, to make a useful contribution to the emergent praxis within the Sesame approach.

I have taught Jung's psychology on the Sesame course at the Royal Central School of Speech and Drama for 11 years. Although I am not trained as a dramatherapist, over the years I believe I have developed an understanding of some of the resonances between the students' practice and the theory I introduce in the weekly seminars in Analytical Psychology.

I first tried to look at the link between theatrical questions and psychological questions in a 2005 paper called 'Theatre and Psyche' (Saban, 2005), in which I brought my own background in acting and performing into dialogue with my new profession of Jungian analysis. In 2010 I delivered a talk called 'Playing the Other' at a conference at Central School of Speech and Drama, in which I focused on ideas about mimesis, and perceptions and experiences of the body.

In this chapter, I further develop some links between therapy (and particularly dramatherapy) and Jungian psychology by focusing on what I have come to see as one of the essential ideas behind analytical psychology: that of the multiplicity of psyche. I try to show how active imagination, the practice that, in as sense, originally initiated Jung into the practice of an archetypal psychology, is a fundamentally dramatic endeavour and thus has much to offer to an understanding of the Sesame Approach to Dramatherapy. In order to deepen and illuminate my theme I introduce some ideas and images of the Greek god Dionysus, and, in tune with the spirit of Sesame, allow mythological and archetypal motifs to echo and re-echo, in the hope that these reverberations will bring some soul-understanding.

Listening to the Other

Jung's work during his early years at the Burgholzli psychiatric hospital bore fruit in the articulation and differentiation of the psychological feeling-toned complexes. I would maintain that this work, and particularly Jung's emphasis upon the self-presentation of these complexes *as persons* laid the foundation for his entire mature psychology. Given the context of this chapter, it would perhaps be more evocative to suggest that his early work *set the stage* on which his mature psychology would subsequently play itself out. It seems to me that the psychic model he fashioned, or which fashioned itself through him, enables us to vision the event we call psychic life as an essentially *theatrical* event in which multiple figures – autonomous and personified – dynamically play out their interrelated roles before, and for, multiple inner witnesses. The dramatic (and dramatising) perspective on the psyche that emerged from this new complex-psychology paved the way for what Jung was to articulate as the 'transcendent function' – a concept that itself was primarily exemplified, according to Jung, in the dynamic improvisations and personifications of what became called 'active imagination' (Jung, 1916).

From an archetypal perspective, to evoke the theatre is to evoke Dionysus, and my hope is to illustrate in this Chapter some ways in which an awareness of the Dionysian can shed light upon its psychological complexities, and, in turn, the complexities of Jung's model of the psyche. It is well known that Dionysus was the most paradoxical of gods, and his position as god of theatre is entirely consistent with this fact, since, as we shall see, the event of theatre is a highly paradoxical event. The fact that the avowed *telos* of Jung's psychological model is that of bringing the opposites together, a paradoxical goal if there ever was one, only lends more emphasis to the fact that the Dionysian is, in this context, a crucially relevant archetypal theme.

Jung's model of the psyche entails multiplicity. Like Pierre Janet, Théodore Flournoy and William James (and unlike Freud), Jung posits, alongside the ego-complex and its hegemonic (though blinkered) form of consciousness, numerous other complexes, each of which possesses a certain autonomy, and even a kind of consciousness of its own. It is appropriate then, according to Jung, that these complexes (refigured in his later theory as *archetypes)* tend to take a personified form – in other words they show up, in fantasy, dream, or hallucination, *as persons* (Saban, 2016). Most of us are familiar with the particular personifications that Jung made famous: the shadow, the animus, the anima, the hero, the wise old man, etc.

According to Jung, it is necessary to psychological life, and essential to what he describes as the process of individuation, that the ego should not only become aware of, but ultimately engage in dialogue with these other figures. However, such a confrontation is not something that the ego tends to enjoy – indeed it is the inveterate nature of the ego-complex to find itself in tension with, resistant to and even in conflict with the other psychic complexes. This is why, Jung tells us, our dreams so often offer us scenes of discord, friction and dispute – scenes which we (or at least our egos) can experience as a succession of attacks, humiliations, rejections and abandonments. This is because dreams, or at least the dreams we best remember, frequently enact scenes in which the ego reveals an inability or unwillingness to engage with or even acknowledge the call of the inner other, in its myriad forms.

Because of this, the therapeutic approach that Jung recommends is 'a dialectical procedure, a real coming to terms with them, often conducted … in dialogue form' (Jung, 1934, para 85).

As Jung often reminds us, all psychologies are highly conditioned by the 'personal equation' of their creators. Given this, it comes as no surprise to discover that Jung himself was intimately acquainted with the experience of inner discord from his earliest years. In the opening chapters of his autobiography he describes his own possession of (or should I say *by*) two personalities. Throughout his childhood, according to his memoir, *Memories, Dreams, Reflections*, (Jung and Jaffeé, 1989) Jung was tossed to and fro between personality no. 1 and personality no. 2, possessed first by one and then by the other. Eventually, in the wake of his 'storm lantern' dream, he came to the realisation that in order to achieve psychic wholeness he needed to find a way to accommodate both of these personalities. However, it was not until the traumatic break with Freud and the psychological crisis that played out in its wake, that the conflict between Jung's two personalities returned to centre stage and he started to deliberately explore, from the inside as it were, the lived implications of his dissociationist theory. The fruit of Jung's years of inner exploration and dialogue was the Red Book (Jung, 2009). In the original German edition of what was translated as *Memories, Dreams, Reflections* Jung uses the term '*Auseinandersetzung mit dem Unbewussten*' to describe his experience during this time (Jung and Jaffeé, 1962, p. 174). In the English translation, the word *auseinandersetzung* was rendered as 'confrontation' – confrontation with the unconscious (Jung, 1989, p. 170) – but it is a word that could also mean dialogue, discussion, involvement or engagement with the unconscious, and these alternative translations perhaps convey better the highly *reciprocal* nature of what Jung is describing. In the Red Book, Jung's ego-complex finds itself in various dramatic settings, many of which entail conversation and debate with the figures it meets. So Jung is never 'confronted' by something called 'the unconscious'; what happens is far more specific: Jung finds himself speaking and being spoken to by various autonomous and personified consciousnesses of which his ego has hitherto been unconscious.

That there is something intrinsically dramatic, not to say theatrical, about Jung's psychodynamic model was obvious to many, not least Jung himself. Not only did he analyse dream structure in the literary terms of classical drama, uncovering in dreams moments of exposition, lysis, and culmination (peripeteia) (Jung, 1945, paras 561ff), and describing the theatre as a 'psychotherapeutic institute where complexes are staged' (Jung, 2013, p. 2) but more interestingly, for our purposes, he also drew a more direct parallel between dream as event and theatre as event:

A dream is a theatre in which the dreamer is himself the scene, the player, the prompter, the producer, the author, the public, and the critic. (Jung, 1916, para 509)

Ostensibly Jung is utilising this metaphor to show us how the dream functions 'on the subjective level' by which he means to suggest that everything in the dream is a portrait of the inner dynamics of the dreamer's psyche. However, Jung is simultaneously, by implication, pointing out the dynamic complexity of the theatrical model: the unique living event of theatre is envisaged here as the dramatic interaction of a multiplicity of persons and energies, and therefore, by extension, not only dream but psyche itself exists as a similarly complex interaction involving a similar multiplicity of inner personalities.

As we have seen, it was during the difficult period following his split with Freud that Jung first found himself confronted by inner pressures that led him to the brink of questioning his own sanity. Eventually, despite strong resistance from the ego (expressed in the form of a powerful sense of shame and humiliation), he eventually bowed to what he experienced as inner necessity. Deliberately loosening the controlling grip of his (personality no. 1) ego, he (re)opened himself to the voices of a multiplicity of personified inner others (personality no. 2). It is worth noting here that the cluster of terms I have found myself using here (madness, loosening, multiplicity) are precisely the terms most often to be found in the vicinity of Dionysus and the Dionysian.

Jung's experience at that time, leading up to and during the writing of the Red Book, has been described by various Jungian scholars as Dionysian. In a recent book, *Remembering Dionysus*, Susan Rowland pays particular attention to the Red Book's fragmentary qualities (Rowland, 2016). For her, whether we regard the work from a literary perspective or a psychological perspective what we find imaged there is dismemberment. In one of the myths of Dionysus the god is torn to pieces by the Titans, but is later reborn. In other myths it is the god himself who brings about the dismemberment of his enemies. His female followers, the wild maenads, are described as tearing apart both animals and men. Images of rending, splitting and subsequent re-membering are characteristic of the complex of motifs that constellate around Dionysus in both his mythology and his rituals. Images and motifs of this kind when approached psychologically seem to speak dissociation and madness, and indeed these themes too are native to the world of the Dionysian. There is much to be said with regard to the psychology of the Dionysian, but my focus here is the Dionysian as it reveals itself in theatre. As a radically decentred form that often features the conflictual interplay of multiple consciousness, theatre carries the metaphor of dismemberment in a direction all its own. Rowland herself brings together the themes of dismemberment and of theatre in the Red Book when she draws attention to the fact that it is Jung himself who emphasises the dramatic aspect of his writing – describing it with the term 'mystery play'. (Jung, 2009, p. 246; Rowland, 2016, pp. 75–76). Indeed, she goes so far as to suggest that 'The Red Book seeks to be a mystery play for our time, re-incarnating the Dionysian spirit in the textures of living' (ibid., p. 76). Nietzsche's *Also Sprach Zarathustra*, a work that is undoubtedly a stylistic influence upon Jung's *Liber Novus*, also shares this highly psychological Dionysian quality. As Graham Parkes puts it, Nietzsche's book:

> is a play of images constituting a consummate picture of the most comprehensive soul, of psyche in totality. It is possible, and enlightening, to read the entire text as a complex image of a single soul — Zarathustra's — and to understand as the major theme the Dionysiac dissolution of the unitary I through multiple overflowings into a plurality of persons … (Parkes, 1996, p. 360)

When it comes to the Red Book, James Hillman has particularly emphasised its Dionysian theatrical dimension. In a dialogue conducted with Sonu Shamdasani on the subject of the Red Book (Hillman and Shamdasani, 2013), Hillman begins by pointing out that even in the pre-Red Book period of *Wandlungen und Symbole der Libido* Jung was already in 1912 depicting the libido in mythical forms and that such a psychology should be described as 'psychodramatics':

> it implies that we're in a different realm of a different God. We're in the realm of Dionysus who was the patron, the God, of the theater. And then we have to use another language altogether for doing psychology. We have to imagine it as a realm of Dionysian life. Of life force, of passion, of tragedy and comedy and not a clarification that you would get from an Apollonic or an Athenian or another perspective of what goes on. (ibid., p. 33)

Hillman goes on to suggest that in the breakthrough Red Book, we find:

> break-ins of the unwanted forces of nature, passion, revelry, violence, and so on, that are supposed to be kept out of the temenos in a way – or at least brought in and held within the vessel – this would be the reappearance of the Dionysian, which is there authentically in the psychodramatics of engaging with the other persons. It's a theater … [Jung's] thought develops in this work as an interplay between characters. They stage positions and also are tremendously cultural and historical. (ibid., p. 34)

Psychotherapeutically, Hillman suggests, the implications of such an approach are profound. A step beyond the Freudian, Jung's multiple, dramatic model of the psyche is crucial because it enables us to see the ego as merely one complex among many. The ego is a:

> member of the dramatis personae. He's in the cast … one among others. Now isn't that a huge insight just to begin with? Isn't that a huge relief for the egocentric human being of our time, who goes to his therapy and tries to work out his problems, when this says you're one among others. There are a lot of people in your house. You don't live alone. (ibid., p. 101)[1]

Acting Imagination

The process or technique that grew out of the experiences described in Jung's Red Book became known as 'active imagination'. In his subsequent work with analysands Jung liked to recommend it as a dynamic means of enabling a meeting with their unconscious inner other(s). Aged 75,

---

[1] Hillman here develops themes he touches on elsewhere in his work. In *Healing Fiction*, for example, discussing the Dionysian, theatrical, approach to psyche, he suggests that:

> The self divided is precisely where the self is authentically located … Authenticity is the perpetual dismemberment of being and not-being a self, a being that is always in many parts, like a dream with a full cast. (Hillman, 2012, p. 39)

and writing his masterwork *Mysterium Coniunctionis* (Jung, 1955) Jung still considered the technique to be sufficiently important to warrant a lengthy description. Significantly, in this account, he chooses to use theatrical terminology to describe this means for bringing about a dialectical meeting of the conscious ego and the personified energies of the deep unconscious, which reveal themselves as autonomous figures that, as Wallace Stevens put it, 'speak because they want to speak' (Stevens, 2011, p. 194).

Jung recommends that we catch a dream or fantasy image and fix it with our gaze until it begins to alter. Thus animated, it takes on its own autonomous life and so it is that a kind of drama begins to be played out. Now, as the images begin to flow, he says, we can either sit back and enjoy the drama as a mere entertainment *out there,* or we may start to see that:

> The piece that is being played does not want merely to be watched impartially, it wants to compel [the imaginer's] *participation.* If [the imaginer] understands that his own drama is being performed on this inner stage, he cannot remain indifferent to the plot and its denouement. (Jung, 1955, para 706)

Later Jung comes back to this image. He talks about the way in which the reality of the psychic process is experienced by an individual:

> Although, to a certain extent, he looks on from outside, impartially, he is also an acting and suffering figure in the drama of the psyche. (ibid., para 753)

So long as you just stare at the pictures, Jung says, nothing transformative happens and nothing will happen. But …:

> If you recognize your own involvement, you yourself must enter into the process with your personal reactions, just as if you were one of the fantasy figures, or rather, as if the drama being enacted before your eyes were real. It is a psychic fact that this fantasy is happening, and it is as real as you – as a psychic entity – are real. (ibid.)

The evident care Jung takes in this lengthy description within his magnum opus is a clear indicator of the central importance of such encounters within his psychology. They exemplify, according to Jung, the so-called transcendent function whereby the opposites are brought together – the alchemical term for which is *mysterium coniunctionis* – a process that constitutes both the essence and the culmination of individuation. And it is highly significant that in order to explicate it, Jung chose the theatrical metaphor as the most appropriate parallel. It takes a form whereby one engages with an inner other, thus creating a relationship of tension and even conflict, and through this enactment, which is somehow simultaneously engagement and observation (one foot in/one foot out, actor/audience), we both meet and are met by something that is experienced as both utterly different and yet also, uncannily, our own inner other. This strange recognition brings about, or perhaps is identical to, an inner movement of transformation.

This place of meeting is precisely the one in which the Sesame Approach to Dramatherapy, as I understand it, finds itself most focused and most effective, because it enables an event to emerge in which several particularly dynamic forms of relationship can simultaneously occur within the crucible of *play*. On its most basic level this dialogical event occurs between client(s) and therapist. On another less apparent but no less important level the dialogue plays out also between personal and archetypal dimensions of both the event itself and its participants. Moreover, all the participants take up positions oscillating in play between that of actor and that of audience. Behind it all unfolds the interplay of self and other through a dynamic field that somehow incorporates both the security of containment and the freedom of improvisation.

Why Dionysus?

When I describe such an encounter as Dionysian, it is not purely because Dionysus is the god of theatre. It is rather because the theatrical is always already essentially Dionysian.

When we examine the cluster of themes, motifs and actions that have been associated with the Greek god Dionysus we can see that they tend to easily fall into oppositional binaries:

He is both very near and yet somehow very far.

He is thoroughly masculine, and yet somehow effeminate.

He takes one out of oneself, and yet leaves one more whole.

He is always a stranger, from afar, and yet is not only authentically Greek but has a place at the centre of Greek culture.

He is a great creator, and yet a terrible destroyer.

He appears in the form of the mask, which emphasises both presence and absence, hiding as much as it reveals.

He has been aptly described as the 'image of indestructible life' (Kereényi, 1996), and yet he is, according to Heraclitus also Hades, god of the dead (Kahn, 1981, p. 81).[2]

The Dionysian holds these opposites somehow together in one place; it is essentially paradoxical. If theatre is Dionysian it is because it too holds together some of the impossible contradictions that characterise Dionysus. Presence and absence, truth and lie, connection and detachment. If Jean-Paul Vernant is right when he says that 'Dionysus is a god with whom man can only make contact face to face' (Vernant, 1988, p. 202), then theatre is most certainly the prime locus for that encounter. It

---

[2] I am not referring to the Dionysus of Nietzsche's *Birth of Tragedy* (Nietzsche, 2008) here, who makes up half of a polar binary with Apollo, but rather the more complex and interesting Dionysus who we actually find in ancient Greek culture in all its multiplicity. The later Nietzsche's Dionysus is paradoxical in this way; through a kind of binary synthesis he has for Nietzsche become a kind of dialectical unity contained in and transcending the tension between both Dionysus and Apollo.

manifests as the face-to-face meeting of the actor with the mask, of one actor with another actor, of actor and audience, and of audience with audience. Through masked fiction we are presented, face to face, with a truth in the shape of a lie.

There is something essentially Dionysian about the mutuality of this encounter. In Euripides' *Bacchae* (perhaps our richest theatrical and meta-theatrical source for the Dionysian) when the young tyrant Pentheus first interrogates the stranger (Dionysus pretending to be one of his own followers) about his god, he asks him, 'How did you see him? In a dream, or face to face?' (line 468) The stranger replies obliquely: *horon horonta*, 'I saw him seeing me.' As Vernant says:

> [This reply] stresses that the god's epiphany … is based on the meeting of two gazes in which (as in the interplay of reflecting mirrors), by the grace of Dionysus, a total reversibility is established between the devotee who sees and the god who is seen, where each one is, in relation to the other, at once the one who sees and the one who makes himself seen. (Vernant, 1988, p. 393)

Intentionally or not, Vernant seems to echo an idea of Merleau-Ponty's here. For Merleau-Ponty *reversibility* is an important aspect of what he calls the *chiasm*, whereby:

> every perception is doubled with a counter-perception … [it is] an act with two faces, one that no longer knows who speaks and who listens. (Merleau-Ponty, 1968, pp. 264–265)

Such ideas seem highly relevant to a model of psyche in which, as Jung emphasises, ego not only meets and sees the autonomous other of the deep unconscious, but also crucially experiences what it is to be in turn met and seen by these autonomous others. As Marie-Louise von Franz puts it:

> One sees oneself for a moment through the eyes of another, of something objective which views one from the outside, as it were. (von Franz, 1998, p. 7)

This is the discomfiting experience of seeing the unconscious seeing us.

But this is also highly pertinent to the realm of dramatherapy wherein both therapist and client(s) are not only seen by each other, but also seen to be seen. A relation of such complexity and subtlety has perhaps been best articulated in Merleau-Ponty's concept of chiasm. With the image/concept of chiasm Merleau-Ponty seeks to avoid a reductive short-circuiting of what is a profoundly delicate and asymmetrical relation: a relation situated on the fault-line between self and other. it is intended, with the lightest step, to tread this fine line, the interface where the otherness of the other gets related back, in paradoxical fashion, to self's own radical otherness, while at the same time allowing for the revelation that the common humanity felt between us is intimately bound up with its own shadow – unassimilable alterity. As Lisa Folkmarson Käll has put it:

> By taking perspective on us, others bring to light our limits and by contesting what we say about them, point to the limits of our own perspectives. I see myself limited by the other and, yet, I nevertheless need the other to give birth to me through dialogue and interaction. I need the other to strengthen and validate as well as doubt and contest my experience of the world and of myself. (Quoted in Celenza, 2014, p. 22)

Theatre – and also therapy – exist on, and exist to reveal, that fault-line, one that holds us apart but also holds us together, because it holds apart our parts, our personae (in Dionysian dismemberment) while providing the space in which they can be held together, maintaining an essential wholeness.

So, in Euripides' *Bacchae*, for example, Dionysus is evidently present in the figure, the role, the person of Dionysus, the stranger, a figure that disrupts, bringing chaos, and catastrophe. But we need to remember that Dionysus is also present in the theatrical event as a whole, which, by presenting it in a form that can be met, though not thereby swallowed up or assimilated, nonetheless contains that chaos – or at least holds open a space wherein the chaos – our chaos – may be encountered and not just undergone. At the end of a Greek tragedy we, and our emotions, are left in a state of fruitful perturbation. This has nothing to do with the smug *schadenfreude* that comes from observing from a distance the safe and tidy packaging of catastrophe visited upon others. It rather reflects the fact that in the theatrical event it is we (audience and actors) who have together shared in, truly participated in, though without being over-whelmed by, this terrible undoing.

Theatre and therapy are both *ec-static* in that they point towards the need to stand outside of ourselves, or rather our ego-selves, thus opening up an awareness that we are more than (or is it less than?) we thought we were, and also more vitally and immediately connected to the other (in the form of inner and outer others) than we knew or perhaps wanted to know.

As Charles Segal puts it:

> In the tragic theatre, as in the Bacchic ecstasy, [and I would add in active imagination, and even in therapy] the participant 'stands outside' of himself: he temporarily relinquishes the safe limits of personal identity, in order to extend himself sympathetically to other dimensions of experi-ence. (Segal, 1997, p. 215)

And this is another Dionysian paradox: we lose ourselves in order to gain a deeper sense of ourselves.

Yet, however terrifying to ego the experience of such ecstatic states may be, it is nonetheless, in both theatre and therapy, somehow *contained*. In both events what gets opened up is an *empty space* (in Peter Brook's sense) for the playing out of the rawest and most violent complexes and emotions in an atmosphere of improvisation and spontaneity, and yet this empty space, the container (and I mean the analytic third, not the therapist), somehow holds these forces in an elastic envelope that works, because it inhabits a world that is not the 'real world', it is animated through a relationship that is not quite a 'real relationship' – though for this very reason it is felt to be more real in a more focused and more visible way than any number of so-called 'real' relationships.

Dionysus in Therapy

The rites of Dionysus, as Richard Seaford points out, are essentially to do with the transformation of individual identity (Seaford, 2006, p. 11). Just as, for the Greeks and also for us today, the theatrical event constitutes a place of transformation and liberation, so too does the therapeutic event. As we have seen, for Jung the psychic dynamics whereby these goals, both of which make up individuation, are achieved, or rather find their achievement through us, may be visioned most fully through the theatrical metaphor. On the empty stage of dream, or active imagination, our inner figures make their exits and their entrances. Through interminable agonistic encounters the heroic ego meets, battles with and is humiliated by its own others, and thus, learning through suffering, we, as 'acting and suffering figures in the drama of the psyche' but also as an audience that is passionately and intimately engaged with what it witnesses, become able to achieve insight on a level that transcends, or burrows beneath, the simply intellectual.

This is exemplified perhaps most clearly in psychotherapy, where client but also crucially (as Jung emphasised) therapist, strut and fret their hour (or 50 minutes) upon the stage. I have already drawn attention to the ambiguity that surrounds the fictive truth or truthful fiction of what occurs on this therapeutic stage. But there is more to be said. In the mysterious events and processes we call transference and countertransference we tend to find and engage with the very figures that we (unconsciously) need to find and engage with. In effect we cast the therapist in the role or roles we need them to play, and insist upon hearing all their lines as making sense, possessing meaning, only within this, our own plot. Our ultimate task is to release ourselves from this singleness of plot by coming to recognise the true otherness of our dialogical partner, a recognition that is, paradoxically, precisely what will enable us to gain knowledge of ourselves. As Folkmarson Käll says, echoing Merleau-Ponty:

> I can neither know the other in the same way as I can know myself nor myself in the same way as the other knows me. There is thus a clear duality at the very heart of the relation between self and other and the issue at stake in understanding intersubjectivity is how to preserve the uniqueness of the other while at the same time bridging the gap between self and other. (Folkmarson Käll, 2009, p. 21)

The 1913 encounter that initiated the succession of highly developed meetings with inner others that we can read in the Red Book also marked Jung's first meeting with what he was later to describe as the 'anima' – the inner feminine aspect of a man. As Jung describes it in his 1925 seminar, while questioning himself about the scientific status of his visions he hears the voice of a woman telling him, 'that is art' (Jung, 1990, p. 42). As Jung points out, this comment, and the conversation that ensued, had a perfectly ordinary feel to it. 'A living woman could very well have come into the room and said that very thing to me.' (ibid.) This was particularly the case since Jung, he tells us in *Memories, Dreams, Reflections*, recognised the voice as that of 'a patient, a talented psychopath who had a strong transference to me' (Jung and Jaffeé, 1989, p. 185). Jung thus associates the dialogue that plays out (once Jung has succeeded in offering her the use of his 'speech-centres') with that of a conversation taking place in analysis – and specifically one taking place in the context of an erotic transference. Interest in the identity of this female patient[3] has obscured the crucial point here: that Jung is identifying the dialogical relationship between his ego and his inner other not just with a clinical relationship but with the sort of highly reciprocal relationship that characterised his erotic bond with Spielrein, and very likely that with Moltzer (and subsequently of course with Toni Wolff). Jung later emphasises the mutuality of the relationship with the anima by noting that he 'was like a patient in analysis with a ghost and a woman' (*Ich kam mir vor wie ein Patient in Analyse bei einem weiblichen Geist!*) (Jung and Jaffeé, 1962, p. 189; Jung and Jaffeé, 1989, p. 186). So, although Jung has informed us that the woman's voice was that of a patient, in the dialogical experience that ensues it is Jung himself who somehow becomes the patient and the woman/ghost the analyst. At times during the Spielrein relationship Jung himself had played the patient role in receipt not only of her penetrating analytical interpretations, but also of her love and support. For example, in his 4 December 1908 letter to Spielrein he writes, 'Give me at this moment something back of the love and patience and unselfishness that I was able to give to you during the time of your illness. Now I am the sick one ... ' (Carotenuto, 1984, pp. 195–196). This ambiguity with regard to who here is the analyst and who the patient gains in focus when we re-place this mutual, dramatic model into its proper context: the clinical world of transference and countertransference from which, as we have seen, it partly derives.

---

[3] Various suggestions have been made (Nietzsche, 2008).

Conclusion

We can now see how three different but related settings, all Dionysian in their own way, may be seen to illuminate each other.

The first is the virtual world of the theatrical event, a world parallel to that of 'ordinary life'. A world of dynamic, complex and reciprocal relationships between audience and actor, actor and role, actor and actor. Here unreality, fiction and mimesis enable the unveiling of truth.

The second is the virtual world of active imagination, another world parallel to 'ordinary life'. A world in which ego engages in reciprocal dramatic and dialogical relations with internal others: a virtual realm that is nonetheless, Jung emphasises (or rather his internal other emphasises), a field of 'objective' psychic reality.

The third is the virtual world of psychotherapy and dramatherapy, yet another world parallel to 'ordinary life'. A world in which therapist and client(s) playfully though seriously co-discover/co-create a subjective/objective reality by standing in for those others (inner/outer) who need to be encountered or re-encountered. Here by (re-)enacting those dramas that need enacting each partner is (re-)acquainted with those psychic parts that have been split off, forgotten, or never met and thus come home to themselves and, in T. S. Eliot's words in *Four Quartets*, 'know the place for the first time'.

It is crucial to remember that the actor is never a characterless nothing who simply pours themself into the role, or hides behind the mask, but is always a complex individual who brings to any role a unique and personal history and sensibility, such that what we see on stage is always an amalgam of both role and actor. In psychotherapy too, as Jung suggests, it is the 'whole person' of the therapist that is engaged with the 'whole person' of the client; indeed psychotherapy is no more than the meeting of these two wholenesses, although the event of that meeting also somehow constitutes, or is constituted by, a third event. This event is transcendent in the sense that it cannot be reduced to a formula of person plus person, any more than theatre can be reduced to the formula of actor plus audience. It is then never accurate to portray the event of therapy as a one-sided projection from client onto the blank screen therapist – an event that adds up to merely a rehash or replay of old patterns, old plots. The living drama of psychotherapy is far more complex, and far more interesting than that. That dynamic interaction possesses the potential for infinite novelty and spontaneity. It is truly an interplay, and it plays between and within the rich events that we soberly describe with the terms transference and countertransference, as if we knew what they were – processes in which both client and therapist enact and improvise a bewildering array of roles in a bewildering array of dramatic genres, moving together and apart, forming anew ever-shifting compounds and amalgams.

The *Dionysian* aspect of all this, as in theatre, resides not just in the chaotic emotional maelstrom which this process can sometimes resemble, but also in the very container – the boundaries and structures – that, on a good day, can hold it. Dionysus – paradoxically – exists in the unstable tension between the two: chaos and container, just as the boundaries that always surround theatre are always in tension with the tragic destructive/creative energies unleashed within them. The essential power of theatre resides in this tension, as it does also the power of psychotherapy.

References

Carotenuto, A. (1984). *A Secret Symmetry: Sabrina Spielrein Between Jung and Freud*. New York, NY: Pantheon Books.

Celenza, A. (2014). *Erotic Revelations: Clinical Applications and Perverse Scenarios*. New York: Routledge.

Folkmarson Käll, L. (2009). *Expressive Space: Encountering Self and Other*. Available at: https://philosophy.columbian.gwu.edu/sites/philosophy.columbian.gwu.edu/files/image/Kall_gwu_presentation.pdf. Accessed 6 December 2016.

Hillman, J. (2012). *Healing Fiction*. Putnam, CT: Spring Publications.

Hillman, J. & Shamdasani, S. (2013). *Lament of the Dead: Psychology After Jung's Red Book*. New York, NY: W.W. Norton.

Jung, C. G. (1916). General Aspects of Dream Psychology. *CW 8* paras 443–529.

Jung, C. G. (1934). Archetypes of the Collective Unconscious. *CW 9i* paras 1–86.

Jung, C. G. (1945). On the Nature of Dreams. *CW 8* paras 530–569.

Jung, C. G. (1955). *Mysterium Coniunctionis: An Inquiry into the Separation and Synthesis of Psychic Opposites in Alchemy CW 14*. London: Routledge.

Jung, C. G. (1990). *Analytical Psychology: Notes of the Seminar Given in 1925*. London: Routledge.

Jung, C. G. (2009). *Liber Novus*. New York, NY: W.W. Norton.

Jung, C. G. (2013). *Dream Analysis: Notes of the Seminar Given in 1928–30*. London: Routledge.

Jung, C. G. and Jaffeé, A. (1962). *Erinnerungen, Träume, Gedanken Von C.G. Jung*. Aufgezeichnet und Herausgegeben Von Aniela Jaffé. Walter-Verlag, Zürich; Düsseldorf.

Jung, C. G. and Jaffeé, A. (1989). *Memories, Dreams, Reflections*. New York, NY: Vintage Books.

Kahn, C. H. (1981). *The Art and Thought of Heraclitus*. Cambridge and London: Cambridge University Press.

Kereényi, K. (1996). *Dionysos: Archetypal Image of the Indestructible Life*. Princeton, NJ: Princeton University Press.

Merleau-Ponty, M. (1968). *The Visible and the Invisible: Followed by Working Notes*. Evanston, IL: Northwestern University Press.

Nietzsche, F. (2008). *The Birth of Tragedy*. Oxford and New York, NY: OUP Oxford.

Parkes, G. (1996). *Composing the Soul: Reaches of Nietzsche's Psychology*. Chicago, IL: University of Chicago Press.

Rowland, S. (2016). Remembering Dionysus: Revisioning psychology and literature. In *C. G. Jung and James Hillman*. Oxon and New York, NY: Routledge and Abingdon.

Saban, M. (2005). Theatre and psyche. *Harvest*, *51*, 88–101.

Saban, M. (2016). Jung, Winnicott and the divided psyche. *Journal of Analytical Psychology*, *61*, 329–349.

Seaford, R. (2006). Dionysos. London: Routledge.

Segal, C. (1997). *Dionysiac Poetics and Euripides' Bacchae*. Princeton, NJ: Princeton University Press.

Stevens, W. (2011). *Wallace Stevens: Selected Poems* (Reprint edition). New York, NY: Random House Inc.

Vernant, J. P. (1988). *Myth and Society in Ancient Greece*. New York, NY; Cambridge, MA: Zone Books; Distributed by the MIT Press.

von Franz, M. -L. (1998). *Dreams*. Boston, MA: Shambhala; Distributed in the U.S. by Random House.

15

The Commodification of Wellbeing

Naomi Bonger

Consumerism and the Pursuit of Wellbeing

The concern for wellbeing – for feeling whole, for becoming one's true self – is a timeless quest. Questions like 'Who am I? How can I come to know myself? How can I live my life more fully?' have their roots in the earliest beginnings of philosophy and religion, and yet remain at the heart of contemporary culture's fascination with selfhood and the pursuit of fulfilment.

The framework around what wellbeing is and how to go about achieving it has no doubt changed, but this very human desire finds itself centre stage in what has been described as the 'massive subjective turn of modern culture' (Taylor in Heelas and Woodhead, 2005, p. 2). This shift away from dogmatic narratives towards the subjective reality of the individual as the 'unique source of significance, meaning and authority' (ibid., pp. 3–4) can be empowering, but it also puts new demands on the individual: to pursue oneself, to find oneself, to experience oneself, in order to give shape and meaning to the disorder of existence. Narratives of wellbeing become more and more important in a culture that emphasises selfhood, and so does the 'tacit assumption that self-realization is the largest aim of human experience' (Lears in Miller, 2005, p. 86). As Maslow's hierarchy of needs reflects, people who are not struggling simply to stay alive, or find work or make families, have more time and energy, more psychological space, for pursuing personal identity and fulfilment as their ultimate goal (Maslow, 1943).

This quest for wellbeing is, however, easily exploited, something that is painfully obvious today in the way it is intensively marketed to us by a consumer culture which explicitly promotes a positive relationship between consumption and fulfilment. In fact it is clear that the wellbeing values of an individualist society fit neatly with the demands of consumer capitalism, where an individual's consuming and investing are seen as the central unit of experience (Foucault in Landers, 2012, p. 202). So, for example, where previously the psychological need for meaning might have been derived from traditional, perhaps more communal, sources such as myth, religion or community life, individuals have increasingly become directed 'to fulfil their needs for meaning, wholeness and belonging through consumption'(Miller, 2005, p. 88): buying stuff becomes the new mythology.

The market model of fulfilment moulds and manipulates socio-psychological anxieties ('Am I good enough? Attractive enough? Popular enough? Safe enough?') so that particular products can be presented as their immediate remedy. Consumption is positioned to address:

> the alienated qualities of modern social life and claims to be the solution: it promises the very things the narcissist desires – attractiveness, beauty, personal popularity – through consumption of the 'right' kinds of goods and services. (Giddens, 1991, p. 172)

So it is that as the subjective turn has seen people become increasingly orientated towards the pursuit of wellbeing, advertising has manipulated this search so that the 'infinite longing of the human heart has been introjected into products' (Kavanaugh, 2006, p. 13). Commodities become associated with states of wellbeing that can be bought and consumed, meaning we are induced to buy not just products but the promise of greater self-worth, deeper relationships and a more profound sense of fulfilment. This is evident in the marketing of consumer items such as cars and perfume, but also more explicitly in wellbeing services and experiences such as retreats, massages and, of course, therapy.

The difficulty with this lies in the fact that the structure of a consumer economy depends on these promises not being fulfilled, on 'people developing both a high expectation of satisfaction from consumer products, and subsequently becoming equally profoundly dissatisfied with these same products' (Conway, 2006, p. 150). This is what enables the cycle of producing, marketing and consuming to keep moving: allowing the expectation and disappointment of the consumer to feed a craving for more. This has problematic implications for the field of wellbeing with its explicit focus on the alleviation of dissatisfaction, and its manipulative edge jars with what therapy might hope to offer, for example a sense of trust between therapist and client. A pessimistic reading might suggest that therapists cynically seek to keep clients unhappy in order to secure their continued employment, but even a less extreme analysis must acknowledge that the character of the market, with its ultimate emphasis on buying and consuming, will have an impact on how therapy works.

Wellbeing and Dramatherapeutic Practice

This is the cultural milieu in which both the providers of and participants in therapeutic practices operate. Dramatherapists are part of a consumer culture in which their services are advertised within the frame of wellbeing, and as such they can come to operate as a marketplace from which clients seek to purchase particular results. Therapy runs the risk of becoming another commodity through which people attempt to buy up their sense of self, just as fast foods offer comfort and perfumes promise individuality.

What's the problem with this? It could be argued that dramatherapists should embrace the market way of working, and that rather than allow themselves to be marginalised by consumer culture, they should use it as a vehicle to promote their work, making it as accessible to as many people as possible. Why not just go with the flow? There are two responses to this: firstly, I think the qualities of dramatherapy make it an uneasy fit with consumerism. By this I mean that things like the embodied nature of the work, its relational basis, its quality of working with the unknown, all butt up uncomfortably against the fast-paced, smooth-lined efficiency of the consumer model, so that dramatherapy would need to modify itself out of all recognition in order to fit the mould. Secondly, what if it is the cycle of buying and discarding that is itself a root cause of human unhappiness? What if wellbeing and the potential for living a fulfilling life are actually obstructed by the pressures and demands of consumerism? Then a market-embracing dramatherapy would simply offer another way of being disappointed by a purchase. The reality is that dramatherapists work within a consumer context, but that doesn't mean they must be subsumed by it. Perhaps it is, in fact, by developing a healthy sense of challenge to the surrounding culture that the practice of dramatherapy can be best upheld, and of most use to those who access it.

So, with this idea of challenge in mind, how might dramatherapy respond to contemporary narratives of wellbeing? I am particularly interested in how the practice of dramatherapy might relate to the underlying human hope of feeling well without competing or colluding with models which ultimately leave people feeling more dissatisfied. In exploring this, I will look at dramatherapeutic theories and practices generally, and then focus in on those aspects of the Sesame Approach to Dramatherapy which I have found particularly helpful in addressing this theme.

My sense is that the critical issue is with the notion of wellbeing as a product that a therapist can sell. The desire for quick-fix wellness can lead to people seeking therapy as a magic bullet, and to therapists claiming they can offer it. However, yielding to the pressure for therapy to conform to our culture's preoccupation with immediate fulfilment will ultimately undermine the genuine potential for wellbeing that therapy can offer.

Dramatherapy needs to resist this pressure and I believe that in the qualities of the dramatherapeutic space a resistance to the consumerist hegemony can take place. That in this space something countercultural, non-market orientated, and honestly fulfilling can happen. So what are the qualities of the dramatherapeutic space and how can they offer such a challenge?

Practising a Cultural Resistance

The Role of Relationship

Dramatherapy is undoubtedly concerned with issues of selfhood and wellbeing. As Phil Jones articulates in his article 'The Active Self: Drama Therapy and Philosophy', as a practice which includes 'dramatic projection, embodiment and role taking, certain aspects of identity … are emphasised by the very nature of the form of the therapy' (Jones, 2008, p. 224). However, while a consumer model might present wellbeing and selfhood as objects which can be bought, the dramatherapeutic space encourages people to explore being in relationship, where relating well is considered essential in both understanding oneself and realising a true sense of wellbeing. Selfhood is seen to develop not as an isolated unit but through relationship to other people, to the world around and ultimately to oneself. We are going to look a little further at these three aspects of the self-in-relation, and reflect on how they form part of dramatherapy's practice of resistance.

The central plank to any process of therapy is the therapeutic relationship. That therapy occurs in the mess and joy and wrangle of actual human encounter, that interaction is in fact its medium, immediately marks it out from the individualism of many wellbeing pursuits, which tend to emphasise an 'intensely private sense of well-being' (Rieff in Miller, 2005, p. 85) as their final goal. While subjective experience of oneself is absolutely part of the process of dramatherapy, it is perhaps not seen as a unit which can be 'accomplished' separate from the process of the relationship. Instead, the selfhood of the client is understood as finding and forming itself in relation to the 'otherhood' of the therapist. As Martin Buber puts it, 'every person discovers the self in relationships with other. One becomes conscious of oneself as a person, an "I" … by dealing with another person, a "you"' (Buber, 1970, pp. 134–135). Therapy cannot exist apart from the back-and-forth give-and-take between (at least) two people; it can only operate in collaboration.

Jones explores how a shift in the understanding of the self 'typified within philosophy as independent, insular and isolated' (Jones, 2008) towards conceptions which emphasise the self in relationship reflects and supports the work of *drama*therapy in particular. The dynamic of the dramatherapeutic relationship, which is embodied and interactive, and where therapists can variously be cast as co-creators, directors, audience or play-things, explicitly seeks to 'establish the nature of identity not just in verbal reflection and self examination, but in the action and relation of enactment' (Jones, 2008). In doing so the practice of dramatherapy seems to be uniquely positioned to reinforce and celebrate identity as a collaborative construct, rather than an interior object.

Fred Landers articulates the way in which this collaborative approach to selfhood might be positioned as a kind of cultural resistance in a paper about 'Urban Play', in which he explores the use of Developmental Transformations as a form of activism. While our culture places high value on the experience and agenda of the individual self, he comments that, 'A commitment to playing in a larger community than the individual subject is the alternative that Urban Play presents to neoliberalism.' (Landers, 2012, p. 204) In a subtle but real way, simply engaging beyond one's own sphere, opening oneself up to be affected and transformed by relationship to another, is itself a form of challenge to a worldview which is concerned with purchase power above all else.

The assumption that therapy is a self-indulgent activity perhaps misses this radical relationality of the process, which sets it apart from the all-consuming drive to 'find oneself', as if oneself is the end goal of all experience. Using the framework of the therapeutic relationship, people are able to explore and discover what the self-in-relation feels like, to try out different ways of being with it, and to practise being in relationship with others. This potential space between client and therapist is 'an intermediate area of *experiencing*, to which inner reality and external life both contribute' (Winnicott, 1991, p. 2). It seeks to validate the personal reality of the client as an intersection between inner and outer worlds. It is concerned with selfhood, but the negotiation of a relationship with another person means learning about oneself as part of something bigger than oneself; it is participating in a story beyond oneself.

The Sesame Approach to Dramatherapy draws on the world of mythology to provide this wider story, which I'm thinking of as the self-in-relation *to the world around*. It works with Jung's concept of the collective unconscious, an understanding that there is a pattern to the human psyche which 'is not individual but common to all men … [and which] is the true basis of the individual psyche' (Jung, 1960, p. 152). Drawing on the archetypal symbols and narratives of the mythologies that underlie different times and cultures can provide an opportunity to look at personal experience from a new angle. It destabilises narratives of selfhood which turn exclusively inwards ('Who am I? How am I?') by refracting them outwards through other stories. In contrast to a postmodern idea of reality where 'the world is draped over the individual' (Tomka, 1999, p. 30), the self is here given a deeper context in which to find its bearings.

Working with myth can enable us to dig inside other ways of thinking about our reality, and put us in touch with a broader set of messages about what it is to be human, messages which run in different directions to the consumer ideology which dominates much of our cultural intake. Because when the identity of an individual is most strongly shaped by the identity of 'consumer', as is perhaps likely in our current consumer context, then the world becomes something to consume. It is to be bent and manipulated to personal tastes, believed to exist in order to fulfil individual requirements. And as we have seen, this assumption leads to inevitable disappointment and disillusionment, as the promise that we can consume our way to contentment fails to deliver. However, when the personal story of an individual is shaped by its relation to other stories, and the individual psyche finds its relation to the collective, there is a sense of a shared journey. The need to form meaning is no longer borne alone, and the desire for wellbeing develops from an individualistic pursuit into a shared exploration.

Engaging with mythology, widening the horizons of our perception and putting our sense of selfhood into relationship with different human experiences stops one powerful set of ideas dictating our identities: it allows different voices to emerge. This principle of being multi-voiced also underlies the final aspect of the self-in-relation: putting the self into relationship *with itself*.

As cultural descendants of Descartes, many people consider their sense of self to be firmly located in their mind: they think therefore they are. This rational part of the self is esteemed in our culture, and although much of the desire for wellbeing is shaped by emotional drives (to which advertising is frequently targeted) our sense of 'me' is still often closely identified with thinking. Dramatherapy, however, offers a different way in. By its nature as a form which uses techniques such as role play, improvisation and witnessing, dramatherapy conceives of 'individual identity as multifaceted … and as reflexive, in that part of the self is able to look at and change another part of the self' (Jones, 2008, p. 230). With this philosophy embedded in its practice, it is able to provide a space to draw together into conversation the thinking, feeling and acting parts of an individual, and acknowledge and appreciate the different voices of the self that emerge, even when they seem to be saying different things.

One of these 'voices' of the self comes from the body, and dramatherapeutic practice aims to acknowledge not only the conceptual narrative of the self, but also the embodied experience that underlies it (Kozak, 1992, p. 150). This attention given to the body and its communications is an important facet of what I'm calling dramatherapy's cultural resistance. Rather than attempting to separate physical and mental health, the psyche and soma are understood to be an integrated whole, such that healthy relationships *within* the self are seen as equally important as healthy relationships with others in the world around.

The Sesame approach has a particular emphasis on embodiment that is markedly different from the familiar consumerist preoccupation with bodies. All around us we see bodies represented in advertising, selling us different notions of wellbeing through idealised versions of attractiveness, fitness or desirability. The dramatherapeutic space seeks to reclaim the body from this kind of commodification, to shift our perspective from seeing it as a *thing*, towards appreciating it as part of our whole self with its own story to tell. Indeed this holistic approach recognises that our perceptions of reality are rooted in the fact of our embodiment. Jung maintained that 'nothing is true until it reaches the body, and that the symbol always needs physical expression' (Kaylo, 2003, p. 111). The Sesame approach aims to make space for this embodied expression of reality, which might simply mean allowing it to move around without any particular agenda. This requires a particular kind of vulnerability, which might mean giving up one's sense of ego-control, peeling back a well-hewn persona and trusting what the body communicates. Crucially, in embracing embodied consciousness as part of its practice, the Sesame approach seeks to appreciate the body not as an object-container for the intellectual self, but as an active contributor to the meaning-making process, that is: the body plays a part in what and who and how a person is, as part of 'a continuum of existence, involving self, objects and other people' (Merleau-Ponty in Jones, 2008, p. 229).

In a simple but significant way, the actual physical presence of bodies in a room together also marks out the dramatherapeutic encounter from the hyper-real, image-saturated interactions many people have over the internet. Dramatherapy cannot be reduced to words or pictures, it can only exist and be experienced in the physical present. This feels important because while much of our interaction is now funnelled through online media, the embodied practice of the Sesame approach seems to naturally resist the consumer model of the internet. Personal relationship is often devalued in favour of speed and cost-efficiency, but the fact that this work happens through the meeting of bodies in space means it cannot be condensed or accelerated for convenience, it needs to respect the pace and depth and integrity of the real-life human beings involved.

The first aspect of dramatherapy's resistance to the consumer narrative of wellbeing is concerned with the idea of the self-in-relation. This principle marks dramatherapy out from other wellbeing activities, because while the 'me-time' emphasis of a spa has its own value, it is very different from a therapeutic process which considers that 'me' to grow and deepen and develop in relationship. It recognises the basic relationality of being human, what has been described as the 'inter-subjective, inseparable relationship formed between our existence and the world' (Kaylo, 2003, p. 122), and is able to acknowledge and work with 'the idea of a tension or active relationship between an individual, their body, their sense of self and the culture they live in' (Jones, 2008, p. 229). This appreciation for relationship – to each other, the world and ourselves – can create a 'freedom from dominant social norms' (Landers, 2012, p. 202), by countering a widely marketed ideal of the self as an independent unit with the apparent power to make itself up according to what it consumes.

Instant Gratification and the Pace of the Psyche

My sense is that it is the desire to buy up fulfilment as an immediate antidote to other feelings that lies underneath the commodification of wellbeing. The instant gratification of our culture is so addictive that everything, even experiences which require time to develop authentically, is induced to happen faster and faster because speed is given such high value.

Dramatherapy's attention to the pre-verbal, its 'active involvement with the images of the psyche' (Pearson, 1996, p. 41), means that it must assert a different sense of time. If we are to acknowledge individual connection to the collective unconscious we need to make space for the ancient pattern and pace of the internal self to emerge, even when it is quite out of step with the increasing speed of external life. I like to think of approaching the psyche from the side, slowly and gently, as one might approach a deer so as not to startle it. This is not to suggest the work itself must be slow. It might be high paced, physical and exuberant, but the psyche itself cannot be hurried, for just as a deer cannot be rushed at without it fleeing, the unconscious self needs to surface into consciousness at its own pace.

Jung recognised the psyche's capacity to self-regulate and to find its own balance between opposites. In fact he proposed that the very structure of the psyche worked 'as a dynamic process which rests on a foundation of antithesis, on a flow of energy between two poles' (Jung, 1995, p. 383). Drawing on this theory, the therapeutic goal of the Sesame approach is to create space for this energy to move, and time to allow the symbols of healing to bubble up, rather than attempting to apply a solution to a given problem as one might seek to fix a computer. The slowness of this approach requires trust, and means holding one's nerve against the expectation of a culture demanding instantaneous results. It also has practical implications. There needs to be a long enough stint of time working together for the therapist and client to build a safe relationship from which to explore. There needs to be freedom from the pressure to succeed. And there needs to be an openness which resists forcing a client to fit with a particular agenda. However, in my experience these kinds of pressures are in fact often at play, and it is not helpful simply to deny them or to demand only perfect conditions: we have to work in the real world with its real-world limitations. So what does it look like for drama-therapists to practise a resistance in a culture of immediacy?

I think it means practising the principle of working at the psyche's pace whatever the circumstances of the therapy. Being responsive to, but not manipulated by, the culture around. Perhaps even when only six sessions are available and specific aims have been set, it means holding to an authentic respect for the speed of a client's internal journey, and recognising that this is what prepares the ground for real and lasting change to take root, even if we only see the beginning of it.

Wellness as a State of Being

Dramatherapy is working with aims that can be difficult to pin down and towards results that can be difficult to prove. In some ways we can see that the materialism of the consumer model has made non-material fulfilment difficult to assert against the commodity way of thinking, so that areas of life unmediated by the market, like solitude or intimacy or love of nature, become marginalised (Kavanaugh, 2006, p. 61). This is evident in the example above of allowing room for slowness; in so far as it goes against a widespread culture of increasing speed and quick results it can seem invalid, almost embarrassing, as a way of working: slowness has no market value.

So, on one hand, uncommodifed, non-material qualities can become sidelined. Perhaps even more dangerous, however, is that attitudes that people display towards consumable items, for example low levels of commitment or an assumption of disposability, can easily start to spread into other areas of life. This means that wellbeing, identity, even human relationships themselves can come to be 'viewed as things to be *consumed* ... subject to the same criteria of evaluation as all other objects of consumption' (Conway, 2006, p. 151). This spread of commodification, which reduces experiences and people into things, can then turn human interaction into another arena for playing out consumerist desire and dissatisfaction, so that these potential sources of genuine fulfilment become warped.

This is particularly relevant for the therapeutic relationship because the context in which it emerges can easily be framed and understood as consumerist. Perhaps a client is seeking a particular outcome from therapy, and is willing to pay the therapist to 'provide' it for them. Then it is easy to see how the consumer lens, which sees even non-material things such as fulfilment as potentially buyable, can start to affect the relationship. It might, for example, invoke an attitude of low commitment or disposability ('If this doesn't work, I'll just go elsewhere'), which gets in the way of actually relating to the therapist and committing to the process. This throwaway culture can feel empowering as it gives an illusion of control, but by ducking out of relationships which are challenging or not immediately rewarding, we miss learning how to negotiate difficulty, and lose the deep satisfaction of seeing change. Equally the consumer lens might raise expectations ('This therapist is the answer to all my problems'), which are necessarily disappointed, leaving the client with a sense of failure (either the therapist's or their own). The consumer cycle, explored above, relies on this dissatisfaction to keep people seeking and buying, but when it's at play in human interaction it can turn toxic, meaning people discard relationships when they fail to satisfy their particular demands.

This is not to begrudge people the goal of feeling well. And it is equally not to let therapists 'off the hook' in the sense of engaging in high quality therapeutic practice. But it aims to reconsider our ideas about wellbeing, and reflect on how the qualities of the dramatherapeutic space might enable a deeper connection with it.

The crucial factor is about what wellbeing is understood to be. The desire for wellness is so pervasive, such a fundamentally *human* desire, that it is easily manipulated and attached to products and services which claim to provide it as if it were a thing that can be owned. Where wellbeing is understood to be a product that can be bought there will be a never-ending desire to buy it. And therapy, operating in this climate, can find itself entangled in these promises to achieve particular results as if those results were on order and awaiting delivery: 'Are you feeling lonely? Depressed? Without meaning? See a therapist and feel better!'

At their best, aims and outcomes provide a framework to monitor the progress of therapy, to identify what is being worked towards, and to observe what is helping and what is not. In a saturated wellbeing market, however, and in a culture of cuts, therapy comes under intense pressure to prove itself as an outcome provider in direct competition with other services. Here, outcomes can easily become distorted, that is, they can be turned into things to be purchased, to be won at all costs, even at the expense of genuine change. But simply to go along with a culture preoccupied with outcomes can imply that a deep sense of wellbeing can be definitively bought and owned, and this is to be complicit in a model whose prime aim is to sell things, rather than work towards authentic change.

In a comprehensive study of the issues and challenges facing the field of dramatherapy research, Jones investigates this tension between the need for dramatherapy to demonstrate its impact and efficacy, while remaining true to its identity as a practice and genuinely responsive to its clients' needs. He comments that 'Dramatherapy may have different ways of understanding its impact than those reflected by standardised methods used by other disciplines' (Jones, 2012, p. 119), and that there is a need therefore to embrace 'values and approaches developed within dramatherapy where "messy" processes such as improvisation and spontaneity are central to its work' (Jones, 2012, p. 135). Here Jones is acknowledging the need to engage with the cultural context of the work, whilst placing explicit value on the very aspects of dramatherapy which mark it as different: its messiness perhaps, its potential slowness, and its emphasis on process over product.

Dramatherapeutic practice needs to be transparent about wellbeing as a process, a state of being that one can participate in rather than possess, and demonstrate how fulfilment, authentic wellbeing and true selfhood are in fact something like by-products of relating well in and with the world. This discovery can itself be liberating, meaning individuals have agency to form their own experiences of wellbeing, rather than believing that they have to purchase fulfilment through a specific product, or perhaps thinking that they have been locked out of it altogether.

In practice this notion of wellbeing as a state of being is perhaps simply a way of speaking and practising which emphasises the role of relationship, which acknowledges the time and space required, and which avoids a sales pitch that promises a list of particular outcomes. For wellbeing is not a tick-box outcome; in fact I am proposing that it's not a *thing* at all, but rather that it emerges as an effect of practising deep relationship with oneself, with other people and with the world around.

Space for Shadow

If true wellbeing can be seen as the fruit which grows from the root of deep relationship, then dramatherapy needs to be concerned with this practice of relating well, even when it appears messier, more time-consuming, or less appealing than the feel-good wellbeing which is advertised to us; even when it means things looking worse before they get better.

Ironically, dissatisfaction with therapy may result precisely because it seeks a deeper sense of satisfaction. By not complying with a quick-fix culture of immediate gratification, therapy can feel like it's not going anywhere, like it's not getting results. And, of course, this may be true. But by looking at the experience of dissatisfaction, by making space to *be in it*, rather than giving up and seeking to buy into something new, therapy can enable people to see what lies beneath their desires, and to gain insight into where they place their hope for wellbeing. The practice of dramatherapy can create this space in unique ways. Dramatherapists can be alongside people as they experience dissatisfaction, offer them tools to create what it looks and feels like, and provide time for them to imagine how it might be different. They can play out fantasies, be kicked against and killed, or hold the space for a cherished hope. This live-action drama can bring to the fore as characters and creations feelings which might usually be hidden away under the surface of consciousness, and make space to see how they can be integrated into a fuller sense of self. Dissatisfaction might be an uncomfortable feeling, but dramatherapy at its best can transform it from an obstacle to be avoided into fertile material from which insight and change can grow.

For me, one of the most exciting 'practices of resistance' that dramatherapy can offer is concerned with making space for shadow. Jung's concept of the shadow refers to the inferior part of the personality, 'everything that the subject refuses to acknowledge about himself' (Jung, 1959, p. 284), and it is clear how contemporary consumerism is culpable in attempting to repress shadow aspects, while simultaneously playing on our anxieties about them. Furthermore, our culturally conditioned idea of wellbeing is heavily influenced by the idea of the pursuit of happiness, so that the concept of being well can merge in our minds with being happy. But it is an unrealistic and perhaps undesirable aspiration to be happy all the time, with no shade to the unrelenting light, for as Jung put it: 'There is no light without shadow and no psychic wholeness without imperfection.' (Jung, 1954, p. 72) The repression of our shadow side, the disowning of the unappealing parts of ourselves, leaves us with a thin sense of what is 'allowed' to be shown. The fullness of our selfhood (the psychic wholeness Jung refers to) is flattened out; it might be rendered acceptable but what remains no longer represents who we really are.

Dramatherapy doesn't have to hide from shadow material, to avoid it or repress it, because it can be weaved creatively into the material of the work. The skeletons in the closet can be exhumed and enacted, seen and explored. In fact, therapeutic work *needs* this raw unconscious matter, for it provides the energy of opposites which sparks movement in the psyche and makes way for real change. There is space for the whole person in the therapeutic relationship; not just those parts which feel acceptable, but the full range of characters which play on the stage of the self. This is exciting partly because it is unusual to be allowed to share all of oneself, or to be present to another who does so, and this warts-and-all vitality can feel something like a rebellion against, or a resistance to, a wellbeing culture which can seem too picture perfect or vacuum-packed.

It is a squeaky clean picture of wellbeing that is so often sold to us: of relaxation and recreation and 'me-time', all of which may be good in and of themselves. But it is not true that authentic wellbeing is only attainable when conditions are perfect. In fact genuinely being well needs to include space for a full range of feelings, which allows an individual to express darkness, as well as enjoy their light. Where only happiness is prized as the ultimate target, then other feelings can easily become repressed and distorted and capable of damage, as 'the less it [the shadow] is embodied in the individual's conscious life, the blacker and denser it is' (Jung, 1975/1958, p. 131).

Acknowledging the material of the shadow, which for Jung contains good and creative aspects as well as the reprehensible, is part of coming into contact with our whole selves. Integrating these rejected aspects of the self enables us not to be dominated by them, or by the need to hide them, and allows us to live more freely and more fully. But it can be a painful and difficult process to honestly acknowledge anger or sorrow or envy or guilt, to uncover and own our darkness, to risk rejection, and therapy is perhaps uniquely positioned to be alongside people as they do so. In offering acceptance and support and tools for exploring the parts of the self usually hidden even from oneself, dramatherapy practises a resistance to the consumer ideal of presenting the most attractive, sellable version of oneself. And in this practice of making space for shadow, it articulates something critical: that wellbeing needs to include the capacity to not be well; that wellbeing is not a monoculture, but is enriched by the depth and diversity brought by being able to feel different feelings.

Perhaps, in conclusion, it is possible to say that dramatherapy is working with the shadow of contemporary society, making space for those parts which are repressed and distorted by a culture of consumerism and commodification. As Fordham puts it: '*The shadow* contains, besides the personal shadow, the shadow of society ... fed by the neglected and repressed collective values.' (Fordham, 1990, p. 5) This is where dramatherapy can practise its challenge.

In placing the practice of relationship at the heart of its work; by asserting the value of a different pace in a climate of instant gratification; by unearthing wellbeing as a state of being which one can participate in rather than a commodity one can own; and by making space for shadow, dramatherapy is enacting a resistance. Under the glare of a consumer way of thinking it can seem outdated or unfashionable in its commitment to these practices, that perhaps it should upgrade its way of working as one might a phone, but that is exactly the point. The treasure of this work is that it offers something countercultural, it resists colluding with the consumer model, and in doing so it enables a different narrative of wellbeing to emerge.

References

Buber, M. (1970). *I and Thou* (trans. Walter Kaufmann). New York, NY: Scribner's.

Conway, E. (2006). The commodification of religion and the challenges for theology: Reflections from the Irish experience. In L. Boeve & K. Justaert

(Eds.), *Bulletin ET Journal of the European Society for Catholic Theology*, Vol.17 (2006/1) Special Issue, *Consuming Religion in Europe? Christian Faith Challenged by Consumer Culture* (pp. 142–163). Leuven: Peeters.

Foucault, M. (2008). *Birth of Biopolitics* (trans. G. Burchell, ed. M. Senellart) Basingstoke: Palgrave Macmillan.

Fordham, M. (1990). *Jungian Psychotherapy: A Study in Analytical Psychology*. London: H. Karnac (Books) Ltd.

Giddens, A. (1991). *Modernity and Self-Identity: Self and Society in the Late Modern Age*. Cambridge: Polity Press in association with Basil Blackwell.

Heelas, P. & Woodhead, L. (Eds.). (2005). *The Spiritual Revolution: Why Religion is Giving Way to Spirituality*. Oxford: Blackwell.

Jones, P. (2008). The active self: Drama therapy and philosophy. *The Arts in Psychotherapy*, 35(3), 224–231. Available at: http://www.sciencedirect.com/science/article/pii/S0197455606000232. Accessed 13 October 2016.

Jones, P. (2012). Approaches to the futures of research Part 2. *Dramatherapy*, 34(3), 116–138. Available at: http://www.tandfonline.com/doi/abs/10.1080/02630672.2012.737630. Accessed 13 October 2016.

Jung, C. G. (1995). *Memories, Dreams, Reflections*. London: Fontana Press.

The Collected Works of C. G. Jung

Jung, C. G. (1980). *The Archetypes and the Collective Unconscious* (trans Hull, R. F. C.). In G. Adler & R. F. C. Hull (Eds.), *The Collected Works of C.G. Jung* (2nd ed., Vol. 9, pt. 1) Princeton, NJ: Princeton University Press (original work published 1959).

Jung, C. G. (2014a). *The Development of Personality* (trans Hull, R.F.C). In H. Read et al. (Eds.), *The Collected Works of C.G. Jung* (Vol. 17) East Sussex and New York, NY: Routledge (original work published 1954).

Jung, C. G. (2014b). *The Structure and Dynamics of the Psyche* (trans Hull, R.F.C). In H. Read et al. (Eds.), *The Collected Works of C.G. Jung* (Vol. 8, pt. 2) East Sussex and New York, NY: Routledge (original work published 1960).

Kavanaugh, J. F. (2006). *Following Christ in a Consumer Society: The Spirituality of Cultural Resistance*. Maryknoll and New York, NY: Orbis Books.

Kaylo, J. (2003). The phenomenological body and analytical psychology. In *Harvest: Journal for Jungian Studies*, 49(1), 111–131.

Kozak, A. (1992). The epistemic consequences of pervasive and embodied metaphor: Applications to psychotherapy. *Theoretical & Philosophical Psychology*, 12(2), 137–154.

Landers, F. (2012). Urban Play: Imaginatively responsible behavior as an alternative to neoliberalism. *The Arts in Psychotherapy, 39,* 201–205. Available at: http://fulltext.study/dl/7KT85883MW6340847. Accessed 13 October 2016.

Maslow, A. H. (1943). A theory of human motivation. *Psychological Review, 50*(4), 370–396.

Merleau-Ponty, M. (1965). *The Structure of Behaviour* (trans. A.L. Fisher) London: Methuen.

Miller, V. J. (2005). *Consuming Religion: Christian Faith and Practice in a Consumer Culture.* London and New York, NY: Continuum.

Pearson, J. (Ed.). (1996). *Discovering the Self through Drama and Movement.* London: Jessica Kingsley.

Tomka, M. (1999). Individualism, a Change in values, the experience society: Converging trends in sociology. *Concilium, 4,* 25–35.

Winnicott, D. W. (1991). *Playing and Reality.* London: Routledge.

Epilogue

As this book has taken shape, it appears to have formed a kind of montage, reflecting the state, the margins and the possible future horizons of Sesame-inspired dramatherapy today. The writing evidences the where, the what and the why of this particular approach and examples of how it is being practised, developed and innovated in diverse settings.

Diversity emerges as a strong current throughout the text. In a forest, diversity is an indicator of the good health of the woodland. The diverse nature of the writing here similarly suggests that the Sesame Approach is in rude health. That Sesame practitioners are testing the edges of practice and exploring the margins of the specialism. Through this it appears they are meaningfully engaged with their roles in the clinical, creative, educational and social settings in which they practise, that the Sesame Approach's ancient roots continue to find traction and relevance in contemporary lands, reflecting an emerging paradigm of interdisciplinary practice and connectivity. This tension between the then and the now ensures the rootedness of new developments, which in turn refresh and replenish its continuity. The Sesame Approach is fundamentally based on play. Play stands as the essential taproot of the method. And play in therapy requires both the characteristics of experimentation and the critical thinking and acting inherent in praxis. These qualities can be found in the style and content of the chapters, through the interplay between existing knowledge and new ideas; rhythm and risk. Rachel Porter's chapter (Chapter 10) is a case in point. She addresses a core process in the Sesame Approach – Movement with Touch and Sound. She critiques the contemporary relevance of the work of Erik Erikson and suggests a new theoretical framework and body of research. In so doing, she revitalises the method while remaining sensitive to its heartland and the intuitive compass it requires of the therapist. As we have worked with the authors we have noticed how chapters appear to speak across to each other. These moments of convergence, where Merleau-Ponty's ideas of the gaze combine with Stern's understanding of mutuality, are exciting and potential fields of further study. We set out to avoid developing another handbook of dramatherapy. Instead we have curated a compendium of thought and reflection on diverse subjects which have a contemporary relevance for the profession. Praxis has an intimate relationship with time and this book seems to mark a timely convergence of knowledge from different fields, which may, in turn, lead to new and unexpected destinations. As Jung says of the moment of insight, 'in no case was it conjured into existence through purpose and conscious willing, but rather seemed to be borne on the stream of time' (1981, p. 92).

In recent times, the current UK government has announced a 'new' policy apparently aimed at turning the clock back to the three-tier academically selective public, grammar and secondary modern schooling system of the post-war past. And this at a time when our already fragmenting world appears to be in especially urgent need of cohesion and connection. Divisive and excluding initiatives such as this challenge and undermine the integrative goals of identifying, supporting and maximising individual human potential. So in what ways is dramatherapy able to ensure its way of linking past, present and future is healthy, progressive, inclusive and relevant? This question appeared alive in the conception of this book; in those course team meetings mentioned in Chapter 1. The team grappled with what it was that really mattered to them in their practice and this in turn appeared to shine particular and often compelling light on why and how dramatherapy is as relevant and urgent today as it has ever been. It occurred to us that the current relevance of dramatherapy is rarely argued for. There was some sense that we dramatherapists might not be understood, as if we speak in a different tongue and so decide to remain and/or feel silenced. However if we turn our gaze to concurrent developments in associated fields we see much to both encourage and support us in our connections with other practitioners. We also see plenty as testimony to our profession's contemporary relevance.

In the field of mental health care and following a period of great and unbridled enthusiasm, the appetite for cognitive and behavioural-focused approaches has begun to wane. Certainly their pervasive dominance and tendency towards a one-size-fits-all philosophy is being more thoroughly questioned. The validity of such approaches' 'evidenced effectiveness' has been called in to question by a meta-analysis of success indicators and claims (Baarseth et al., 2013). These criticisms have been underscored by questions relating to the declining effectiveness and comparatively high dropout rates of those receiving cognitive behavioural therapy (CBT). The underlying philosophies of cognitive and behavioural approaches, and CBT in particular, are also coming under increasing scrutiny. It is of note that in very recent Care Quality Commission inspection reports, care programmes that provide a more rounded therapeutic approach, without adhering to a strict CBT doctrine, are being acknowledged as good practice in recognising, assessing and meeting the diversity of patient need.

As we enter a time of potential re-evaluation in this sector, it will be helpful for dramatherapists to consider how best to evolve their approach and to be clear in the ways in which they position the practice alongside those of other therapeutic interventions. Clearly, cognitively based approaches will not disappear but we may be looking forward to a time of more healthy co-existence and compatibility between approaches. Our hope is that the articulate and evidenced voices alive in these pages will inspire and support the voices of practitioners in practice settings, to speak, argue, dialogue and be heard in shaping future clinical practice.

We've been similarly intrigued and encouraged by recent and emergent trends in theatre practice: perhaps most notably, the great surge of interest in those immersive theatre forms which fuse place, sound, light and shadow to stimulate the sensory, foster participation and oil a more intimate encounter between performer and audience. This apparent thirst for immediate and visceral human contact; the hope of meeting an other as promised by a carefully boundaried 'play space'. As if awoken by the tsunami of online, virtual, remote, social networking, the notion of offline, actual and immediate personal contact dawns: the shared lineage of Artaud, Grotowski and Bachelard et al. The use of ritual forms and the common curiosity of haptic and noetic forms of knowledge provide the connecting tissue between the two disciplines of immersive theatre and dramatherapy. Drawing from these shared sources, immersive theatre may be seen to manifest in the outer empty spaces of site, street, field and tunnel. Dramatherapy meanwhile turns the immersive enquiry mostly inwards and towards travails and serendipitous stumblings within interior landscapes, and potentially towards profound and intimate encounters with the Self.

This encounter with the Self was something which Jung positioned at the centre of Analytical Psychology. This Self, as the totality of the personality, contains both the unconscious and the conscious psyche and within it a cultural inheritance. The paradox here is how the contemporary relates to tradition, how the archetypal touches the everyday. The tensions between traditional and new forms of understanding and practice go to the heart of Jung's work, where the contemporary narrative should connect with the myth, where religious symbols appear syncretically and evidence the collective unconscious and our collective humanity. In this way Jung opened up his challenge to live a symbolic life, and we can note the current dangers of literal interpretations. The increasing interest in Jung's writing reflects the desire and indeed the imperative to understand the psyche more fully. And Jung led the way in drawing on philosophy and mythology as well as the natural sciences to develop a psychology which moved away from the behavioural. The voices here develop these studies, sometimes directly and sometimes through the underlying, tangential and subsequent theoretical and philosophical thinking. This dialogue, the clarity and the mess of it all, rumbles on and speaks back to both cross-cultural experience and universal themes. These are voices examining historical perspectives on the nature of the psyche, commenting on the philosophical, artistic and theoretical considerations which underpin dramatherapy practice today. These are voices which unearth and scrutinise the immaterial evidence that establishes the existence of dramatherapy in corners both local and remote.

In all of this, one question seems to recur and it strikes us now that the question's recurrence is vital and healthy and key to the continuity of this as a living, burgeoning thing: how does dramatherapy practice respond and position itself in relation to the ever-emergent, often uncertain and increasingly swift change, trend, renewal and reinvention of the current milieu? Critically, not just *how it responds,* but how it is irrevocably *shaped* by the perpetual ebb and flow of all that surrounds it. Honouring the spirit of this book's origin, authors have been encouraged to trust their own distinctive voice and to speak back to the uncertainty and transitory nature of our times. To write following their curiosity and passion in the here and the now. To invest belief that in so doing, in mining what matters, that something enduring will be revealed: that there is a base, a foundation, a cornerstone and some marrow to this seemingly ephemeral profession of ours. We asked them to mark in these pages what appears to matter: to them, their clients, their practice and profession. As such the writing here arises from doing: clinical practice, training, direct contact, encounter and relationship.

And so this is what our book has become. Looking back, only now do we see and discover the land which we have traversed and the path our footsteps have made – seeing the praxis of it all. At times, in reading and editing these chapters, we've been quietly struck by the ever-wider meanings these writings may offer. There is a febrile and creative discrepancy between the *fact* of writing about and describing praxis by the writer and the meanings drawn and felt by the reader; tensions between the facts and fictions of the word written down and its aliveness in being read and reconsidered. These unbidden responses, mediated and evolved by personal experience, feed our earlier hopes that the work will resist being overly circumscribed, prescriptive or nailed down. We hope instead that it serves to test, disrupt and provoke assumptions around this profession and gives some sense of why we do what we do.

References

Baarseth, T. P., Goldberg, S. B., Pace, B. T., Wislocki, A. P., Frost, N. D. et al. (2013). Cognitive-behavioural therapy versus other therapies: Redux. *Clinical Psychology Review, 33*, 395–405.

Jung, C. G. (1981). *Psychological Types*. Oxon: Routledge.

Index

Druck:
Canon Deutschland Business Services GmbH
im Auftrag der KNV-Gruppe
Ferdinand-Jühlke-Str. 7
99095 Erfurt